CHAPTERS OF BRAZIL'S COLONIAL HISTORY

HISTORY

1500–1800

OXFORD

CHAPTERS OF
BRAZIL'S COLONIAL
HISTORY
1500–1800

CAPISTRANO DE ABREU

Translated from the Portuguese by
ARTHUR BRAKEL

WITH A PREFACE BY FERNANDO A. NOVAIS

AND AN INTRODUCTION BY STUART SCHWARTZ

New York   Oxford
Oxford University Press
1997

Oxford University Press

Oxford   New York
Athens   Auckland   Bangkok   Bogotá   Bombay
Buenos Aires   Calcutta   Cape Town   Dar es Salaam   Delhi
Florence   Hong Kong   Istanbul   Karachi
Kuala Lumpur   Madras   Madrid   Melbourne
Mexico City   Nairobi   Paris   Singapore
Taipei   Tokyo   Toronto   Warsaw

and associated companies in
Berlin   Ibadan

Copyright © 1997 by Oxford University Press

Published by Oxford University Press, Inc.
198 Madison Avenue, New York, New York 10016

Oxford is a registered trademark of Oxford University Press

Library of Congress Cataloging-in-Publication Data
Abreu, João Capistrano de, 1853–1927
[Capítulos de historia colonial, 1500–1800. English]
Chapters of Brazil's colonial history, 1500–1800 /
by Capistrano de Abreu ; translated by Arthur Brakel ;
with a preface by Fernando A. Novais,
and an introduction by Stuart Schwartz.
p. cm. — (Library of Latin America series)
Includes bibliographical references and index.
ISBN 0-19-510301-7 (alk. paper)
1. Brazil—History—To 1822.
I. Brakel, Arthur. II. Title. III. Series.
F2524.A2413 1997   981'.03—dc20   96-43461   CIP

135798642
Printed in the United States of America on acid-free paper

Contents

Series Editors'
General Introduction

The Library of Latin America series makes available in translation major nineteenth-century authors whose work has been neglected in the English-speaking world. The titles for the translations from the Spanish and Portuguese were suggested by an editorial committee that included Jean Franco (general editor responsible for works in Spanish), Richard Graham (series editor responsible for works in Portuguese), Tulio Halperín Donghi (at the University of California, Berkeley), Iván Jaksić (at the University of Notre Dame), Naomi Lindstrom (at the University of Texas at Austin), Francine Masiello (at the University of California, Berkeley), and Eduardo Lozano of the Library at the University of Pittsburgh. The late Antonio Cornejo Polar of the University of California, Berkeley, was also one of the founding members of the committee. The translations have been funded thanks to the generosity of the Lampadia Foundation and the Andrew W. Mellon Foundation.

During the period of national formation between 1810 and into the early years of the twentieth century, the new nations of Latin America fashioned their identities, drew up constitutions, engaged in bitter struggles over territory, and debated questions of education, government, ethnicity, and culture. This was a unique period unlike the process of nation formation in Europe and one which should be more familiar than it is to students of comparative politics, history, and literature.

The image of the nation was envisioned by the lettered classes—a minority in countries in which indigenous, mestizo, black, or mulatto peasants and slaves predominated—although there were also alternative nationalisms at the grassroots level. The cultural elite were well educated in European thought and letters, but as statesmen, journalists, poets, and academics, they confronted the problem of the racial and linguistic heterogeneity of the continent and the difficulties of integrating the population into a modern nation-state. Some of the writers whose works will be translated in the Library of Latin America series played leading roles in politics. Fray Servando Teresa de Mier, a friar who translated Rousseau's *The Social Contract* and was one of the most colorful characters of the independence period, was faced with imprisonment and expulsion from Mexico for his heterodox beliefs; on his return, after independence, he was elected to the congress. Domingo Sarmiento, exiled from his native Argentina under the presidency of Rosas, wrote *Facundo: Civilización o barbarie*, a stinging denunciation of that government. He returned after Rosas' death and was elected president in 1868. Andrés Bello was born in Venezuela, lived in London where he published poetry during the independence period, settled in Chile where he founded the University, wrote his grammar of the Spanish language, and drew up the country's legal code.

These post-independence intelligentsia were not simply dreaming castles in the air, but vitally contributed to the founding of nations and the shaping of culture. The advantage of hindsight may make us aware of problems they themselves did not foresee but this should not affect our assessment of their truly astonishing energies and achievements. It is still surprising that the writing of Andrés Bello, who contributed fundamental works to so many different fields, has never been translated into English. Although there is a recent translation of Sarmiento's celebrated *Facundo*, there is no translation of his memoirs, *Recuerdos de provincia (Provincial Recollections)*. The predominance of memoirs in the Library of Latin America Series is no accident—many of these offer entertaining insights into a vast and complex continent.

Nor have we neglected the novel. The Series includes new translations of the outstanding Brazilian writer Machado de Assis' work, including *Dom Casmurro* and *The Posthumous Memoirs of Brás Cubas*. There is no reason why other novels and writers that are not so well known outside Latin America—the Peruvian novelist Clorinda Matto de Turner's *Aves sin Nido*, Nataniel Aguirre's *Juan de la Rosa*, José de Alencar's *Iracema*, Juana Manuel Gorrit's short stories—should not be read with as much interest as the political novels of Anthony Trollope.

A series on nineteenth-century Latin America cannot, however, be limited to literary genres such as the novel, the poem, and the short story. The literature of independent Latin America was eclectic and strongly influenced by the periodical press newly liberated from scrutiny by colonial authorities and the Inquisition. Newspapers were miscellanies of fiction, essays, poems, and translations from all manner of European writing. The novels written on the eve of Mexican Independence by José Joaquín Fernandez Lizardi, included disquisitions on secular education and law, and denunciations of the evils of gaming and idleness. Other works, such as a well-known poem by Andrés Bello, "Agriculture in the Torrid Zone," and novels such as *Amilia* by José Marmol and the Bolivian Nataniel Aguirre's *Juan de la Rosa*, were openly partisan. By the end of the century, sophisticated scholars were beginning to address the history of their countries, as did João Capistrano de Abreu in his *Capítulos de história colonial*.

It is often in memoirs such as those by Fray Servando Teresa de Mier or Sarmiento that we find the descriptions of everyday life that in Europe were incorporated into the realist novel. Latin American literature at this time was seen largely as a pedagogical tool, a "light" alternative to speeches, sermons, and philosophical tracts—though, in fact, especially in the early part of the century, even the readership for novels was quite small because of the high rate of illiteracy. Nevertheless the vigorous orally transmitted culture of the gaucho and the urban underclasses became the linguistic repertoire of some of the most interesting nineteenth-century writers—most notably José Hernandez, author of the "gauchesque" poem "Martín Fiero" which enjoyed an unparalleled popularity. But for many writers the task was not to appropriate popular language but to civilize, and their literary works were strongly influenced by the high style of political oratory.

The editorial committee has not attempted to limit its selection to the better-known writers such as Machado de Assis; it has also selected many works that have never appeared in translation or whose work has not been translated recently. The Series now makes these works available to the English-speaking public.

Because of the preferences of funding organizations, the series initially focuses on writing from Brazil, the Southern Cone, the Andean Region, and Mexico. Each of our editions will have an introduction that places the work in its appropriate context and includes explanatory notes.

We owe special thanks to Robert Glynn of the Lampadia Foundation, whose initiative gave the project a jump-start, and to Richard Ekman of the Andrew W. Mellon Foundation which also generously supported the project. We also thank the Rockefeller Foundation for funding the 1996 symposium, "Culture and Nation in Iberoamerica," organized by the editorial board of the Library of Latin America. The support of Edward Barry of Oxford University Press has been crucial as has the advice and help of Ellen Chodosh of Oxford University Press. The first volumes of the series were published after the untimely death, on July 3, 1997, of Maria C. Bulle who, as an associate of the Lampadia Foundation, supported the idea from its beginning.

—*Jean Franco*
—*Richard Graham*

Preface

When, in 1876, a young man by the name of Capistrano de Abreu was making his way from the northern province of Ceará (by way of Pernambuco) to Rio de Janeiro, Francisco Adolfo de Varnhagen's *História geral do Brasil* had been published in its entirety. This important work brought together an entire generation of research that had begun with the founding of the Instituto Histórico e Geográfico Brasileiro (Brazilian Institute of History and Geography) in 1837. One of Abreu's first undertakings as a journalist in the imperial capital was a series of articles that definitively situate and evaluate Varnhagen's work as the canonical and factual foundation of Brazilian history. This starting point is of extreme importance for the present endeavor—an attempt to evaluate Abreu's contribution to Brazilian historiography and to evaluate *Chapters of Brazil's Colonial History* in Abreu's lifelong production.

Indeed, beginning in 1876 and continuing until Abreu's death in 1927, this great historian's activity was always split simultaneously in three directions: historiographical criticism aimed at evaluating and integrating studies on Brazil; wide, persistent documentary research that yielded important discoveries as well as critical editions of basic texts; and historical work itself—be it in monographs, or be it in synthetic works. Studies on Varnhagen, Eduardo Prado, and Alfredo de Carvalho stand out among the works in the first vein, which were gathered and published (1931) in the three volumes of *Ensaios e estudos* (*Essays and Studies*). In the research sector, of special notice are: Abreu's discovery and annotated edition of the 1618 *Diálogos das grandezas do Brasil* (*Dialogues on the Grandeurs of Brazil*); his critical edition of Friar Vicente do Salvador's 1627 *História*; and his sensational identification of the author of *Cultura e opulência do Brasil* (1711) as the Jesuit João Antônio Andreoni. Abreu's 1899 *Caminhos antigos e povoamento do Brasil* (*Old Roads and Brazilian Settlement*) is a masterpiece of monographical research whereas *Chapters of Brazil's Colonial History* (1907) was his main effort toward synthesis.

Seen in this light, *Chapters* occupies a high point in Abreu's total output, although chronologically speaking, it appears more or less at the midpoint of his career. Putting *Chapters* both in the center and at the apex of Abreu's output allows historians to apprehend the profound significance of this book within the author's work. It also facilitates the description of Abreu's career as a historian. Above all, one must point out this author's remarkable identification with his object of study.

Beginning with the critical evaluation of Varnhagen, Abreu immediately understood that Brazilian historiography was at an incipient stage, that the gathering of documents had not reached a point where synthetic work could be written. At the same time, however, Abreu understood that an overall vision of a country's history is indispensable in guiding topical research. This is the paradox that is expressed in the oft cited phrase from Abreu's correspondence with Lúcio de Azevedo—Brazilian history, so he maintained, was a "house built on sand." This explains the permanent tension among the different types of work Abreu simultaneously undertook. It also explains the essence of this book, which appears unfinished, as if it were the abandoned framework of a building. Yet, at the same time, this book is fundamental within the totality of Abreu's work. It is almost ironic that although Abreu (along with Rodolfo Garcia) provided dense annotation for all of Varnhagen's writing, he nonetheless left his own work unfinished. Only years later, in 1954, would José Honório Rodrigues supply the rigorous annotation for *Chapters of Brazil's Colonial History*—a book that reveals its author's greatness as well as his shortcomings.

In the same way that *Chapters* occupies a central position in Abreu's work, Abreu occupies a central position in the history of Brazilian history, i.e., in "Brazilian historiography" strictly speaking. Students of the history of Brazilian history, however, have not always taken certain indispensable premises into account concerning the limits of their endeavor. Thus, when Brazilian history is considered as a whole, there are two possible criteria for putting works into categories. If one considers the subjects of this discourse (i.e., Brazilian historians and authors), one lumps together all the work of Brazilian historians—even if they happened to write about the European Middle Ages or about Egypt and the pharaohs. If, on the other hand, the criterion is the object of study (i.e., Brazil), the works by Brazilian historians dealing with other subjects are of necessity left out. However, to compensate for that exclusion, foreign historians' work on Brazilian history should be included. The vast production of foreign "Brazilianists" joins the cast in the latter case, but is absent in the former. When Brazilians speak of "Brazilian Historiography" strictly speaking they mean the body of work by Brazilian historians on Brazil, and it is in this context that Abreu sits at center stage. That is so if we take for granted the solution to another preliminary problem.

This extremely thorny problem is whether or not colonial chroniclers should be considered to belong to Brazilian historiography. There was no such thing as Brazil when they were writing, and for that reason those chroniclers should be left out. But Brazil was emerging as an entity, and in this sense the same chroniclers are expressions of that process.

While I tend toward the second point of view, it seems that, in the interest of pinpointing Abreu's importance, it would be most strategic to consider Brazilian historiography in its strictest sense, which includes only those writings on Brazilian history done by Brazilian historians once Brazil had become an independent nation state. In this strictest sense, Brazilian historiography begins with the 1837 founding of the Instituto Histórico e Geográfico Brasileiro (IHGB)—itself a venerable institution which has recently become the object of some excellent studies.

The IHGB was created during a tumultuous period of the Regency, i.e., the period from 1831 to 1840, when Brazil's second monarch, Dom Pedro II, was still legally a minor. That is, it was founded at the crucial juncture in Brazil's consolidation as a nation state. Its legitimizing function can be seen in its name: it was intended to build national awareness on two foundations—geography and history. Or, in the words of the sixteenth-century chroniclers, on the "land" and on the "people."

Of course, the "sin" of anachronism is inherent in all historiographic discourse, but no historiographic subsection is more susceptible to anachronistic temptations than national history. In the famous words of Julien Benda, one always tends to tell the story of a people in order to demonstrate their "desire to become a nation." This was nowhere so explicit as it was in the case of Brazil. The IHGB, a government bureau supported by the Crown, began by sponsoring a contest to learn "how Brazilian history should be written."

The contest, won by the German naturalist K. F. Ph. von Martius, turned out to be a disaster. Martius maintained that Brazil's history could be seen as the result of contributions from white Portuguese, from native Americans, and from black Africans. One does not need much critical spirit to conclude that this absolutely sinister notion of "contributions" is aimed at obliterating the whole intrigue associated with domination, exploitation, and conflict—that together brought the Brazilian nation to term. The notion of "contributions" caused a particular, somewhat ill-mannered critic by the name of Pedro A. Figueira to claim that with the founding of the IHGB early Brazilian historiography rejected a commitment to the Truth and opted instead for a pact with the Throne.

To repeat, Varnhagen's monumental production distills and consolidates all the work in that first phase of Brazilian historiography. As is to be expected, his entire account emphasizes the sphere of politics and deals with the upper classes and the ruling elites. Abreu brought that phase to a close when he criticized Varnhagen and argued for getting beyond the latter's vision of history. Abreu cleared the way for what might be called modern Brazilian historiography, which began in the 1930s.

Critical observations such as Abreu's insistence that the monotonous spread of cattle up the São Francisco River Valley was much more important than the heroic battles to drive out the Dutch have become famous and have put him at the center of Brazilian historiography. But, still, historians do not pay heed to the deeper meaning of Abreu's critique, which can be apprehended in his work as a whole. Abreu did not merely suggest different themes; he argued for transcending sectional history in favor of global history, for going beyond purely narrative history, and for writing history that, while still narrative, would also be explanatory or, at least, comprehensive.

Comprehensive history, with its integrating dialogue with the social sciences, is the distinguishing trait of modern Brazilian historiography, which began in the 1930s with the work of a particular generation: Gilberto Freyre, Caio Prado Jr., and Sérgio Buarque de Holanda—as well as with the founding of universities. Capistrano de Abreu built a bridge between the first (IHGB) and third (university) phases of Brazilian historiography. His bridge precluded a break in continuity. This is the meaning of his work and his activity in all its grandeur and in all its shortcomings.

—*Fernando A. Novais*
University of Campinas, Brazil

BOOKS BY CAPISTRANO DE ABREU

Caminhos antigos e povoamento do Brasil (1889). 2d ed. Rio: Ed. Briguiet, 1960.

Capítulos de história colonial (1907). 3d ed. revised and annotated by José Honório Rodrigues. Rio: Ed. Briguiet, 1954.

O descobrimento do Brasil. Rio: Ed. Anuário do Brasil, 1929.

Ensaios e estudos (crítica e história). 3 vols. Rio: Ed. Briguiet, 1931.

Correspondência. 3 vols. Introduction and footnotes by José Honório Rodrigues. Rio: Instututo Nacional do Livro, 1954.

WORKS ON CAPISTRANO DE ABREU

Câmara, José Aurélio Saraiva. *Capistrano de Abreu, tentativa biobibliográfica*. Rio: José Olympio, 1969.

Carmo, J. A. Pinto do. *Bibliografia de Capistrano de Abreu*. Rio: Instituto Nacional do Livro, 1942.

Lacombe, Américo Jacobina. *Introdução ao estudo da história do Brasil*. São Paulo, Ed. Nacional, 1974.

Rodrigues, José Honório. *História e historiadores do Brasil*. São Paulo: Fulgor, 1965.

———. *Teoria da história do Brasil*. 3d ed. São Paulo: Ed. Nacional, 1969.

———. *História da história do Brasil*. São Paulo: Ed. Nacional, 1979.

Vianna, Hélio. *Capistrano de Abreu, ensaio biobibliográfico*. Rio: MEC, 1955.

A House Built on Sand: Capistrano De Abreu and the History of Brazil

> The history [historiography] of Brazil gives the impression of a house built on sand. If anyone leans on a wall, no matter how sturdy it seems, it crashes down in bits.
>
> *A história do Brasil dá a idéia de uma casa edificada na areia. É uma pessoa encostar-se numa parede, por mais reforçada que pareça, e lá vem abaixo toda a grampiola*
>
> —C. DE A. TO J. L. DE AZEVEDO
> 17 APRIL 1920
> *CCA*, 1, 161

Brazilians, like other Latin Americans in the nineteenth century, sought in the writing of their national history the foundations of their existence as a nation and the patterns of social, cultural, and economic life that had given their country its distinctive character. History would explain the past, legitimate the present, and plot the future. History's role in nation-building was serious business and in 1838 under the auspices of Brazil's young monarch Dom Pedro II, the Brazilian Institute of Geography and History (Instituto Histórico e Geográfico Brasileiro) was established in Rio de Janeiro, the first such institution in the Americas. The study of history was not yet professionalized as an academic discipline and was written by amateurs, educated men (almost exclusively) who wrote history as a pastime or avocation. They assumed the task or, some would say, they seized the opportunity to construct a narrative of Brazil's past that would make sense of the present.

The importance of history as a form of nation-building had been made clear in 1844 in a remarkable essay by a foreigner who knew the country well. In the previous year the Brazilian Institute of Geography and History, in order to promote the study of national history, had sponsored a contest on how to write the history of Brazil.[1] The winner was Karl Friedrich Philipp von Martius, a German naturalist and scientist with considerable experience in Brazil who had previously written on Brazilian linguistics, botany, and ethnography and had traveled widely in the country.[2] The account of his travels from 1817–20 in the company of another German scientist, Johann Baptist von Spix, is still read with profit today for its acute observations on social and economic conditions.[3] Martius saw no benefit in localized chronicles of unimportant administrators and their actions. Instead, he suggested that the real history of Brazil was the mixing of its human elements: Indian, European, and African. He believed that each group had made a contribution and that each had a history worthy of study. He believed that: "The history of Brazil will always be primarily a branch of Portuguese history. However, if Brazilian history is to be complete and to deserve the name history, it can never exclude the roles played by the Ethiopian and Indian races." Here was a forward-looking formula that would wait almost a century before it was taken up again seriously in the works of Gilberto Freyre and other scholars of his generation.

But Martius's essay won not because of his novel emphasis on racial mixing but rather because while it recognized the centrality of the social and geographical diversity of Brazil it subsumed that diversity within a project to create an integrated nation and a national history. Brazil had just passed through a decade of violent provincial rebellions in which the centripetal forces of regionalism had threatened the monarchy and the unity of the country. Martius's project was a centralizing one. The object of his history would be to "spread noble patriotic sentiments" to Brazil's "politically immature population." While Martius's emphasis on the contributions of three distinct cultures was novel and seemingly radical, he was at heart a political conservative, very much a supporter of the Brazilian status quo of constitutional monarchy. He wanted a history that would show the dangers of republicanism, of an unrestrained press, and of irresponsible free speech about politics. This history would demonstrate that in a country based on slavery, monarchy was a necessity. The history of a Brazil entering an age of progress would serve to emphasize its unity and to create a sense of conservative patriotism among all its inhabitants. Martius's objectives, if not his precocious multicultural approach, resonated among an elite hoping to create a national history as part of creating a nation. The challenge was accepted.

During the nineteenth century, Brazil was blessed with a number of talented historians, but two figures dominated historical studies and the role that history played in the creation of a national identity. Quite different in background, opinions, and accomplishments, the lives of the two chronologically overlapped and their lives and work became curiously intertwined. Together, they became the fathers of modern Brazilian historiography. One was Francisco Adolfo de Varnhagen (1816–1878), author of a factfilled, compendious, general history, and the other, João Capistrano de Abreu (1853–1927), whose classic outline of Brazil's colonial past is translated here in English for the first time.

Given their backgrounds and political sentiments, the two historians would have been somewhat unlikely companions. Francisco Adolfo de Varnhagen and João Capistrano de Abreu were quite dissimilar in many ways, but despite their differences, their desire to establish a firm basis for a national history, a passion to uncover lost, forgotten, or unknown sources on which to build that history, and an underlying sense of nationalism united them. Their work became inextricably braided together.

Francisco Adolfo de Varnhagen, born in Sorocaba (São Paulo), son of a German mining technician, handsome, privileged, argumentative, and proud, left Brazil at an early age, received his education and some military experience in Portugal, and then applied for Brazilian nationality in 1841.[4] Always sensitive about his German father, he later claimed to be a Brazilian by both birth and choice. In truth, he spent most of his life abroad in the Brazilian diplomatic service where he was able to dedicate much of his time to investigation in foreign archives. A tireless researcher, influenced by the currents of nineteenth-century Romanticism and Liberalism, he eventually became very much an exponent of the critical methods being developed by German historians like Leopold von Ranke, and like him was a believer in facts as ascertainable entities that could reveal truth. He was later to claim that he wrote, " . . . with the love of truth which guides me above all other human considerations, and thus should be written all history which hopes to pass on to posterity."[5] He wrote a number of important historical studies but his great work, the *História geral do Brasil* was first published between 1854 and 1857. This was a national history in the positivist vein, crammed with information, revealing many previously unknown facts, and based on newly discovered sources, many of which he had uncovered himself in European archives. No one before had ever produced such a complete history and none would equal it. This was especially true of the much improved second edition (Vienna, 1877), and of later editions that included Varnhagen's history of Brazilian independence (published posthumously), and even more so after Abreu edited Varnhagen's work with many notes, additions, and corrections.

The *História geral do Brasil* was a magnificent accomplishment and for it Varnhagen sought recognition from the monarchy almost as tirelessly as he had carried out his research. He became something of a sycophant at the Brazilian court. At one point he wrote to Dom Pedro II, "I fell on my knees, giving thanks to God . . . for having inspired in me an idea of such great service to the nation and to other nations. . ."[6] Such appeals finally secured for him the title of baron and then later (in 1874), Viscount of Pôrto Seguro in recognition of his great achievement. The title of Pôrto Seguro was chosen because it was the place of the first European landfall on the Brazilian coast.

A treasure trove of information, Varnhagen's history was neither innovative in the way in which he divided the history of Brazil into periods, nor in his ability to synthesize that history into a cogent story. He did not write the kind of sprightly, popular, and colorful history that Martius had called for, but his political sentiments and proclivities would have pleased the old naturalist. Varnhagen, both because of his dependence on the monarch Dom Pedro II for patronage and because of his naturally conservative and centralist disposition, wrote a history with no sympathy for republicanism or democracy in which he saw, like Martius, the seeds of despotism. His treatment of the early elite movements for independence like that of Minas Gerais in 1788 or of Pernambuco in 1817 at first received slight and unsympathetic notice while those of the lower class were either completely ignored or condemned.[7] He altered this attitude somewhat in the second edition.

Although sometimes thought of as an archconservative, such an evaluation of Varnhagen is not entirely fair. Varnhagen wrote against the slave trade and slavery as early as 1850, and while he shared the belief of many contemporaries that the hope for Brazil's future lay in European immigration and the "whitening" of Brazil, he did recognize the contributions of Africans to Brazilian history and culture and argued for the improvement of their social condition, although he believed that they would always remain dependent. He had certain populist pretensions. He signed the second edition of the *História geral* as a "son of the people (*filho do povo)*" and at one point, he advocated the creation of "a true *people*, free and independent, instead of classes of rich and poor, plebeian and patrician, slaves and masters. . . ."[8] Still, his was basically an upper-class vision of Brazil, one in which history was made from the top down by great men and leaders.

Above all else, Varnhagen was moved by a vision of Brazil based on its unity and progress, and any elements in the nation's history that seemed to threaten these ends received his condemnation. Thus he wrote a history that defended what he considered to be "civilization:" the Europeans, the Portuguese colonial system, monarchy, law and order, and especially, the Bragança royal family in which he saw the key to the continuity of Brazilian unity. He had no patience for regionalism or separatism, which he saw as the bitter fruits of republicanism, and he was particularly negative toward what he called "*caboclo* Brazilianism," the attempt to make the Indian the symbol of Brazilian identity. The Indians, he argued, "can in no way be taken as our guides in the present or past in sentiments of patriotism or in representation of our nationality."[9] Such attitudes led him into acrimonious debates with Brazilian Indianophiles just as his negative assessments of early republican movements also earned him the criticism of more radical nationalists who saw his attachment to Portuguese culture and the monarchy as retrograde beliefs.

Throughout his life, Varnhagen remained a conservative nationalist, or a patriot, as he would have it. In 1874 he published an important book on the Dutch occupation of Brazil (1630–54). He had begun the book in order to stimulate the patriotism and morale of his countrymen who at that time were engaged in a long and bitter war against neighboring Paraguay (1865–70). His historical judgments in the *História geral* were often made in relation to his sense of patriotism and his preoccupation with Brazilian unity, a unity that, whatever its failings, had been created by Portuguese government, culture, and colonialism. His history was the intellectual side of nineteenth-century nation-building, and it left little room for deviance or opposition, for voices from below, or for groups that refused to ride the tide of the mainstream. In terms of its method, its content, and its detail, the *História geral* became the baseline of Brazilian historiography for the rest of the century, but as the political and social context of Brazil began to change and as the context of monarchy and slavery were increasingly questioned, dissident voices were raised on how the nation's past should be considered.

On Varnhagen's death in 1877, João Capistrano de Abreu, a young man recently arrived in Rio de Janeiro from the provinces and already beginning to make a mark as a historian, was asked to write an evaluation of the scholar's life and work.[10] Abreu was a different kind of man and historian. Born in 1853 into a large family on a rural estate or *fazenda* near the cattle market town of Maranguape in the northeastern province of Ceará, his upbringing was rustic, among the cattle, the sugar mills, and the slaves. In his later years he could still recite the rhymes he learned in childhood from the slaves on the estate where he grew up.[11] Educated in provincial schools, a quick but irreverent student, his passion for reading soon became apparent. He continued his schooling in Recife in neighboring Pernambuco province in a more cosmopolitan atmosphere and then returned to Ceará where he spent much of his time involved in local intellectual life and writing for local periodicals.

It was also a time of incessant reading—philosophy, literature, history, and natural history—in English, French, and Portuguese (he later learned German, Dutch, Swedish, Latin, and Italian). Like many of his generation, he became an admirer of the social Darwinism of Herbert Spencer (1820–1903), finding in Spencer's biological analogies a way of explaining Brazilian society.[12] The metaphor of Brazilian society as a developing organism becoming more complex as it matured stayed with Abreu for most of his life. Like Spencer, he was a strong believer in "progress," but he was not greatly influenced by the evolutionary racial concepts of Spencerian thought. The Positivism of the French philosopher Auguste Comte (1798–1857) also attracted his interest in the 1880s. Its emphasis on the application of "scientific" principles to social development and on education caught his fancy. He was very friendly with some of the leading Positivists of his day, such as Miguel Lemos, but he eventually rejected Positivism as an intellectual "strait-jacket" when his own experience and judgments led him away from its deterministic theories. Above all, Abreu became a great admirer of German scholarship on natural history, economics, and society. The German school of human geography and natural science, especially as it related to Brazil, influenced Abreu for most of his life. He read books like J. E. Wappoeus's study of the physical geography of Brazil and A. W. Sellin's general geography of Brazil with admiration and translated some of their most important works into Portuguese.[13] Their influence on his conception of history and human society was deep and he always placed great attention on the geographical setting and environment and its impact on human action.[14]

The historians who most influenced Abreu at first were men like the Frenchman Hippolyte Taine (1828–1892), and the Englishman Henry Thomas Buckle (1821–1862). They were the leading exponents of Comtian Positivism as applied to historical studies and both sought to apply "scientific" principles to history.[15] But by 1900 Abreu was far less interested in "laws" of history and far more attracted to the critical methods of Leopold von Ranke and German historical scholarship: the discovery, internal criticism, and interpretation of historical texts as a way of setting history on firm ground. This became his historical passion, but he continued to read incessantly, always seeking to find an interpretative framework for the new information his critical scholarship revealed.

He consumed books. We know he liked to read in a hammock. He later reported that his great accomplishment in Rio de Janeiro had been to learn German well enough that he didn't have to get out of the hammock to look up words in a dictionary. He admitted toward the end of his life that he would be content to be buried in a hammock, like the poor folks of Ceará. One author believes that the hammock explains why Abreu read so much and wrote relatively little.[16]

In 1875, this erudite and enormously well-read twenty-two-year-old provincial had left Ceará for Rio de Janeiro, his voyage apparently paid for by the sale of a slave who had been willed to him by his grandfather.[17] He fell in love with Rio de Janeiro almost immediately. He called it on first sight, "the fatherland of the sun (*pátria do sol*)."[18] He lived there the rest of his life, traveling widely in Brazil, but never leaving the country. He thus watched the enormous changes in Brazil, lifting his eyes from his beloved historical documents and texts to witness from the vantage point of the capital the abolitionist movement, the end of slavery, the fall of the monarchy, a military coup, the establishment of a republic, and various political crises. His last trip to Ceará was in 1884 when he attended the celebrations of the province's abolition of slavery. But he never forgot his provincial identity and roots. He treasured friendships from his boyhood and his northeastern upbringing. In his extensive correspondence with the Portuguese historian João Lúcio de Azevedo, he always called him *xarapim*, the Ceará term for someone with the same name. He once wrote in the midst of Rio's heat, that as a *cearense* he could not complain.[19] He had a strong sense of his origins and he valued them. He envisioned a Brazilian unity but always recognized its regional variations and he celebrated his own distinctive background.

Employed first as a journalist and tutor, he secured a position in the National Library in 1879 and then as a professor at the elite Colégio Dom Pedro II where he taught from 1883 to 1898. He tutored students privately and married one, a daughter of an admiral, in 1881. Throughout much of his life he supported himself as a journalist, translator, and editor in the fields of his interest: literary criticism, history, geography, ethnography, and the natural sciences. He became a well-known and respected figure in the intellectual world of turn-of-the-century Rio de Janeiro.

When Abreu was asked to write that evaluation of Varnhagen's works on the occasion of his death, the essay he produced, rather than a typical laudatory necrology, was a balanced and critical evaluation. It recognized Varnhagen's great contributions, the fact that he had done his work without the aid of able generations of predecessors, his contribution in finding and using a wealth of new sources, and his dedication to establishing a factual basis for the Brazilian past; but he also chided the deceased Varnhagen for his lack of literary style, his jealousy and begrudging attitude toward contemporary historians, his colorless presentation, and his inability to synthesize or periodize the flow of the past. While doing this Abreu suggested his own vision of Brazilian history and the topics that lay unstudied: the expeditions that opened the interior and histories of the roads of Brazil, the municipalities, elite dynasties (such as the Casa da Torre of Bahia), the gold mines, cattle, and the Jesuits. He saw that archaeology, geography, linguistics, and anthropology were needed to make their contribution to historical studies. Varnhagen would remain the guide, said Abreu, only until a new generation changed the basis on which that history could be written.

Perhaps Abreu's most radical departure from Varnhagen was in terms of periodization. Instead of Varnhagen's plodding governor-after-governor approach and a periodization based on political and military events, Abreu suggested another plan to conceptualize Brazilian history within six periods: The first period, 1500–1614, encompassed the years from European discovery to the time the coast was fully under Portuguese control. The second phase, from 1614 to 1700, included the years of occupation of the interior, using the rivers as the routes of penetration. The third period, from 1700 to 1750, took in the years dominated by the discovery of mines and the settlement of Minas Gerais and the Brazilian west. The years 1750–1808, the fourth period, witnessed the consolidation of the colonial regime; and after the arrival of the Portuguese court in Brazil in 1808, the fifth phase began, the time of colonial "decomposition," which lasted until 1850. The sixth period, from 1850 to his own day, Abreu saw as the age of the empire, a period of political centralism and industrial development.[20] Here was a way of thinking about the Brazilian past in which economy, settlement, and occupation of the national territory weighed as heavily as Varnhagen's view of administration and politics.

But if Abreu had ideas about how to write the great general history of Brazil and dreamed about doing so, his life during the next 30 years was filled with other activities. Like his predecessor Varnhagen, he became fascinated with the discovery and publication of long lost sources of Brazilian history. He believed that the knowledge of the Brazilian past was incomplete and unstable. It was, in fact, like "a house built on sand" and, until its walls could be supported by a fuller record of the past, generalizations and syntheses were impossible. His correspondence with friends in Portugal is filled with petitions for copies of archival materials and inquiries that could help him identify authors or the provenance of manuscripts. He published many documents in short articles in ephemeral publications, such as the *Gazeta literária*, but any historian working on colonial Brazil today would recognize that some of the most important and extensive texts now considered indispensable were discovered, attributed, or edited by Abreu. A few important examples should suffice: Fernão Cardim's *Do princípio e origem dos índios do Brasil* and his "Do clima do Brasil e de algumas cousas notáveis;" José de Anchieta's "Informações do Brasil e suas capitanias;" Ambrósio Fernandes Brandão's *Diálogos das grandezas do Brasil;* João Antônio Antonil's *Cultura e opulência do Brasil;* and the records of the first Inquisition visit to Brazil, the *Primeira visitação.* Perhaps most important was his 1887 publication with extensive notes and long model introductions of the long-forgotten first history of Brazil (1627) by Frei Vicente do Salvador. It is hard to conceive what Brazilian colonial history would look like today without Abreu's discoveries and contributions.

But with all his fascination for historical documents, Abreu was no pedant. His correspondence is filled with observations and judgments about contemporary politicians, events of the day, social customs, and even the regional variations of sexual slang. A bit near-sighted, a late-riser, a chain-smoker, enormously erudite but with a taste for a naughty story, he avoided using honorific titles, disliked giving or hearing lectures, and sought no membership in academies or institutes with the exception of the Instituto Histórico e Geográfico Brasileiro in which he became a member in 1887. He was humble, sometimes signing his letters "João Ninguem (John Nobody)" and threatening his friends late in life that he would refuse to participate in any formality honoring his work. A bit lazy, he treasured the beach, a swim in the ocean, and the hammock. José Honório Rodrigues, a historian and Abreu's most knowledgeable biographer and in some ways his intellectual successor, said Abreu loved "knowledge, his children, and his friends." A man of simple tastes and pleasures, he celebrated the "delirium" of his discovery of the true authorship of the *Cultura e opulência do Brasil* with a few beers, a good dinner, and a long conversation well into the night. He lived in the midst of Rio's belle epoque and was a well-known figure but he had little to do with the style and cultural fashions of the time.[21] Not really a bohemian, devoted to his family, and rather conventional in many ways, he nevertheless had a bit of the character of a person whom Brazilians today would call a *boa vida*. He knew how to live a good life and was comfortable with his priorities.

Meanwhile, Abreu continued to produce articles and essays on a variety of topics, to translate works, to write introductions to newly revealed documents, and to work and read in the areas of human geography, ethnography, political economy, and linguistics, fields in which he was especially influenced by German scholarship.[22] His insights were sometimes profound. In his introduction to the Inquisition records of Brazil, he characterized the Brazilian family as, "taciturn father, a submissive wife, and terrified children," a phrase that has been often repeated. He gave attention to Brazilian society in a way that no one had done before. Some of the essays broke new ground. A series begun in 1889 later published as *Caminhos antigos e povoamento do Brasil* traced the history of the roads, the settlement of the interior, and the frontiers, themes that in his critique of Varnhagen he had shown were previously neglected. His emphasis on the backlands or *sertão*, its people and the changing history of both altered the way in which Brazilians came to think about their history. It has been suggested that Abreu's essay was to Brazilian historiography what Frederick Jackson Turner's *The Frontier in American History* (1893) was to the study of the United States.[23]

We can tell a great deal about Abreu's developing vision of history and of Brazil from these writings and from the extensive correspondence he maintained.[24] Like Varnhagen, Abreu saw historical study as a way of creating a nation. He realized that Brazilians themselves had to invent Brazil, as the "Dutch had created Holland after God created the world." To do this, Brazil needed to know the reality of its past. Discovering this past was the most important role of the historian, but this invention had to be based on evidence.[25] As he put it: "the questions depend on the present but the answers depend on research, otherwise the historian would become tendencious and without scientific foundation."[26]

A strong sense of nationalism informed his interpretation of the past and his fears for Brazil's present. He read Portugal's historical dependence on England as a cautionary tale that Brazil needed to remember in its relations with the United States. Abreu divided the history of Portugal after it had regained its independence from Spain in 1640 into two periods, the first characterized by gravitation toward England until the

Methuen Treaty of 1703 and the second by which Portugal had "sold its soul for a mess of pottage of colonies and enslaved itself to England." "Next to Ireland," said Abreu, "no nation had been as vilified by England and thus reduced to an absolute passive dependence."[27] He feared that a similar relationship would exist between Brazil and the United States When Brazil was allowed three representatives at the Paris Peace Conference after World War I, Abreu saw this as proof of a growing and dangerous United States patronage. He warned, "I believe as much in the friendship of the United States for Brazil as in that of England for Portugal."[28] As Portugal had become the docks (*cais*) of England, he feared that a Brazilian foreign policy based on alliance with the United States would turn Brazil into the docks or springboard for North American penetration of South America. In this he was an opponent of the "unwritten alliance" between Brazil and the United States that was a cornerstone of the foreign policy forged in the period by the Baron of Rio Branco, Brazil's great diplomat and Foreign Minister, whom Abreu knew well.[29] His respect for German scholarship and culture and his anti-English sentiments and fears led him to hope for a German victory in World War I.

Along with his nationalist sentiments, Abreu held beliefs like other authors of his age about national or ethnic characteristics that we might classify as prescientific racism. He spoke of the "taciturn" Portuguese, of the "melancholy" Indians, and of the good humor, sensuality, and affectionate nature of Africans as though these were inherent features. But race per se was not a major factor in his interpretation of the Brazilian past and he was far less inclined than many of his contemporaries to ascribe negative results to racial origins or to miscegenation. In fact, he believed that when mulattos combined daring with talent and good luck they could reach the highest positions and that the charms of mulatta women had made them the queens of Brazil. Here we see sexual and racial stereotypes that were part of a Brazilian national myth that Abreu both embraced and helped create.

Although sharing some of the ideas of his generation and social class about racial characteristics, Abreu was far from espousing the racism that many of his contemporaries had. This is shown clearly in his refusal to simply denigrate the Jews or to side with the forces of the church in historical interpretations of their role in Portuguese and Brazilian history. Here, too, he shared some of the prejudices of his time and ascribed to the Jews certain inherent characteristics. He could not believe, for example, that Jews had been among the pathfinders who had opened the interior or *sertão* because they were "not that fiber." He once even referred to them as a "foreign element," but he also joked that perhaps the name Abreu came from the word *hebreu* (Hebrew).[30]

Whatever the prejudices of his age, they did not become the basis of his historical judgment. His friend and correspondent, the Portuguese historian João Lúcio de Azevedo, had written extensively about the converted Jews or New Christians, always from a negative viewpoint. When Azevedo defended the Inquisition and sought to lay Portugal's ills on the New Christians, Abreu could not hold back.

> I see the misfortunes of Portugal—not in the New Christians—*vae victis*—but in the angelic Holy Office [of the Inquisition], whose clemency I read celebrated by the person whom I least expected it from, in the English who reduced it to an open state of regifuge, in Camões who atrophied and imprisoned the intelligence of the people, and in an abject, abject noble class.[31]

Race, as he understood it, was not a debilitating element in terms of negative attributes or characteristics that it introduced into the body politic of the nation, but because it divided society and limited the formation of unity. He wrote in the *Chapters of Brazil's Colonial History* of "three irreducible races" with nothing to bring them together and of how the distrust of each other created centrifugal forces that precluded a sense of unity that only joint collaboration against foreign enemies like the Dutch had begun to overcome.

For Abreu, it was not race, but culture and environment or geography that were the keys. We can see this most clearly in his view of the Indians. He had long recognized that the opening of the Brazilian interior had been greatly influenced by the Indians and that both in terms of their contributions and their opposition to European penetration they had been a factor in Brazilian history. In fact, perhaps his most serious scholarly work was a linguistic study of an isolated Indian language that had included many ethnographic observations. It was long considered the best work ever done on a South American Indian language. To write this he had brought two Indian informants to live and work with him in Rio de Janeiro. He had read widely in the history and ethnography of South American Indians and made a major contribution to that literature.[32] But in his conceptualization of an integrated Brazilian nation and people, he saw little participation for the Indian and little in their culture that could contribute to the construction of a modern nation. In the *Chapters*, Abreu's interest in them is limited and he is not above an occasional ironic or disparaging remark: "Some tribes ate their enemies, others their friends and relatives, here was the difference." But he also recognized their sensibility toward nature, their artistic talents, and the fact that their own history had been forgotten or stolen and this was a great loss. As he put it: "Concerning their legends, whose telling could at times keep them awake and attentive all night long, we know very little. One of the missionaries' primary concerns was and is to eradicate and replace native lore." Abreu noted with apparent approval the remarks of the eighteenth-century Benedictine author Loreto Couto who praised the Indians and pointed out that their seemingly savage or barbaric practices were no worse than those of the ancient Portuguese. Ultimately, however, indigenous cultures provided no models for the Brazilian future, although Abreu saw as a positive contribution the integration of the Indian like that of the natural environment into a Brazilian sense of distinctiveness.

Although Abreu was widely known as Brazil's most knowledgeable historian of his time, he continued to work primarily as an editor, annotator, and essayist. His youthful dream of writing a general history remained unfulfilled.

In 1906, the Centro Industrial do Brasil, a trade group, approached him to write a brief overview of Brazilian history for a broad public as part of a project to make Brazil better known in the world. Since 1902, Capistrano de Abreu had been working sporadically on preparing notes and an introduction for a new revised edition of Varnhagen's *História geral* and so he had been thinking deeply about the sweep of Brazilian history. Rather than seeing this new invitation as a chance to write the great history of which he had long dreamed, he saw it as an opportunity but to lay out a broad outline and highlight certain aspects that had been long ignored. Originally designed to include contemporary Brazilian history as well, by January 1907 he had written 300 pages to cover the period up to 1800. The pressures of space and deadlines, and even perhaps, personal inclination caused him to stop writing. The *Chapters of Brazil's Colonial History* were originally published in 1907 as part of a larger work *O Brasil—suas riquezas naturais . (Brazil—Its Natural Resources)* to provide historical background for understanding contemporary Brazil.[33]

A separate edition of *Chapters* appeared later that year. Versions in Italian and French were published soon after but it never appeared in English. In the same year that *Chapters* was published, Abreu suffered a major disappointment. Almost the entire edition of his revision of Varnhagen's *História geral* went up in flames at the printer's offices. Only a few copies of the first part of Volume One, which was already in print, survived. The manuscripts with his extensive notes, revisions, and corrections for the remainder of the work were lost. He could never bring himself to work on it again and turned his notes over to his friend and assistant Rodolfo Garcia. The year 1907 proved to be one of both triumph and tragedy for Abreu.[34]

Chapters of Brazil's Colonial History is Capistrano de Abreu's single integrated attempt to lay out the history of Brazil. Although written by a scholar, it was not written for a scholarly audience. It is a synthesis written for the general public. Abreu did not employ the six-part periodization he had suggested previously in his critique of Varnhagen, but there are traces of its conceptualization and of his favorite themes: the interior, the roads, and the ranching frontier. In Chapter 9, "The Backlands," this material is presented in an imaginative and innovative way. Here we see him at his best, envisioning the great sweep of history but paying attention to the details of daily life, what people ate, how they confronted their environment, how the rivers were crossed, and how the corrals were built. His characterization of the ranching frontier and the backlanders' dependence on their livestock for everything as "the age of leather" reveals his insight and his powers as a historian.

Unlike the histories of Brazil that preceeded it, *Chapters* is not essentially administrative or diplomatic history. Instead, Abreu uses geography, ethnography, and social and economic history to create a fuller image of the Brazilian past. Often Abreu inverts the relative weight given to certain themes, the traditional favorites, devoting far less time to discussing episodes such as the Dutch invasion or the pre-Independence movement of Minas Gerais, while devoting more time than anyone had before to issues like the society of the frontier. *Chapters* marked out new territory. Some of the great themes that subsequent generations of Brazilian historians would take up—miscegenation, racial prejudice, the evils of export agriculture, and social history—are all traced in its pages. Above all, Abreu gave the interior of Brazil, its people and its ways, a central role in the nation's history.

Chapters makes no attempt at thoroughness and surprisingly leaves out important events and participants, but what it does treat it sketches with a rare perception and an ironic and sometimes poorly-disguised pain at the debilitating effects of Brazil's past and the failures of Abreu's countrymen. The Indians with their Stone Age culture and warring divisions could provide no leadership or model; slavery condemned Brazil to "immobility and backwardness"; export monoculture ignored the needs of the country; education was minimal and designed to stamp out any spark of spontaneity, producing intellectual sloth. The Brazilian people, the protagonists of the book, had been, in his much quoted phrase, "castrated and bled, bled and castrated." At the end, "there was no such thing as social life—there was no society." He ends the book on a note of despair. The diverse ethnic groups of five different geographic regions were linked by religion and language and by their dislike of the Portuguese but had little use for each other. "After three centuries, this is how we were."

This pessimism had a deep effect on Brazilian thinking and set the tone for the generations that followed. His student Paulo Prado picked up the theme and made it the central idea of his popular *Retrato do Brasil* (1922), a book filled with condemnation of the past that claimed that Brazil did not develop but "rotted." Similar attitudes can be found in the extremely influential Marxist account of Caio Prado Júnior published in 1942 that placed the blame for Brazil's condition on colonialism and a dependent export economy that produced "incoherence and instability in [its] settlement, poverty and misery in the economy, dissolution in its customs, ineptitude and corruption in its civil and ecclesiastic leaders."[35] This was a critique that echoed Abreu's pessimistic analysis. But Abreu's negative evaluation of the colonial past never undermined his hope for the future: "I love, I admire Brazil. I have hopes for it. The bad Brazilians will pass away, Brazil remains."[36]

Capistrano de Abreu never wrote the great general history of his nation, the work that would build on Varnhagen but surpass him. He is remembered instead for some brilliant essays, for his discovery and edition of long-forgotten but essential historical documents, for his additions and annotations to Varnhagen's *História geral*, and probably most of all for *Chapters*, a work he conceived as "a modest history, with great strokes and long spans" which said some new things and broke the iron framework that Varnhagen had created for thinking about Brazil's past.[37] After his life and work, and that of his predecesor Varnhagen, the house of Brazilian history no longer rested on sand. Its documentary foundation was more secure, its form better defined. Abreu, however, always realized that facts and documents were in themselves not enough. As he liked to say, "working is easy, thinking is difficult."[38]

—*Stuart Schwartz*

NOTES

Abbreviation:

CCA *Correspondência de Capstrano de Abreu*, ed. José Honório Rodrigues, 3 vols.(Rio de Janeiro: Civilização Brasileira, 1977).

1. "How the History of Brazil Should Be Written," in *Perspectives on Brazilian History*, ed. E. Bradford Burns (New York: Columbia University Press, 1967), 21–41.

2. A concise appreciation of Martius is found in José Honório Rodrigues, *Vida e história* (Rio de Janeiro: Civilização Brasileira, 1966), 151–162.

3. See Johann Baptist von Spix and Karl Friedrich Philip von Martius, *Travels in Brazil in the years 1817–1820 undertaken by command of His Majesty the King of Bavaria*, 2 vols. (London: Longmans, 1824). (The original German edition was dated 1823). See also Alice Piffer Canabrava, "Varnhagen, Martius e Capistrano de Abreu," *III Colóquio de estudos teuto-brasileiros* (Pôrto Alegre, 1980), 215–235.

4. An excellent appreciation of Varnhagen's life and work is found in José Honório Rodrigues, "Varnhagen, mestre da história geral do Brasil," in *História e historiografia* (Petrópolis: Vozes, 1970), 123–149.

5. Cited with a fuller discussion in Stuart B. Schwartz, "Francisco Adolfo de Varnhagen, Diplomat, Patriot, and Historian," *Hispanic American Historical Review*, 47, no.2 (May 1967): 185–202.

6. Varnhagen to Dom Pedro II, Madrid, 14 July 1857, in Francisco Adolfo de Varnhagen, *Correspondência ativa*, ed. Cláudio Ribeiro de Lessa (Rio de Janeiro, 1961), 242. He was so sure of his book's benefit to the nation that he paid the cost of the second edition himself to keep the price in reach of his compatriots. See Schwartz, "Francisco Adolfo de Varnhagen," 191.

7. Rodrigues, "Varnhagen," 131–132.

8. Francisco Adolfo de Varnhagen, *O tabaco da Bahia: De que modo se ha de melhorar* (Caracas, 1863), 6.

9. "Discurso preliminar. Os índios perante a nacionalidade brasileira," in Varnhagen, *História geral do Brasil*, 2d ed., vol. 2 (Rio de Janeiro, 1857).

10. Abreu also penned a later version that is available in a fine English translation. See "A Critique of Francisco Adolfo de Varnhagen," in *Perspectives on Brazilian History*, ed. E. Bradford Burns (New York: Columbia University Press, 1967), 142–155. The best outlines of Abreu's life and work available in English are José Honório Rodrigues, Capistrano de Abreu and Brazilian Historiography," in Burns, *Perspectives*, 156–80; and Robert Conrad, "João Capistrano de Abreu, Brazilian Historian," *Revista de historia de América* 59 (1965), 149–164.

11. José Aurélio Saraiva Câmara, *Capistrano de Abreu* (Rio de Janeiro: José Olympio, 1969), 22.

12. On Spencer's influence in Brazil, see Richard Graham, *Britain and the Onset of Modernization in Brazil* (Cambridge: Cambridge University Press, 1968), 232–251.

13. For example, J. E. Wappoeus, *Handbuch der Geographie und Statistik des Kaiserreiches Brasilien* (Leipzig, 1871), translated as *A geografia física no Brasil* (Rio de Janeiro: G. Leuzinger e filhos, 1884).

14. The best study of the various influences on Abreu's thought is Arno Wehling, "Capistrano de Abreu: a fase cientificista," in *A invenção da história* (Niteroi: Editora Central da Universidade Gama Filho and Editora da Universidade Federal Fluminense, 1994), 169–216. See also José Honório Rodrigues, "Capistrano de Abreu e a Alemanha," in *História e historiografia* (Petrópolis: Vozes, 1970), 175–190.

15. James W. Thompson, *A History of Historical Writing*, 2 vols. (New York: Macmillan, 1942), 2, 446–449; On Ranke's influence see, Stephen Bann, *The Clothing of Clio. A study of the representation of History in nineteenth-century Britain and France* (Cambridge: Cambridge University Press, 1984).

16. Saraiva Câmara, *Capistrano*, 142–143.

17. Saraiva Câmara, *Capistrano*, 91.

18. Pedro Gomes de Matos, *Capistrano de Abreu. Vida e obra do grande historiador* (Fortaleza, 1953), 57–60.

19. Abreu to J. L. de Azevedo, 1922, *CCA*, vol. 2, 234.

20. See the discussion in José Honório Rodrigues, *Teoria da história do Brasil*, 2 vols. (São Paulo: Companhia Editora Nacional, 1957), 1, 165–168.

21. Cf. Jeffrey D. Needell, *A Tropical Belle Epoque* (Cambridge: Cambridge University Press, 1987).

22. His most important essays have been published in collections. See *Caminhos antigos e povoamento do Brasil*, 2d ed. (Rio de Janeiro: Livraria Briguiet, 1960); *Ensaios e estudos*, 3 vols. (Rio de Janeiro: Livraria Briguiet, 1931–33).

23. José Honório Rodrigues, "Capistrano de Abreu and Brazilian Historiography," in *Perspectives*, ed. Burns, 157–180.

24. *Correspondência de Capistrano de Abreu*, 3 vols., ed. José Honório Rodrigues (Rio de Janeiro: Civilização Brasileira, 1977); J. A. Pinto do Carmo, *Bibliografia de Capistrano de Abreu* (Rio de Janeiro: Imprensa Nacional, 1943).

25. Rodrigues, "Introdução," in *CCA*, vol. 1, xxxv.

26. Cited in José Honório Rodrigues, *Teoria da história do Brasil*, 2 vols. (Rio de Janeiro: Companhia Editora Nacional, 1957), 1, 15.

27. Abreu to João Lúcio de Azevedo, letter, 2 June 1925, *CCA*, vol. 2, 331–332.

28. Abreu to Domício da Gama, letter, 3 June 1918, *CCA*, vol. 1, CA , 264; Abreu to João Lúcio de Azevedo, letter, 1925, *CCA*, vol. 2, 335.

29. See E. Bradford Burns, *The Unwritten Alliance. Rio Branco and Brazilian-American Relations* (New York: Columbia University Press, 1966).

30. *CCA*, vol. 2, 252.

31. Abreu to João Lucio de Azevedo, letter, 2 June 1925, *CCA*, vol. 2, 331–332.

32. João Capistrano de Abreu, *Ra-txa hu-ni-ku. A língua dos caxinauás do Rio Ibuau, afluente do Muru* (Rio de Janeiro: Prefeitura de Tarauaçu, 1914). On the appreciation of this work see the comments in Canabrava, "Varnhagen, Martius, and Capistrano de Abreu," 225.

33. The work appeared as *Breves traços da história do Brasil colônia, império, e república*, in *O Brasil. Suas riquezas naturais*, vol. 1: *Introdução. Indústria extrativa* (Rio de Janeiro: M. Orosco & Co., 1907), 1–216, and later in the same year as a separately published book, *Capítulos de história colonial.* The edition used for this translation was João Capistrano de Abreu, *Capítulos de história colonial e os caminhos antigos e o povoamento do Brasil*, ed. José Honório Rodrigues (Brasília: Editora da Universidade de Brasília, 1982).

34. A good discussion of the publication history of *Chapters* is provided in Hélio Vianna, *Capistrano de Abreu. Ensaio biobibliográfico* (Rio de Janeiro: Ministério de Educação e Cultura, 1955), 55–59.

35. Caio Prado Júnior, *The Colonial Background of Modern Brazil*, trans. Suzette Macedo (Berkeley: University of California, 1967), 414.

36. Abreu to Urbano de Oliveira, 9 July 1895, *CCA*, vol. 1, 63.

37. Abreu to the Baron of Rio Branco, 1890, *CCA*, vol. 1, 130. See also, Conrad, "Capistrano," 152.

38. *CCA*, vol. 3, 419.

CHAPTERS OF BRAZIL'S COLONIAL HISTORY

1500–1800

1

Indigenous Antecedents

Almost all of Brazil lies in the Southern Hemisphere. Its greatest mass can be found between the equator and the tropic of Capricorn.

It is surrounded on the south, southwest, west, and northwest by the continent's Spanish-speaking nations—except for Chile and Panama, which are bordered Bolivia and by Colombia respectively. Future negotiations will determine whether or not Brazil is to share a border with Ecuador. From the headwaters of the Rio Branco to the coastline, one finds British, Dutch, and French colonies bordering Brazil.

Along its nearly 8.000 kilometers of eastern coastline, Brazil is bathed by the Atlantic Ocean. Cape Orange, which forms Brazil's border with French Guiana, is 37 degrees north of the Chuí River, which marks our border with Uruguay. A glance at a map demonstrates the insignificance of the maritime periphery. Just as it does along the coasts of Africa and Australia, the sea does not encroach on the land of Brazil, nor does the land invade the sea. There are no inland seas and no peninsulas, gulfs, or islands of any size or importance. Sea and land exist side by side without transition or penetration. On their own, Brazilians can do no more than venture out to sea on fishing rafts.

The sea coast stretches out in two main directions. It runs northwest to southeast from Pará to Pernambuco, and northeast to southwest from Pernambuco to the far south.

The northwest-southeast coastline is low, almost straight, and broken by dunes and sheets of sand. North of the Amazon River it is low, muddy, and irregular—all the way to the Oiapoque River. Shoreline and river sediments make the coast seem static. Ports are rare. Ports (*barras*) on rivers are real but precarious inlets. Economic development or administrative exigencies rather than the lay of the land have restricted large-scale shipping to the ports of Belém, São Luís, Amarração, Fortaleza, Natal, Paraíba, and Recife. The other ports are only open to small, coastal trading vessels. The port of Tutóia allows ocean-going ships to enter the Parnaíba River.

From Pernambuco to Santa Catarina, the southeast coastline is bordered by the mountain range known as the Serra do Mar. It is extremely varied. At times the coast consists of sandy expanses, red barrier reefs, woody hillsides, or mountains that contend directly with the ocean's waves. On this coastline Brazil's major bays are found: All Saints Bay, Camamu, Rio de Janeiro, Angra dos Reis, Paranaguá. Ocean-going vessels come to port at all the capitals of coastal states, save Sergipe's and Paraná's. They also dock at Santos, Paranaguá, and São Francisco do Sul. Along this section of the coast, one also finds the majority of Brazil's islands, as well as its largest ones. Originally they were all part of the mainland.

Beginning at Santa Catarina, the coastal mountains disappear once more. Rio Grande do Sul's coastline is dominated by lagoons whose extensive internal shores will only prosper once our skill permits us to surpass nature and open passages to the ocean.

The islands of volcanic origin—Fernão de Noronha (due east of Rio Grande do Norte) and Trindade (due east of Espírito Santo), are of little importance today. Trindade seems unfit for permanent habitation. England recently wanted it because it was useful for mooring transatlantic cables.

The coastal band is of variable width. In general, it is widest between the states of Pernambuco and Pará, and in Rio Grande do Sul. In the remainder of the country, its width is subject to the whims of the Serra do Mar. We call this section the harmonious coast or *costas concordantes.*

In the north the coast joins the Amazon lowlands, which are quite extensive at the river's outlet, relatively narrow between Xingu and Nhamunda, and extremely wide west of the Madeira and Negro Rivers and all the way to the base of the Andes. The northernmost waterfalls of the Tocantins, Xingu, Tapajós, and Madeira Rivers form the outer limits of the southern Amazon lowlands. In the north, east of the Rio Negro, a few dozen kilometers from its mouth, one approaches the falls area of the rivers flowing south from the Guianas. From east to west the descent is not noticeable. The São Francisco River drops a greater distance at the Paulo Afonso falls than the Amazon does in the 3000 kilometers between Tabatinga and the sea.

The coastal lowlands are further linked to the south by the Paraguayan lowlands, which begin at the River Plate estuary and continue northward into Mato Grosso. The city of Cuiabá, at the very center of the continent, may be slightly higher than 200 meters above sea level. The banks of the main river are quite high in the southern parts, but become progressively lower as one proceeds northward into a region that on a yearly basis is extensively flooded. This area is what the early explorers called Lake Xarais. There are also abundant riverside lakes known locally as *baias* or "bays." Brazil's border with Bolivia passes through a string of these bays.

The Amazon and Paraguayan lowlands are contiguous with ocean lowlands and approach one another in the west. Very few kilometers of dry land lie between the Aguapeí River (which flows into the Jauru, itself a tributary of the Paraguay River) and the Rio Alegre (flowing into the Guaporé, one of the rivers making up the Rio Negro). The Portuguese government considered cutting a canal through this portage and linking the Amazon and the Plate. From the Amazon travelers could follow the Casiquiare River to the Orinoco all the way to the Island of Trinidad and the Caribbean Sea.

Scarcely had the work begun when it was halted. The project seems totally unfeasible because an interceding strip of highlands extends all the way to Chiquitos, Bolivia. The difference in altitudes between the two lowlands does not favor the building of a canal.

The Amazon and Paraguayan basins with their myriad of rivers, their numerous islands, their large lakes, and their countless channels make up for Brazil's scantly developed sea coast—to a certain extent. They are, in fact, Brazil's inland seas. The Paraguayan depression joined with that of the high Amazon River separate the Andes Mountains from the Brazilian highlands, which are also separated from the Guiana tableland by the Amazon lowlands. The coastal lowlands lie east of Brazil's plateau. After the Jauru River, the Paraguay River receives no tributaries worthy of mention from Brazilian territory on the right.

North of the Uruguay River the Brazilian plateau is bordered on the east by the Serra do Mar. The Serra is rugged and wooded on the coastal side but softer on the inland slopes. Its width is varied, between 20 and 80 kilometers, and its peaks are rarely higher than 2000 meters. It divides the rivers into those that flow directly into the Atlantic and those that eventually flow into the Plate. The former are generally quite short. The Iguape and the Paraíba are the only ones that cut through the range. The rest run along the coast or down the mountains. The rivers emptying into the Plate are of much greater length and importance. The Uruguay River flows through Brazilian territory up to Peperiguaçu, on the Argentine border. Argentina borders Brazil along the Uruguay River from Peperiguaçu to the Quaraim River, which forms the northern border of Uruguay. The Iguaçu river also flows westward. Where its left bank forms the border with Argentina, it has mavelously beautiful falls and rapids. The Ivaí enters the Paraná above the Guaíra Falls or Sete Quedas area. The other important eastern tributaries of the Paraná River include the Paranapanema and the historically important Tietê.

The Mantiqueira Mountain Range [*Serra da Mantiqueira*] emerges from the northern part of the Serra do Mar. The Mantiqueira runs inland from the state of Paraná to Minas Gerais. This mountain range contains Brazil's highest peak, Itatiaia, which is nearly 3,000 meters in height. Then comes the Serra do Espinhaço, which borders the São Francisco on its right, up to the point where the river curves toward the northeast before plunging to the sea. Both ranges produce unremarkable watersheds: the Mantiqueira, between the Paraíba do Sul River and the upper Paraná; and the Espinhaço, between the São Francisco River and those on the eastern side: the Doce, Jequetinhonha, Pardo, Contas, and Paraguaçu— all of which empty into the ocean. The Serra do Espinhaço narrows the São Francisco river basin on the eastern side, just after forming the Rio das Velhas. These ranges separate the former rivers from those on the eastern side.

From the highlands around Barbacena begins an east-west transversal ridge that is known by several names and that has some truly mountainous areas, as well as other parts that are bereft of vegetation. This is the plateau's major watershed. The illustrious Eschwege[1] called it the Vertentes [spilling] Range, which is an excellent coinage, if one pays no mind to the formation's structure but considers the part it plays in Latin America. On one side the waters run toward the Paraná and Paraguay rivers, both of which begin in this area and, like the Uruguay, flow into foreign lands. On the other side of the ridge, flow the Madeira's tributaries. The Madeira has been the object of protracted arguments ever since Manuel Félix de Lima traveled it from the mines in Mato Grosso to its mouth. These tributaries include the Tapajós River, which people from Cuiabá (in Mato Grosso) traveled to buy guaraná [a tropical fruit] from the Maué Indians and the Xingu River, whose poor navigability detoured exploration for many years and, until recently, left numerous indigenous tribes living in the Stone Age. These people, nonetheless, provided powerful motivation for study by South American ethnographers. Other rivers fanning out from this ridge include the Araguaia-Tocantins, the Parnaíba, and the São Francisco.

The São Francisco River is of great historical importance. It begins in the Serra da Canastra in Minas Gerais and is joined at Pirapora by the Rio das Velhas. In its upper reaches, its most important tributaries can be found between its two headwaters, which eventually join one another. Beyond the waterfall at Pirapora, the Tocantins watershed becomes more and more distant, which allows the Paracatu, the Urucuia, the Carinhanha, the Corrente, and the Grande to develop. On the right hand side of the São Francisco, however, the Serra do Espinhaço encroaches. Beyond Barra, where the Grande joins the São Francisco, this river has no more tributaries worthy of note. Navigation becomes more and more difficult, to the point where a series of waterfalls causes river traffic to stop and goods to be transported overland by rail.

The São Francisco is, in a manner of speaking, similar to all Brazilian rivers. On the plateau, once the amount of water makes it possible, it is navigable by vessels of greater or lesser size, often for hundreds of leagues on end. Then, down a series of falls and rapids, it leaves the plateau—just like the treacherous parts of the Rio Madeira, the Augusto [area falls?] on the Tapajós, the Itaboca area on the Tocantins, the Paulo Afonso Falls on the São Francisco, and so many others. After this, the waters grow calm and deep. The rivers become navigable once more, as long as they have sufficient current to prevent the formation of sand bars in the ports.

The Amazon and its tributaries are totally different. The former's stormy region ends in its headwaters, well before entering Brazil. Its tributaries situated west of the rivers Madeira and Negro, in the area known as Solimões, all originate in relatively low-lying regions and then, almost level, they disperse in the great lowland area. The same situation prevails along the Paraguay River and its tributaries, but on a smaller scale. The Parnaíba River and those rivers in the State of Maranhão flow smoothly down a graded slope all the way to the sea. They are a type midway between the rivers of the high tableland and those of the great lowlands.

The mountains prepare and the rivers carve four distinct regions out of the Brazilian plateau: the Amazon lowlands between the Guaporé and Tocantins Rivers; the Parnaíba plain between the Amazon area and the São Francisco plain, which is more extensive and attains its greatest length along the left edge of this basin. Finally there is the Paraná-

Uruguay plateau between the Serra do Mar and the Guaiás Mountains. The disposition of these flatlands has affected their settlement.

The Guiana plateau is another high tableland, with some granite peaks, but few are higher than 1,000 meters.

In the west there are a few tributaries of the Amazon, and they begin outside Brazil. The Içá, Japurá, and Negro Rivers flow parallel to the Amazon in their lower stretches. Some very short and scarcely navigable rivers coming south from the Guiana highlands flow into the Amazon east of Manaus.

The Amazon River drains a basin with an area of seven million square kilometers. It is the biggest river system in the world, and approximately the same size as Brazil itself. Huge sections of the Brazilian, Andean, and Guianese plateau send it water. And, because the rainy season does not occur at the same time in all these regions, when the tributaries from one area begin to narrow, those from another start to swell. So the draining never ends. At times the Amazon (half river, half sea) gets so big it stops its tributaries' flow and breaks through land to send water into the tributaries above the point where they normally reach the Amazon. The lakes along the Amazon's banks, the many islands, the seasonal channels, and offshoots [*paranamirins*] have permitted vessels to sail from the ocean to the far reaches of the country's backlands without ever entering the Amazon channel itself. The river can rise twenty meters when it floods. At that time, vessels can pass over forests whose tree tops, only a few weeks earlier, could not be seen from the boats' decks. The Amazon flows from west to east along the equator, and its climate may be described as similar all along this genuinely tropical stretch. There is little variety in temperature and humidity. The abundant rainfall is greatest along the coast and in the Andes. Winter and summer are distinguished by greater or lesser amounts of rain. Temperature, that is, a slight cooling at night, is the Amazon winter's most prevalent characteristic.

South of the Amazon, between the Parnaíba and the São Francisco Rivers, lies a region that regularly suffers from droughts. When the seasons are normal, it has light showers that the inhabitants call "cashews." These occur as the sun goes southward. More abundant rains fall around the March equinox, and no rain falls after winter solstice (June 21 in Brazil). When this pattern does not obtain, except at a few springs or in extremely deep areas, the rivers run dry. Pastures wither. Trees fail to sprout leaves. Cattle die from thirst or exhaustion. And people die of hunger, if they have to rely only on local resources. To survive such calamities, people have built reservoirs; they have cultivated areas along rivers and reservoirs; they have brought their cattle together and fed them leafy twigs; and they have emigrated en masse.

Along the coast between the Oiapoque and the Parnaíba Rivers, as well as between the São Francisco River and the southern state of Santa Catarina, the climate is predominantly tropical. In some areas it rains almost year round. In other areas there are dry spells, which, in the main, are governed by the sun's movement.

Distance from the equator increases differences in temperature, and great differences may occur in parts of the country that are close to one another. Around the June solstice, temperatures plunge and precipitation tapers off.

In Rio Grande do Sul, the hot and cold seasons are well defined, variations in temperature are more noticeable, and the rainy season tends to coincide with low temperatures.

What has been said is valid for the coastline. Beyond the coast, a tropical climate continues to prevail, but it is modified, more or less, by local conditions, and it can assume a sort of inland or continental mode. As a rule it rains less in the backlands than it does on the coast. The dry and rainy seasons are more clearly separated from one another. The plateau air is easily heated during the day owing to its thinness, and it cools off quickly at night for the same reason. There can be drastic temperature differences in the course of a single day.

In this area rains are also governed by the sun. In several places there are minor rains before the December solstice, followed by major rains in the coming months.

In the Amazon lowlands heat and humidity go hand in hand. Plant life thrives, and the great earthly forest exults.

The struggle for light and air impels plants upward. Tree tops vie with one another on high. Powerful trees from other regions become climbing vines. Swinging vines get tangled with one another. Social plants, such as the imbaúba and the monguba, are exceptions. As a rule, on any given surface, the greatest possible number of different plant species intermingle.

Distance from the ocean has very little to do with local plant life. The nearness of a river is much more important. On the *caa-igapós*, an Indian term for land subject to yearly floods, grow numerous palm trees, many of which are thorny. At the same time in these areas, tree sizes diminish. In the *caa-eté*, which is higher ground, giant plants and triumphant dicotyledons and other types of plants grow. Beyond this area xerophytic (dry land) plants prevail.

The drought-ridden region also has forests, albeit isolated ones located on mountain ranges, capable of condensing water vapor from the atmosphere. There are also forests along rivers and in places favored by the presence of ground water. These forests are small, but are otherwise similar to those of more fortunate regions. They are not, however, particularly abundant.

Beginning in the state of Bahia, a continuous virgin forest occupies the eastern side of the Serra do Mar. In this forest, tree trunks are straight, with high branches and green leaves year round. Many different parasitical species (*espífitos*) grow in a single area. The varied topography produces a striking variety in the landscape and stands in direct contrast with the unending monotony of the Amazon Basin.

Beyond the Serra do Mar fields are open, and vast areas are covered with grassy plants and scrub vegetation.

Altitude permitting, Paraná pines appear. From time to time, one finds clumps of trees. The native word for these clumps also denotes a circular form. Some students of ecology use the low temperatures during sprouting time to explain the treeless southern fields. In the north, similarly, there are treeless fields whose treelessness seems to be explained by their hot, dry soil, that burns the seeds of trees and saps their vitality.

Words like *caatinga*, *carrasco*, *cerrado*, and *agreste* are used to indicate the water-seeking scrub vegetation often characterized by their deep roots whose bulbs retain water. These plants have rough, craggy, exiguous, branching trunks that seem to grow sideways rather than vertically. Their leaves are on the small side and fall off during the dry season to help the plant survive the drought by minimizing its loss of water.

In the arid regions of Brazil, this type of vegetation almost reaches the seashore. Almost all the states evince some effects of the continental climate. The Brazilian people began to settle in the eastern part of the territory. They concentrated in the *zona da mata*, i.e. the coastal forests, which provided Brazil wood, lumber, fields for planting sugar cane, tobacco, and finally coffee. The Amazon forest also provided clove, cacao, sarsaparilla, Brazil nuts, and, most important, rubber. The fields of the south produce *maté*. On the northern fields with their scrub vegetation, one grazes cattle or plants cereals or cotton. Pieces of land known as *capoeiras* are the results of human intervention. They have been cleared of their original vegetation and have been taken over by alien, opportunistic plants, whose appearance has yet to become well defined. Bigger capoeiras [*capoeirões*] can appear to be real forests.

Brazil is rich in insects, reptiles, birds, fish, and small quadrupeds.

Typical species are its rheas, parrots, hummingbirds, edentates [such mammals as armadillos and anteaters], marsupials, and platyrrhinian monkeys.

On the coastal lowlands there are many mollusks, fish, and birds common to all the south Atlantic. Many have colors so much like the color of sand that it is hard to see them unless they move.

The forest fauna, on the other hand, especially butterflies and birds, display remarkable color schemes. In addition, the butterflies can be enormous. Most of these animals are arboreal, and some, like the ancient sloth, are becoming extinct as the forests are felled.

Goeldi[2] reminds us that:

> the backland fauna are more pale in color and more scanty in number. A showy dress uniform in the open fields would not be desirable or adaptive. For the backland animals their monotonous off-white garb is advantageous because, with the grass as a background, their color is halfway between the color of the soil and that of the sun-drenched scrub.
>
> On the one hand, along the coast long wings for protracted flights are useful appendages. In the forests feet for climbing are helpful. On the other hand, long legs capable of responding to great demands are precious attributes for animals who run on the ground. For proof just look at the regal Sariema [a bird of the backlands] and the gigantic rhea. Even the Brazilian wolf has long, almost greyhound-like legs, in addition to its large ears similar to those of a desert jackal.[3]

Among all these animals not one seemed worthy of participating in native society. They provided no milk, clothing, or transportation. Natives domesticated a few species, usually birds and of them mainly parrots, which they kept as pets. They were called *mimbabas* in the coastal language [*língua geral*]. Natives fished and hunted for food. They had an incipient form of agriculture—planting manioc, corn, and different types of fruit. Because they had no metal, fire (produced by friction) performed most of the tasks for which iron is used. Planting, harvesting, cooking, pottery-making, and brewing were all women's work. Men engaged themselves in clearing land, fishing, hunting, and warfare.

There were constant wars. Captive women joined victorious tribes. There was a widespread notion that women were neutral as far as procreation was concerned, just as the land was neutral in the growing process. In many tribes men were eaten during ritual celebrations. Cannibalism was not disdained and seems to have been the rule: some tribes ate their enemies, others ate their friends and relatives. That is the main difference.

Natives lived in small communities. It was hardly difficult to sink a few posts and thatch a roof, or to transport a few gourds and utensils. So they were constantly on the move owing to the scarcity of animals needed for food.

From minuscule disagreements arose definitive separations. Tribes were constantly splitting. A common explanation for great migrations could be a dispute over a parrot.

Native chiefs possessed power in name only. Spiritual power was stronger. People believed in luminous beings, good and inert, who did not require worship. They also believed in evil, shady, vindictive powers. The souls of their ancestors demanded offerings to ward off their wrath and curry their favor and protection. One source of power was the shaman, known as the *pajé* or *caraíba*. He was lord of life and death and had risen after dying, to perish nevermore.

Natives' senses were sharper; their ability to perceive nature's signs was beyond civilized man's conceptions. They were not short on artistic talent, which they revealed in their ceramics, their weaving, their painted gourds, masks, body decorations, dances, and songs.

Concerning their legends, whose telling could at times keep them awake and attentive all night long, we know very little. One of the missionaries' primary concerns was and is to eradicate and replace native lore.

They spoke several different but related languages. Both verbs and nouns had past and future forms. Intransitive verbs doubled as nouns. A transitive verb demanded two pronouns, an agent and a patient. The first person plural forms at times could be inflected for exclusivity or inclusivity. In ordinary speech parataxis was the rule. The abundance and flexibility of supine forms aided the translation of certain European ideas.

Based on linguistic evidence, modern ethnographers have succeeded in grouping certain more or less intimately related tribes. The first group consists of those who spoke the coastal language, known as the *língua geral* (general language) because of its distribution. This was the largest native group living along the coast. They came from the backlands in three distinct migrations. The Carijós or Guaranis were located in Cananéia and Paranapanema and to the south and west of that area. The Tupiniquins settled along the Tietê River, the Jequitinhonha River, the Ibiapaba mountain range, and on the coast and backlands of Bahia. The Tupinambás settled around the area of present-day Rio de Janeiro. They also settled along the lower banks of the São Francisco River, in Rio Grande do Norte, as well as in Maranhão and Pará. The point of origin for these three groups is the area between the Paraguay and Paraná Rivers.

The other groups spoke related languages. They include the Gés, represented by the Aimorés or Botocudos, living close to the sea and still numerous in the interior today. The Cariris lived throughout the backlands, from the Paraguaçu to the Itapecuru and even to the Mearim River. The Tremembés lived on the beaches of Ceará. The Caraíbas, whose easternmost representatives are the Pimenteiras of Piauí, can still be found on the tablelands and in the Amazon basin. The Maipures or Nu-Aruaques, who originated in Guiana and migrated as far as the Paraguay River, still live in the area near their ancient homeland and in the upper reaches of the Purus. There were also the Panos and the Cuaicurus, as well as other tribes.

If we leave out the Amazon region, where there were many Maipures and not a few Caraíbas, we are left with only the Tupis and the Cariris as tribes that were incorporated into Brazil's present-day population.

The Cariris, at least in Bahia and in the old captaincy of Pernambuco, were already situated on the coast when the speakers of língua geral arrived. Pushed into the interior by the recent arrivals, they fiercely resisted the invasion of European colonists. Nonetheless, missionaries were able to group many of them in villages, and the advent of cattle ranching helped reconcile more of them to the new order. The "flat head" [*cabeça chata*] typical of backlanders from the Northeast might be a Cariri legacy.

If we now examine the environment's influence on these natives, indolence is not their primary characteristic. Indolent they doubtlessly were, but they were also capable of great feats. The main effect geography had on natives was to preclude cooperation.

What common preventive measures could be taken against the heat? What incentives did they have to form alliances? How can there be progress in communities made up of half a dozen families?

The same lack of cooperation, the same incapacity to act in a wise and single-minded fashion, with division of labor and its consequences, seem to be the legacies these forebears passed on to their descendants.

2

Exotic Elements

At the beginning of the sixteenth century, Portugal was struggling in its transition from the Middle Ages into the modern era. In its breast two different societies coexisted, each with its own hierarchy, its own legislation, and its own courts. But lay society no longer believed in the church's transcendent superiority, nor would it allow itself to be absolutely dependent on the church. Indeed, the church had been divested of many of its historic prerogatives and had been obliged to reduce its claims.

The state recognized and abided by the laws of the church. It carried out its courts' sentences. It declared itself incompetent in clerical matters and debates. It would only punish a cleric if, after having been condemned by the church, he was turned over to the state by his ecclesiastic superiors. The state honored the right of criminals, even those wanted for capital crimes, to seek asylum in temples and monasteries. And it did not tax the clergy.

Owing to baptism, which was as important for day-to-day life as it was for the saving of one's soul; owing to marriage, which it could permit, sustain, or annul with ecclesiastic diriment; the church reigned supreme. Its powers also included the sacraments, which were administered throughout a person's life. Excommunication stopped people from receiving the sacraments. The interdict separated entire communities from communication with the saints. The church regulated death by permitting or denying specific rights, by allowing bodies to rest in hallowed ground, among their families, or by making them rot in garbage heaps along with animals. It controlled teaching, limited and defined beliefs, and separated what one could and could not teach or learn.

To counter the church, in the still narrow domain in which it had become competent, the state used the *placet* on documents emanating from the papal throne. The Crown's judges used it to protect certain branches of government essential to the exercise of full sovereignty. They used amortization laws to limit the church's acquisition of buildings, and they imposed temporalities when they met resistance. On the other hand, the state shared its jurisdiction with the other power in cases that became known as *mixti fori*. It lent its arm to execute, at times violently, people condemned by ecclesiastic judgment. It severely punished certain acts only because the church considered them sinful. That is, similar to today's governmental or economic interests, at that time religious and ecclesiastic considerations carried weight.

In spite of everything, church and state frequently came into conflict. The church was not eager to let go of its age-old privileges, while the state was bent on conquering or assuming new powers to cope with growing problems—onerous holdovers from the medieval way of life, pressing demands in a new state of affairs owing to a strengthened merchant class, red tape, reborn industry, new ways of thinking, the struggle between money and barter economies, and the expanding world horizons.

Like the pope, who was the head of religious society, the king had become the lord and master of secular society. As an absolute monarch, his powers would not be subjected to definable limits. They were invoked as a principle of superior equity, as solutions for exceptional, grave, and unforeseen dilemmas. The king could use other, more definable powers to a greater or lesser extent, and he could withdraw them.

It was the king's right to coin money, to commission army or naval officers, to appoint judges at the peaks and valleys of their careers, to declare war and call the people to arms and demand the necessary supplies. The king could commandeer his subjects' carts, beasts of burden, and ships. He owned all the highways and streets, the navigable rivers, the rights to cross rivers, the seaports, and the tolls paid to use them. He owned the offshore islands, the incomes from fisheries, marinas, means of producing salt, gold, silver, and other mines, the ownerless assets, as well as the stolen goods possessed by specific criminals. The entire legislative branch was centered on the king. The votes of the Cortes were only valid with his acquiescence and when they suited him. He could set aside the most explicit directives or apply them selectively. All courts and judges were extensions of the throne.

Below the king was the nobility, which was numerous in families and in the degrees that separated different ranks from one another. It was made up of grantee lords possessing titles, private grounds, and jurisdictions; grand masters of military orders whose title the king finally saw fit to appropriate; as well as ordinary knights and squires. Its authority had been extensive, but now it contented itself with its monopoly on government offices, with its prevalent role in times of war or in the Crown councils, and with its privileged place in penal matters, where a title of nobility warded off torture or guaranteed a reduced sentence. The nobility was not an exclusive caste. It could be entered through a number of doors, including the door of letters.

Below the nobility were the common people, the great bulk of the nation. They had no individual rights and were only defended by the worthy people who took them in: farmers, workers, and merchants. Those who were better off were known as good people [*homens bons*], and they met in town councils, organs of local administration whose importance, then as always, was trivial. The common people never weighed in decisively on momentous occurrences, neither in Portugal nor in Brazil. In spite of what some of our contemporaries might argue or write, deceived as they are by fleeting appearances, or blinded as they may be by preconceived ideas, that is how things were.

There were many worthy people with whom the common folk could affiliate: guilds, such as the coiners' and the bombardiers', or greater entities, such as the [society of] citizens of Oporto. The privileges citizens of specific cities enjoyed were awarded to several cities in Brazil: Maranhão, Bahia, Rio de Janeiro and São Paulo, at least. When one examines them closely, these privileges appear to be the result of bargains struck with people whose only asset was their status as human beings.

Dom João II exempted those lucky citizens of Oporto from torture for any evil deeds they may have committed or might commit in the future—except for those deeds and characteristics and that behavior for which the nobility and lords should also be tortured. They should not be imprisoned for any crime, but should be kept under house arrest or on their own recognizance as is the case and befits the nobility. They should be permitted in all their properties and domains to bear whichever and however many defensive and offensive arms they may care to—both at night or during the day. They should not be forced to allow the nobility [*infanções e ricos-homens*] to dwell with them, to take their houses and dwellings, cellars, stables, saddle animals, or anything else belonging to them; and the nobility could no longer seize their houses and do what they wanted both within and around them. Farm laborers need go to war only when their masters go.[1]

Below the third estate were the serfs, slaves, and so forth. Their only right was to pass, in certain favorable circumstances, to the next highest class, since, although they were sharply divided into social classes, they never became social castes.

The Cortes consisted of three branches: the clergy, the nobility, and the common people. They were called to meet on solemn occasions and at arbitrary intervals. Were these convocations for consultation or were their members supposed to deliberate issues? Portuguese scholars take pot shots at one another on this matter. Doubtlessly the Cortes only mattered when kings considered ruling to be their job and they needed pecuniary resources beyond those offered by their copious royal rights.

Brazil's prosperity and settlement proved fatal to this venerable institution. Owing to an in no way fortuitous coincidence, the last Cortes convened in 1697, when the gold from Minas Gerais was beginning to dazzle the world. They only reconvened with the French Revolution, the Napoleonic Wars, and Brazil's actual independence, once the Portuguese monarchy was transferred here.

In 1527 there were approximately 280,528 households in Portugal. Considering that each one contained four people, the nation's population that year must have been somewhere around 1,122,112 souls. With such a scanty crew, which was not even adequate for the country itself, how was Portugal going to populate the world? How else, but to commit itself to miscegenation?

Portugal's agriculture was behind the times. In 1541, Damião de Góis explained to Europe's literate elite the reason behind Portugal and Spain's backwardness. He maintained that the natural fertility of the soil was such that during the greater part of the year slaves and poor men could feed regally on wild fruit, honey, and herbs, and that made them little inclined to field work.[2]

A few traits taken from Costa Lobo's book point out the main characteristics of the Portuguese common people at the beginning of the age of discovery.[3]

The fifteenth century Portuguese were hard-working and abstemious. They had ardent imaginations and were given to mysticism. They were not ill-at-ease with discipline nor restricted by convention. They spoke their mind without subterfuge or euphemisms. They were rigid in character, and their hearts were hard. Their penal comminations knew no pity. Crimes such as the theft of a single silver mark were punished by death. Counterfeiters were burned at the stake, and their property was confiscated.

Given the crude customs that characterize those times, one's safety, family, and possessions largely depended on one's personal strength and resourcefulness. This explains the frequent flights, attacks, woundings, and deaths people regularly executed as reactions to the habitual violence and pain they inflicted on one another. The Portuguese were not upset by scenes of suffering, because no one put much stock in physical pain. Acts of cruelty that today would indicate the vileness of some perverse individual had no such meaning during those times. Whatever damage they caused was not considered excessive, and everyone was susceptible. But if physical or moral pain could mollify the rigidity of dispositions unaccustomed to patience or reflection, or if passion inflamed that rigidity, sentiments were expressed in shouts, wails, and contortions that resembled the writhing typical of raving dementia.

This harshness of character was in line with the Portuguese's rustic nature, which held physical strength in high esteem. A backhand blow from a broadsword that cut a steer's leg in two at the middle of the thigh, or that lopped off its head at the base of the neck were deeds worthy of historical record.

To the Portuguese, who were not native to Brazil, it is necessary to add the blacks, who were also foreign. Their importation began with the founding of captaincies and assumed huge proportions in the following centuries—first because of the planting of sugar cane, then because of tobacco, then the mines, cotton, and coffee. Once the slave trade was halted, in 1850, coffee brought about significant internal migrations, as did abolition.

The first blacks came from the west coast of Africa and in the main belonged to Bantu tribes. Later on they were brought from Mozambique. Their robust constitution and their ability to work hard made them ideal for the arduous labor to which the native population succumbed. Brought in for farm work, they entered colonists' domestic life as wet nurses and household servants. Because of their affectionate nature, they became indispensable to their masters' home life. Racial mixture with the African population, contrary to that with the natives, was frowned upon, and it disqualified people from certain roles in society. Mulattos were barred from the priesthood, for example. And that is why people wanted to have a priest in their family, to prove their blood was clean. As time passed, mulattos were able to improve their lot and assert themselves in society. When they combined daring with talent and luck, they went very far indeed.

Put alongside the taciturn Portuguese and the melancholy Indians, blacks added a note of mirth to colonial society. Their sensual dances, tolerated from the beginning, became a national institution. Their sorcery and their beliefs spread beyond the slave quarters. *Mulatas* found men who appreciated their wily charms and who set them up as queens. Brazil is Hell for blacks, Purgatory for whites, and Paradise for mulattos, concluded the illustrious Antonil in 1711.[4]

3

The Discoverers

Portugal's location destined it to the seafaring life, and its familiarity with the islands to the west dates from Roman times. Arabic tradition has preserved the memory of the *Mogharriun*, who sailed out of Lisbon in search of adventure. When Christians recaptured Lisbon, they produced a national navy that gave life to the port on the Tagus and made it prosper as a port of call on the route to Flanders. Catalans and Italians, in response to a call to teach nautical science and technique, gathered there as well. The 1415 expedition against Ceuta brought together hundreds of ships and thousands of sailors.

After taking Ceuta from the Moorish infidel, the conquerors set off toward African lands. Ships dispatched from the Algarve, in southern Portugal, traveled along the Moroccan coast, exorcised the terror associated with Cape Nun or the point of no return, and mapped out the Sahara while navigating the dense fogs of the dark sea. They discovered mighty rivers, tracts of land where people lived, and the Cape Verde Islands. These islands were truly verdant, even though they lay in the torrid zone. This region's name implied it was uninhabitable because of the heat. It was uninhabitable according to a unanimous proclamation made by philosophers of antiquity, who were now for the first time caught in a flagrant falsehood. This heroic phase reached its peak under Prince Henry the Navigator, the son of Dom João I, and Grand Master of the Order of Christ. The age was dominated on the one hand by a desire to widen the frontiers of the known world, on the other by a hope of reaching a point where the power of Islam might not be felt. Perhaps at that point, Prester John, the legendary high priest and emperor, might reign. Allied with Prester John's forces, the Portuguese would bring about the supreme crusade against Christianity's hereditary enemies. Although these enemies had been expelled from almost all of Spain, they were more powerful than ever in the lands and seas of the East.

As the discoveries continued, the muddled aspirations of their early days became more precise. During the last years of Prince Henry's life the problem of India became clearer. On earlier maps, it had been just one of the many vaguely drawn geographical entities beyond the opening of the Red Sea—from the kingdom of Cathay all the way to the island of Cipango. But now there were all sorts of possible routes to India. The powerful rivers of the now known continent promised routes of infinite penetration. The southward direction of Africa's coast was another likely means of shortening the distance to India. The many declarations on prestigious geographic charts seemed to mark the way. And a new route was urgently needed, because in German and Latin Europe there was a strong demand for spices, silk, fine pearls, precious stones, exotic wood—in a phrase, Indian goods. However, Muslim powers were located along the historic roads that led to the Mediterranean. On a daily basis they increased their demands. They refined their insolence as they despoiled the middlemen engaged in commerce with the Levant. They tormented consumers in the West.

After a few half-hearted attempts, the idea of reaching India by crossing Africa was abandoned. The next plan was to get there by sailing around Africa. Nevertheless, Ptolemy's notion that Africa and Asia were joined to one another stood in the way. He had claimed that in the south the two continents were connected by an isthmus similar to Suez in the north. That land mass made the Indian Ocean an inland sea. But during the life of Prince Henry the Navigator an Italian cartographer protested against the categorical pronouncements of the Alexandrine astronomer. In addition, the discovery of Cape Verde and direct contact with the torrid zone had begun to open people's eyes and show them the simple fact that just because a particular idea had been handed down from antiquity did not mean it was protected from reexamination.

While these tentative notions were being strung together, another solution to the problem was formulated. It had been suggested by Greek and Roman scholars and supported on sacred and pagan grounds. This solution maintained that the ocean to the west of Europe and the one to the east of Asia were one and the same. According to Scripture, seas covered only a small fraction of the earth's surface and dry land predominated. And, seeing that our planet is round, the logical and shortest route to India could be traveled by sailing fearlessly into the ocean, by going so far west that one ended up in the East. Such a voyage, in addition to being shorter, would be more comfortable, since there were islands scattered en route, some of them the size of Antilla, which appeared in the most trustworthy navigation manuals.

Christopher Columbus presented this plan as a new idea to the Portuguese, who rejected it. Less experienced in these matters, the Spaniards received the Genoan sailor and provided him with the means to carry out his plan.

He set sail in 1492 and discovered a few islands and, years later, the sought-after continent, the kingdom of the great Khan, or so he believed.

After the death of Prince Henry and during the reign of Dom Afonso V (1460–1481), the quest for new lands did not die down, but it went on less brilliantly. When Dom João II assumed the throne, it regained momentum. The known world ended at 2° south latitude, Cape Saint Catherine. A few years later it had been extended to the tropic of Capricorn. In 1487 Bartholomew Dias returned and announced he had reached the tip of Africa. On the way back, in the far south, he had almost floundered near a cape that he called the Cape of Storms. The king protested, saying it would not be called the Cape of Storms, it was to be, rather, the Cape of Good Hope.

More than hope, the king was sure he was about to reap the benefits of so much hard work. Dom João II was so confident that the route to India had been found that he asked for no more proof. He calmly prepared for a voyage by having ships built for the stormy oriental seas. He had artillery built that would be a match for that of the Indian potentates and the Arab warships. He sent emissaries to the Red Sea, the Persian Gulf, the eastern coast of Africa, and the Malabar Coast. They inquired, observed, and gathered new and trustworthy information on trade and navigation. One of them, Pero de Covilhã, reached the kingdom of Prester John, who had originally been sought in Asia, but whom he met as the ruler of Abyssinia.

Dom João II left nothing to chance. Columbus's triumphal return in 1493 had little influence on the king's plans. He protested against the division of the world promulgated by Pope Alexander VI. He seems to have sent some clandestine expedition westward. But the appearance of the inhabitants of this new land, their visible primitivity, the artifacts brought back, the countries discovered, all of which were entirely different from what his experts had learned in the East, convinced him that the India the Portuguese sought was not to be confused with the one the Spaniards had found. When he died in 1495, the Perfect Prince left to his successor, Dom Manoel, the simple task of enjoying the ripened fruit. Similarly, Vasco da Gama did little more than follow the path (1497–99) that Bartholomew Dias had opened ten years earlier.

The return of Vasco da Gama and his ships loaded with legitimate Indian products demonstrated Dom João II's vision and wisdom, which had preferred the route marked by the Cape of Good Hope over any other. Dias' discovery does not appear to have made the same impression on the Spaniards, because they stuck to their original endeavor of reaching the East by sailing west.

We have, thus, two well-defined historical trends, both of which began on the Iberian Peninsula. One looked westward, one to the south. Both reached Brazil. The Spaniards, personified by Vicente Yáñez Pinzón, as they began to explore the lower latitudes, crossed the equator and entered the Southern Hemisphere. The Portuguese, heading southward, but far out to sea in search of more favorable winds to help them round the cape, caught the trade winds and, with Pedro Álvares Cabral in command, ended up in the Western Hemisphere. Both events happened in the same year.

We shall concern ourselves solely with Pedro Álvares.

In command of a fleet of 13 ships, he left Belém on Monday, 9 March 1500. Sunday had been a day of celebration. The king had brought the commander to his side, and had placed on his head a holy skull cap made of gold and sent by the pope. He had given him a flag with the royal coat of arms and the cross of the Order of Christ, Henry the Navigator's order. The importance of this fleet was felt all around. It was the largest yet of all the expeditions sent to distant lands.

Fifteen hundred soldiers, adventurous traders, adventurers, a wide range of merchandise, and coined money illustrate the dual nature of this expedition. It would be a peaceful one if in India people preferred openness and honest trade. If they resorted to armed resistance, the expedition was prepared to fight. Some Franciscans, under the leadership of Henrique de Coimbra, added a religious element to this voyage's totality.

On March 14 they sighted the Canary Islands, on March 22, Cape Verde. A month later, on April 21, they encountered long strands of floating seaweed—signs of land close by. The following day these signs were confirmed by the appearance of birds, and, in the afternoon, the sighting of land. Pero Vaz de Caminha, an eyewitness and the scribe of the trading post to be set up in Calecut wrote:

> On that day, around vespers, we caught sight of land: at first a great mountain, wide and high and other, lower mountains to its south, then we saw level land covered with trees. The tall mountain was given the name Mount Pascual. At sundown they found secure anchorage at a depth of 23 fathoms.

From sea, Mount Pascual, in the State of Bahia, can be spotted at a distance of 60 miles.

On Thursday, slowly and carefully, they continued on their course, with the smaller ships in front, keeping track of the depth.

A half league out from the mouth of a river, they dropped anchor. Nicolau Coelho, who had been on Vasco da Gama's expedition, came ashore and spied some natives whose curiosity had brought them out and who offered and received gifts.

A southwest wind accompanied by squalls made the Portuguese seek a sheltered port. On Friday, with their larger ships farther out to sea and their smaller ones close to the shore, they sailed northward. At sunset, after traveling 10 leagues, they found a reef sheltering a port with a wide entrance. Pero Vaz de Caminha recounted:

> Saturday morning the captain ordered us to set sail and we headed for the entrance, which was wide and some six to seven fathoms deep. All the ships came in and anchored at depths of five to six fathoms. This port is so big and well apportioned and safe that it can accommodate more than two hundred ships of different sizes and shapes [*navios e naus*].

The name the commander gave this area, Porto Seguro, "Safe Port," sums up his impression and is preserved today in the name of a nearby town.

On a cay in the bay, once an altar was built, a Mass for Low Sunday [Pascoela, the Sunday after Easter], 26 April, was sung. Friar Henrique de Coimbra preached the gospel of the day. The Savior's Resurrection, His disciples' mysterious sightings of Him, Thomas' doubting, the Apostle of the Indies—all boded well for these strange circumstances. At the end of his sermon, the friar "dealt with our arrival and with our discovery of this land. He ended with the sign of the Cross, under whose guidance we had come." Christ's banner, with which the commander had taken leave of Belém, remained on the gospel side during the homily.

The captains of all the ships met on the flagship, where the commander proposed sending the supply ship back to Lisbon with the news of their finding, so that His Majesty might announce the discovery. All agreed. The following days were spent transferring stock from the supply ship and building a cross with which they would indicate their taking possession of the land in the name of the Portuguese Crown.

The cross was erected on May 1. On the second, the supply ship headed for Portugal, and the powerful fleet set sail for India, leaving behind two tearful criminals charged with learning as much as they could about the land and the local language. It seems that some sailors deserted at this point.

The following words of Pero Vaz de Caminha are typical of a noble spirit's reflections in the face of those remarkable days and events:

> Up to now we have not been able to find out if there is gold, silver, iron, or any thing made of metal on this land, for we have seen none. But the land itself has cool and temperate air, as good as the air between the Douro and Minho Rivers [in northern Portugal]. At least at this time that is how we found them. Its waters are unending and the land itself is so gracious that if one wished to cultivate it, anything would thrive because of its water. But by far the best fruit that can be harvested in this land seem to be the souls of its inhabitants. And this appears to be the main seed that Your Majesty should sew in the new land. That is, this place is a fitting stop-off on the route to Calecut. However, a greater reason [for settling here] is to carry out Your Highness's most desired mission, which is to increase the membership in our holy faith.[1]

The new land's advantageous location along the route to India, the transplanting of old world crops as a means of integrating it into the kingdom, the native question, and the natives' deliverance into the Christian fold are precisely articulated in this passage.

En route to the Cape of Good Hope, the commander's fleet sailed a long way down the coast of the new land, some two thousand miles according to one member of the expedition.

The supply ship sailed northeast, of course not losing sight of land along the way and perhaps going ashore from time to time. It may have met up with Diego de Lepe or some other Spanish traveler. This Portuguese discovery can be found on Juan de la Cosa's map, which he finished in October 1500.

Halfway through the following year, a fleet of three ships left Portugal to explore the recently discovered Island of the Cross, or Vera Cruz. In Beseguiche it met up with Pedro Álvares Cabral, who was on his way back from India. If the discoverer and the future explorers exchanged impressions, they must have recognized that the "new" land was an entire continent instead of an island. Was it a separate continent? The answer to this question could not have been clear because the Pacific Ocean had yet to be discovered. Duarte Pacheco, the hero of Cambay and a member of Cabral's fleet, some years later still believed in the traditional view of the world: vast land masses separated by inland seas which, like great lagoons, opened diverse routes.

After a stormy crossing, the exploring expedition reached the coast around Rio Grande do Norte and sought more temperate regions. The explorers used the calender to name the places they discovered: São Roque, São Jernimo, São Francisco, Baía de Todos os Santos, or "All Saints Bay," Cabo São Tomé, Angra dos Reis, i.e., "Epiphany Cove." They named others for particular incidents or the impressions they made: Rio Real "Royal River," Cabo Frio, "Cold Cape," Baía Formosa, "Beautiful Bay," etc. The explorers, so it seems, never lost sight of the Serra do Mar. For many years the southernmost point to appear on maps was Cananor, which might well be present-day Cananéia, in São Paulo. They estimated that their coastal journey covered 2,500 miles. This more thorough exploration almost entirely confirmed Caminha's words. However, in the eyes of these explorers, the natives seemed more like savages—loathsome, bloodthirsty cannibals more suited to slavery than to Christianity.

After this fleet returned, the Crown decided to lease the land for three-year terms. The lessees agreed to send out six ships per year, to explore 300 leagues, and to set up and maintain one fortress. They banked on making money from the slaves, exotic animals, and brazilwood the first explorers would bring back in their holds. They also clung to the vague hope of finding a route to India.

In 1503 six ships set out together for Brazil. They were reduced to three after the destruction of the flagship off the island later called Fernão de Noronha. Vespucci, the man whose name would be applied to the new world, defected. One of the ships may have begun exploring Cape São Roque in search of the equator. Nothing is known for sure. From this venture along the coast, only two names have escaped oblivion: João de Lisboa and João Coelho e Costa. The lack of ports, the sailing difficulties owing to the prevailing winds, and the sterile impression the land made on the sailors did not motivate them to make frequent landings on their northward course. Notations on maps of the time are either few and far between, or they merely indicate observations from afar.

In 1506 Brazil had been leased to Fernão de Noronha and other New Christians. It regularly produced 20,000 *quintais* of redwood, which sold for 2 1/3 and 3 ducats per quintal [approximately 60 kilograms]. It cost half a ducat to get a quintal of redwood to Lisbon. These lessees paid the Crown 4,000 ducats.

A few years later, the Crown decided to let anyone who wanted to go to Brazil do so and try their luck. The Crown would be entitled to one fifth of whatever they brought back. This may have been the deal struck with the financiers of the *Bretoa*, which was outfitted by Bartolomeu Marchioni, Benedito Morelli, Fernão de Noronha, and Francisco Martins, who sent it to Cabo Frio early in 1511. There are documents on this expedition.

The *Bretoa* had a captain, a scribe, a boatswain, and a pilot—all of whom were responsible for its order and discipline. There were thirteen seamen, fourteen deckhands [*grumetes*], four servants, and a supply officer [*dispenseiro*]. Neither on the way to Brazil nor on the way back could they stop at any port, except in cases of storms, disrepair, or lack of victuals. The crew was allowed to bring knives, scissors, and other tools aboard once the outfitters' cargo had been stowed. With the outfitters' permission, these items could be traded for parrots, cats, and also slaves. Crew members were not allowed to sell arms of war.

Once the cargo was brought ashore, it was handed over to the head [*feitor*] of the outpost. All barter was done under his authority. Traders were to observe the utmost care so as to do no evil or harm to the natives. They were to bring back no free people because, were these natives to die en route, their relatives would assume they had been eaten, since that was their custom. They were not to let people from the ship go inland or stay ashore, as some had already done, which was an execrable act, as far as royal service and dealings were concerned.

The *Bretoa* left the Tagus on February 22 and anchored at All Saints Bay from April 17 to May 12. On May 26 it arrived at Cabo Frio, from where, on June 28, it left for Portugal. It carried five thousand logs of brazilwood, twenty-two lovebirds, sixteen monkeys, sixteen cats, fifteen parrots, and three macacs—all together valued at 24$220, i.e., 24,220 réis. They had forty individual slaves, most of them women, worth an average of 4,000 réis each. On the entire live cargo, the royal fifth was paid while the ship was still in Brazil.

The name Brazil was already well known and appeared in navigation manuals prior to the Portuguese discoveries. Just like Antilla, it was a name waiting for a place. And this explains the rapidity with which it appeared and became current and supplanted other names, such as Land of the Parrots, Vera Cruz, or Santa Cruz. The name was, of course, also propounded by the abundance of and the immediate trade in a highly valued dyewood that up to then had come from the Levant.

Brazilwood was immediately spotted on the coast of Paraíba and Pernambuco, in the vicinity of the Real River, and from Cabo Frio to Rio de Janeiro. Naturally, in the early days, these areas would become those most often visited by the Portuguese traders. Later on brazilwood was discovered in other places.

To aid shipment, trading posts were established, preferably on islands. The posts were little more than pens or fences built to safeguard the items of barter. Some seeds from across the sea might be planted outside the posts, and some animals requiring little care might be let loose. One trading post was set up along Guanabara Bay (present-day Rio de Janeiro) and stood for several years until it was destroyed by the natives, who were at odds with the commander and his companions' dealings. Sugar cane must have been one of the crops traders planted and abandoned, because Ferdinand Magellan found it there in 1519.

In 1513 a fleet of two ships extended the geographic horizon further south into the temperate zone. According to one contemporary, the fleet investigated between 600 and 700 leagues of unfamiliar lands. At the mouth of a mighty river it found metal objects. It learned of snowy mountains to the west. It claimed to have found a strait and the southern tip of the continent. The captain, perhaps João de Lisboa, brought back a silver hatchet and the name Prata, "silver," which he applied to the majestic river. And this act, even today, is a testimonial to the Portuguese' primacy in exploring the South—just like the name of the Amazon River is a legacy of the Spaniards' presence in the North.

The voyage of these ships, outfitted by Nuno Manuel and Cristóbal de Haro, coincided with the discovery of the Pacific Ocean by Vasco Núñez de Balboa.

The Spaniards grasped the importance of these events and in 1515 sent out an expedition to search for the strait the Portuguese had reported finding. They commanded Juan Días de Solís to sail along the new route shouldering the lands of Castilla de Oro. Barely ashore along the River Plate, Solís was killed. His companions returned to Spain without delay. In 1520 Ferdinand Magellan explored the great southern estuary in search of the coveted strait, which he later discovered farther south. He then sailed upon the Pacific Ocean and finally reached the Molucca Islands, the Spice Islands *par excellence.*

Thus, Columbus's plan of reaching the East by sailing west had finally been carried out. On this singular expedition, Magellan sailed in the company of João Lopes de Carvalho, the *Bretoa*'s pilot, and a *mamaluco*, that is, the mestizo offspring of a union Magellan had had with an Indian woman in Rio de Janeiro. Brazilwood, parrots, slaves, and mestizos were the products of the first decades of Brazil's colonization. As for Indian women, their desire to have children belonging to a superior race explains their union with white men. They believed that the father determined their children's status. In addition, these millionaire purveyors of marvelous items, such as fishhooks, combs, knives, scissors, and mirrors, were probably irresistible. Concerning the outsiders, they must have been moved to miscegenation by the scarcity, if not the total absence, of white women. This phenomenon can be observed in all overseas migrations. It survives today even after the advent of steamships and their rapid, safe means of crossing the oceans.

The first colonists who took up residence in Brazil, the criminals, deserters, and castaways, were of two widely different sorts. Some succumbed to their surroundings and pierced their lips and ears, killed their prisoners according to established rites, and ate them. Others, like the lawyer [*bacharel*] of Cananéia, resisted and prevailed. He assumed the responsibility of furnishing 400 slaves for Diogo García, one of Solís's companions, and one of the discoverers of the River Plate.

Diogo Álvares or Caramuru is the midpoint between the two extremes. He lived in Bahia among the natives from 1510 to 1557, the year he died.

4

The First Conflicts

The arrival of the Portuguese in Brazil was closely followed by that of the French, who immediately began to barter with the natives. Given the vastness of the littoral, the French and Portuguese could have spent years without coming into contact with one another. But they were fated to meet, and the meeting would not be friendly.

Because of papal concessions, the border treaty with Spain, and their primacy in the land, the Portuguese considered the new territory to be the direct and exclusive property of the Crown. The king received a percentage of all goods brought out, and the outfitters wanted profit from their efforts and investments.

The presence of intruders hurt them all in every way. The French sold Brazilian commodities in European markets at lower prices, because they did not have to pay a royal fifth. They brought them directly to markets since they did not have to stop at Lisbon. In Brazil, if they could get on well with the natives, who might receive them better, they would be spared the natives' treachery and fraud. Indeed, they might be given preference in trade, and the natives would get used to and prefer French merchandise. Furthermore, as a matter of principle, Portugal did not want the sons of other nations setting foot on Portuguese overseas possessions.

From Paraíba in the north to São Vicente in the south, the coast was populated with tribes who spoke the same language, who shared a common origin and similar customs. Irreconcilable hatred, however, divided them into two separate groups. They called themselves Tupiniquins and Tupinambás. The Tupiniquim migration was the older of the two. At several places, such as Rio de Janeiro, All Saints Bay, the area north of Pernambuco, part of São Paulo, Porto Seguro, Ilhéus, and around Olinda; the Tupinambás had pushed the Tupiniquins into the backlands. There were, however, Tupiniquins living on the coast around the Ibiapava mountain range.

Why the Tupinambás were always on the French side and the the Tupiniquins allied with the Portuguese, no one knows. But the fact is incontestable and was important: for years Brazil teetered between becoming a possession of the Peró (the Portuguese) or of the Maïr (the French).[1]

During the last years of Dom Manuel's reign, protests had begun against the Maïr presence in Brazil. The situation became worse when Dom João II assumed the throne. Once the Crown recognized the futility of sending emissaries to the French court and the worthlessness of promises for which they paid dearly, the Portuguese king resolved to take revenge. A coast guard fleet came to Brazil in 1527. It was under the command of Cristóvão Jacques, who had been in Brazil before and had left a trading post near Itamaracá on his way back from an expedition to the River Plate. From Pernambuco to Bahia and maybe even to Rio de Janeiro, Cristóvão Jacques hunted down the interlopers. According to interested parties, his wrath knew no bounds. He was not satisfied by mere executions; he needed to torture his victims, then he handed them over to the natives, who devoured them. Even so he brought 300 prisoners back to Portugal. He must have done enormous damage to the French.

The coast guard was little more than a palliative. Only by settling the land could the Portuguese cut off the evil at its roots. Cristóvão Jacques offered to bring 1,000 settlers. João de Melo da Câmara, the brother of the commandant of the Island of São Miguel, made a similar offer. He was upset by the Portuguese settlers, who, until then, had come to Brazil, eaten the local produce, and taken Indian women as concubines. He offered to bring many families, oxen, horses, seeds, and so forth.

Instead of acting on these reasonable and practical suggestions, a new and more powerful fleet was outfitted and put under the command of Martim Afonso de Sousa. It would be a compromise between a coast guard fleet and a settlement expedition. Hardly did it reach the coast of Pernambuco in January 1531, than it began its task. In a few days it had captured three French ships.

With two caravels, Diogo Leite was sent from Pernambuco north along the coast running east to west, which was less well known at that time than it was 30 years earlier when Vicente Yáñez Pinzón explored that region. With the other ships the commander headed south. He spent time in All Saints Bay, in Guanabara Bay, and in Cananéia. He was on his way to the River Plate and probably had in mind following it upstream for he had brought unarmed brigantines from Europe. They would be well-suited for this type of exploration. However, the loss of the flagship made him double back to São Vicente. There he waited for his brother, Pero Lopes, whom he would send in his place to the Plattine waters.

Beginning in 1514, the first specimens of precious metals found in the waters of the mighty river reached Europe. They had been brought back on Dom Nuno Manuel's fleet. Some of Solís's companions, who had escaped the Indians' wrath and later on had been allowed to live, supported these tenuous intimations of wealth. On the coast of Patos, some of them even waxed enthusiastic.

Around 1522 Cristóvão Jacques gathered this information in the Patos area or at the river itself and took it to Portugal. In the trading post at Itamaracá rumors of precious metals were so much the topic of conversation that in 1526 Sebastian Cabot, when he reached Pernambuco and heard them, immediately decided to set sail for Santa Catarina to pick up the survivors of the Solís expedition and find the source of the metals everyone persisted in talking about with such conviction. He had been sent to the Moluccas, but he knew that if he were successful in this endeavor no one would fault him for going astray. Indeed, so sure was he of the mines' existence that he did not hesitate in disobeying the strictest of orders.

In spite of Cabot's ultimate failure, the belief in Plattine treasures could not be shaken. Because of this, in Cananéia, Francisco de Chaves, the heathens' great mouthpiece, requested men for an inland expedition, promising to return in ten months time with four-hundred slaves loaded down with silver. Martim Afonso acceded on the spot.

The idea seemed practical. The expedition would not have to go down the coast to the mouth of the River Plate, then go up the river to the fortress Cabot had built to base his exploration in the West, where these treasures lay. The commander gave Chaves forty crossbowmen and forty musketeers who, under the command of Pero Lobo, set off on 1 September 1531. There are vague indications that they died by the hands of Indians. Around the same time, using a more direct route, Francisco Pizarro reached the land of the Incas, which up to then had been sought from the East.

After losing the flagship, Martim Afonso took up the second part of his mission: settling the land. At São Vicente he founded the first town [vila], along the shore. Some leagues inland, on the other side of the Serra do Mar, he founded the second town at the edge of the plain of Piratininga, on the banks of a river flowing westward. Pero Lopes wrote:

> He divided the people into these two towns, and he appointed officials, and established rule of law, which was very reassuring to the townsfolk. They were glad to see towns populated, having laws and restrictions, carrying out weddings, and living in a civilized manner [*em comunicação das artes*], with each person in charge of his own property and [able to] redress offenses and having other benefits vouchsafed and transferable.[2]

These towns owe their location to the proximity of the famous and coveted riches, and to their suitability as points of departure for inland expeditions, that would only take ten months, as Francisco de Chaves guaranteed. Dazzled by these advantages, Martim Afonso forgot about the French, or he felt there was no reason to fear them after Cristóvão Jacques's zealous campaign, which he sustained with tremendous vigor and success.

Diogo de Gouveia, a Portuguese residing in France, had been following the negotiations in that kingdom for a long time and had a singular idea. In disturbing letters he sent to the Portuguese king, he pressed for a royal solution. The problem of the French could not be solved by building a town off the beaten track, but by making several settlements in the contended brazilwood region. Lopes concluded:

> When there are seven or eight settlements in that area, they will suffice to stop the natives from selling brazilwood to anyone else, and with no brazilwood French ships will no longer go there just to return with empty holds.[3]

If one didn't know better, one would believe the French had read these insightful words. Up to then they had been content to barter and had set up at most a trading post or two. They were now about to set up a fort with cannonry and many soldiers. Only then did the Lusitanian court take seriously "the initiative with which the people in the fort would work, once they had settled there and expended some effort, as they had already begun to do in Pernambuco."

The French trading post became known in Portugal thanks to *La Pèlerine*, a ship out of Marseilles that stopped in Málaga on its way back from Pernambuco, where it had left men and cannons. A fleet of ten Portuguese ships bound for Rome happened to be in Málaga at that time.

Dom Martinho, the ambassador to Rome, learned that a lack of food had caused the ship to come to port. He gave the French 20 *quintais* of biscuits and offered to escort them to Marseilles. Five miles out of Málaga they were becalmed. On the pretext of deciding which route they should follow, the French captain and pilot were invited aboard the Portuguese flagship. They were put in irons and *La Pélerine* was sent to Lisbon.

The French fortress in Pernambuco fared no better. Pero Lopes, once he finished his exploration of the Plate region and was on his way back to Europe, bombarded the fortress for 18 days, obliging it to surrender. Part of the garrison was hanged. Another part was brought back to Portugal and these troops spent long months imprisoned in a jail in the Algarve.

5

Hereditary Captaincies

The capture of *La Pèlerine*, the French trading post in Pernambuco, and the news of preparations for building more trading posts jolted the king's inertia. In a letter to Martim Afonso de Sousa dated 28 September 1532, the king announced that he had decided to demarcate Brazil's coast from Pernambuco to the River Plate and award it to people in captaincies, i.e., in 50-mile sections.[1] Martim Afonso would have 100 miles of coastline, and his brother, Pero Lopes, would be one of the donataries.

The victorious young warrior's arrival in Pernambuco once more had shown how imminent the danger was. This may be the reason why certain measures were immediately taken, or at least discussed. Among them were ample freedom to emigrate to Brazil and the preparation of a fleet of three caravels, each of which would carry 10 to 12 men condemned to death. These convicts would be "made to go ashore and tame that country so as not to subject decent men to danger," assured a Venetian by the name of Pietro Caroldo in a letter dated 16 June 1533.[2] Did this fleet actually come?

Its coming would explain many obscure details.

The oldest documents on the awarding of captaincies date from 1534.

The delay between the project's inception and its realization can be explained by the king's wish to wait for Martim Afonso's return, or by the difficulty in composing the captaincies' charters and their accompanying regulations [*forais*], or, finally, by the lack of people seeking virgin lands that were ill-suited for trade right from the beginning. It is actually quite amazing that there were 12 men willing to undertake such a chancy endeavor. No lord of high degree was tempted by the prospect of starting villages in the new world.

In general the donataries emerged from the petty nobility. They were people seasoned by India, used to living well by conquests, perhaps hindered by urban pragmatism. Many never set foot in Brazil, or they gave up with their first setback. The king ceded some royal privileges to the people to whom he awarded captaincies. He had become eager to stimulate the system he had set up. Many of the concessions he granted as administrator and as Grand Master of the Ordem de Cristo.

All in all, he acted

> in consideration of how much of God's work, as well as my own, [would be accomplished] and how advantageous it would be for my kingdom and domains as well as for my subjects and the natives living in them, if my land and the coastal areas of Brazil were more populated than they have been. In such circumstances the divine cult and offices would be celebrated, and our holy Catholic faith would be elevated and would attract the unbelieving, idolatrous natives of said land. Much good would come to my kingdom and domains and to my subjects and the natives living in them, if said land were settled and exploited.

Donataries would be by rights heredity lords of their lands. They would have civil and criminal authority, and in civil matters they could levy fines of up to 100,000 reis. In criminal cases they could condemn to death slaves, Indians, foot soldiers, and free men. They could banish people of higher status for up to 10 years or fine them up to 100 cruzados. In cases of heresy (if the heretic had been handed over by an ecclesiastic), treason, or sodomy; donataries could order the death penalty no matter what the status of the prisoner might be. Prisoners could only appeal or file grievances if their sentences were not capital.

Along the coast and up the navigable rivers, donataries could found towns with boundaries, jurisdictions, and insignias. They would be in charge of offshore islands within 10 leagues of the coast. They would appoint their own magistrates as well as public and judicial notaries. And they would be able to make land grants to people other than their wives or heirs.

So that donataries might maintain their status and noble norms, they were given 10 leagues of land along the coast of the captaincy, from one end to the other. This land would be exempt from any duty or tax other than the tithe. It would be broken up into four or five lots so that between any two lots there would be a distance of at least two leagues. They were entitled to a *redízima*, or a tenth of the tithe on the income going to the Crown and to the Ordem de Cristo [*mestrado*]. They received a *vintena* or a twentieth, after-expenses, tax on brazilwood (which, like spices, had been declared a royal monopoly). They got a tenth of the *quinto* or 20 percent paid to the Crown for any type of precious stones, for pearls, seed pearls, gold, silver, coral, copper, tin, and lead. They would own all the water mills, salt beaches, and other facilities or factories of whatever type that might be built in their captaincy and under their jurisdiction. They would collect the fees paid by notaries and the payments for passage on boats that charged for travel on rivers. They were entitled to a certain number of slaves who could be sold, tax free, in Portugal. And they got a *redízima* of the duty paid on export products.

The codices guaranteed the manorial lords land grants whose only tax was the tithe to the Ordem de Cristo. They had mining privileges (for which they paid a royal fifth), use of brazilwood in Brazil itself, the freedom to export products to Portugal. Slaves and certain controlled substances, brazilwood and spices, were restricted, however. They were given preferential rights that would protect them from foreign competition, free entry of supplies, arms, cannonry, gun powder, saltpeter, sulfur, lead, and any other matériel. And there was to be free contact among the captaincies in Brazil.

The only agents of royal power were the heads of trading posts, keepers of warehouses, and scribes in charge of the accounts of the Crown's stores. For several captaincies we have the names of vicars and chaplains. The king was always present alongside the Grand Master of the Ordem de Cristo.

No magistrate, judicial officer [*alçada*], or other royal authorities could enter donataries' lands to exercise their professions. Nor could there be transfer taxes, impositions, soap factories [*saboarias*], or taxes on salt.

In sum, convinced as he was of the need for this feudal system, Dom João III was less interested in protecting his own authority than he was in providing the donataries with sufficient power to withstand challenges from future manorial lords, which would be similar to the historic challenges during the Portuguese Middle Ages. The *ouvidor* of the captaincy had original jurisdiction within ten leagues of his seat and appellate jurisdiction in his whole district, with the same historical role that the *juíz de fora* magistrates had overseas.

To avoid struggles, such as those proliferating between the still weakened Crown and the despotic vassals, the king absolutely forbade:

> dividing, trading, dismantling, or in any other way alienating [captaincies and their governance]—be it by the marriage of a son or daughter, by gift to another person, even to ransom a father, son, or any other person, or for any more pious reason. It is my intent and will that they remain always whole and that they never be divided nor given away ever.[3]

The 10 or more leagues of land given in blocks to the donataries and saleable in strips must have corresponded to the Lusitanian *reguengos*, i.e., plots of vacant land at the king's disposal.

There were 12 captaincies, which were divided into a larger number of lots. They began at the shore and with the same width proceeded westward to the dividing line between Portuguese and Spanish possessions, which had been established at Tordesilhas. Of course that line had not yet been fixed, nor could it have been, given the knowledge of the time. The northern and southern limits tacitly ended on the coast of Maranhão and Santa Catarina respectively. The sea coast under command of donataries was approximately 735 leagues long.

In the original plan captaincies were to extend from Pernambuco down to the River Plate, which was 12 degrees farther south. That plan did not include the Brazilian coast north of Pernambuco which runs east to west and that had been sectioned off. That area must have been included owing to the information given by Diogo Leite, who had been charged with exploring it. One can only explain Brazil's tacitly determined southern boundary at 28 1/3° south latitude by thinking internationally. The River Plate had been a Portuguese discovery, but the Spaniards had been there, shedding blood and risking their necks for some time. From the Treaty of Tordesilhas on, they had every right to that area.

Division of donatary lands has yet to be described as concisely and in as geographic terms as those set down by D'Avezac, the only one who has been able to make some sense out of this essentially refractory material.

> The southernmost limit of the southernmost captaincy, awarded to Pero Lopes de Sousa, is determined on the award charters [or "maps," cartas in Portuguese] precisely at 21/3° south latitude. A little north of Paranaguá, it bordered on the São Vicente Captaincy, reserved for Martim Afonso de Sousa. It, in turn, extended more than 100 leagues up the coast, north past Cabo Frio, to Macaé. It [was divided] into two sections that surrounded [the area] from São Vicente to the mouth of the Juquiriquerê (at

Santo Amaro), [which] had been deeded to Pero Lopes, Martim Afonso's brother.

North of these domains was the São Tomé Captaincy, whose 30 leagues would end at Itapemirim. This belonged to Pero de Góis, the brother of the famous historian Damião de Góis.

Next came the Espírito Santo Captaincy, granted to Vasco Fernandes Coutinho. Its northern border was marked by the Mucuri River, which separated it from the Porto Seguro Captaincy, designated for Pero do Campo Tourinho. Porto Seguro continued 50 leagues north to Ilhéus, under Jorge de Figueiredo Correia, and was also 50 leagues wide. It bordered the captaincy of Bahia.

This captaincy, awarded to Francisco Pereira Coutinho, extended northward to the São Francisco River, beyond which lay Pernambuco, allotted to Duarte Coelho. This captaincy ran 60 leagues north to the Iguaraçu River, after which Pero Lopes owned a third parcel 30 leagues wide that ended at Traição Bay and formed the Itamaracá Captaincy.

Begining there, and extending 100 leagues of coast north to Angra dos Negros, lay the Captaincy of Rio Grande, which had been given to the great historian João de Barros and his associate Aires da Cunha. From Angra dos Negros to Rio da Cruz 40 leagues had been conceded to Antônio Cardoso de Barros. From Rio da Cruz to All Saints Cape, next to Maranhão, 75 leagues had been allotted to the overseer of the Fernando Álvares de Andrade Fazenda [ranch]. Beyond this came, finally, the Maranhão Captaincy, which was a second parcel belonging to the João de Barros-Aires da Cunha partnership. It was 50 leagues wide along the coast and went up to Diogo Leite Cove, near the mouth of the Turiaçu River.[4]

Of the 735 leagues of coastline sectioned into captaincies, we can set aside right at the start the 265 awarded to João de Barros, Fernando Álvares, Aires da Cunha, and Antônio Cardoso de Barros. The efforts to occupy them came to naught. They were settled later on, by people born or living in other parts of Brazil. Their settlement represents a second stage in the country's history. We should also set aside the 235 leagues between the boundary of the Ilhéus Captaincy at All Saints Bay and the Curupacé River, as well as 40 more leagues from Cananéia to Santa Ana. In this area settlements were attempted, and even today there are some towns founded during the fourth decade of the sixteenth century, but the colonists had to contend with virgin forests, falls in the rivers, and impassible mountains. They could not surmount these difficulties, and only after surmounting them would they move Brazil ahead. The first decisive victory was in Rio de Janeiro, in the eighteenth century, and was won with the help of São Paulo. From that point on, Rio became a more and more important factor. Other ports, such as Vitória, Porto Seguro, and Il-héus had to wait, or are still waiting, for rail connections.

We are left with the 140 leagues running from Traição Bay to All Saints Bay, the 150 leagues between the Curupacé River and Cananéia: Duarte Coelho's captaincy, part of Martim Afonso de Sousa's captaincy, parts of Pero Lopes de Sousa's allotments in the vicinity of Duarte Coelho's (and inside of Martim Afonso's), and the Bahia Captaincy, after the death of its original donatary.

Brazil's history during the sixteenth century took place in locales scattered along 195 leagues of littoral: Itamaracá, Pernambuco, Bahia, Santo Amaro, and São Vicente.

Martim Afonso remained in the town of São Vicente waiting for the people he had sent off to the mines, who, according to tradition, slaughtered the Carijós Indians of Iguaçu on their way back. A letter from the king brought by João de Sousa informed him of the new plans for colonization, leaving it to Martim Afonso to decide whether to stay in Brazil or return to Portugal. In the early part of 1533 he returned to Portugal. From that point on, his attention was directed to other parts of the world.

In civil matters Father Gonçalo Monteiro, a vicar, took over—granting plots of land and providing jobs. In military matters Pero de Góis and Rui Pinto assumed command. Góis tried to expel some Spaniards who had come from Paraguay and settled in Iguape. He failed. The Spaniards defeated Góis's soldiers, they captured their commander, and they invaded and sacked São Vicente. The Portuguese may have found some way to escape, or the enemies may have been satisfied by this warning. However it was, the Portuguese were back in the old world in 1536, as one can see from their captaincy charter dated February 26.

From Bertioga to Cabo Frio, the Tupinambás were implacable. Allied with the Maïr, by land and by sea they went on attacking the Peró. In one of the battles Rui Pinto was killed. Cunhambebe, the truculent Tamoio warlord, added Pinto's habit and crucifix to his trophies.

Among the imprisoned settlers appears Brás Cubas, a young servant of Martim Afonso. Cubas came to São Vicente in 1540. More than once he governed the land, made war against the Tamoios, fortified Bertioga (the entrance favored by the Tamoios). He founded the town of Santos, whose port was better and which quickly surpassed São Vicente. Later on he was engaged in the search for mines, and the records show he found some gold.

Around these towns some sugar plantations were founded by the Portuguese, by a Flemish family by the name of Schetz, whom the locals called *Esquertes*, as well as by the Dórias, who came from Genoa. It is said, although it is probably not totally right, that the sugar cane planted in other captaincies came from this area. Owing to their remoteness and the scarcity of ties in communication, the original plantations cannot have amounted to much.

Concerning the town founded in Piratininga we have news of its existence and little more. Its location on the open plain made enemy surprise attacks difficult. River traffic on the Paraguay livened it up a bit. On the other side of the Serra, where the waters flowed toward the River Plate, the huts belonging to João Ramalho and his relatives and half-breed offspring heralded victory over the coastal virgin forests. And the victory was won here more quickly than anywhere else in Brazil because the colonists merely built on the work of the Indians. They had found a gap above Paranapiacaba and then followed the Tupiniquins' trail.

In the Pernambuco Captaincy, after establishing Iguaraçu, Duarte Coelho went some leagues farther south and set up the headquarters of his domains in Olinda. Its meager port was sufficient for the small boats that landed there, and the nearby presence of the Tabajaras (Tupiniquins) offset the Petiquares' (Tupinambás) constant incursions. The donatary's willpower kept the turbulent colonists in check. Cane fields and *engenhos* (plantations with sugar mills) arose along the lowlands. On the high points foodstuffs were grown. There was brazilwood on the coast and in the backlands. And, because this was the easternmost of all the captaincies and thus the closest to Portugal, here more than any place else was where the ships from across the sea would stop. Commerce flourished. The sea was full of fish, and this abundance stimulated coastal navigation. Bigger caravelles [*caravelões*] frightened off the French, who from that time on began to avoid those parts. The name Nova Lusitânia, which the donatary gave to his colony, on the one hand symbolizes hopes for the future and on the other hand indicates pride in the undertaking itself. On the coat of arms Dom João III assigned on 6 July 1545 five castles represent the five centers of population created by Duarte Coelho. Unfortunately all that remain of them are Igaraçu, Olinda, and, perhaps, Paratibe.

The Itamaracá Captaincy sent help to Pernambuco when the Petiguares' siege threatened Igaraçu. Later on the relations between the two captaincies became strained. Duarte Coelho complains of constant insubordination. A captain had to leave Itamaracá because Duarte Coelho had sent out orders for him to be stabbed. The captaincies' proximity to each other created dissension. Nonetheless, Pero Lopes's colonists were able to keep the Tupinambás in the Serra. As they did not go up the coast to the area around the Paraíba River, which was Petiguar country and friendly to the French, their development was steady and peaceful for some time.

Ample natural resources made Francisco Pereira Coutinho's work easy. The bay was as vast as an inland sea. Numerous waterways facilitated access. Swift rivers moved water wheels. Virgin forests grew next to grassy lands where cattle could thrive according to nature's laws. And this captaincy was located at the center of all the others.

There was no brazilwood in the area, but the French lack of interest in the region made up for its poverty. And because they were not agitated by the French, the Tupinambás were less malevolent. Why then did Francisco Pereira Coutinho fail to prosper?

He was not able to control the people he brought with him, nor did he prevail over the local Indians. His hardships were such that he would have perished without the help sent from Ilhéus.

He later retired to Porto Seguro. He was old and worn out and had little desire to go on. But humors calmed in Bahia and he returned full of hope, only to be killed when he came ashore. In his struggles with the Indians, he had ordered one of the chieftains killed. As a prisoner of the Indians, he was ritually sacrificed—killed by the chieftain's younger brother, who was five years old at the time. He was so small that, according to the written account of a Jesuit, other Indians had to steady the sacrificial cudgel for him.

6

Crown Captaincies

With the first news of Francisco Pereira Coutinho's death, politicians in Portugal should have stopped and meditated on the colonization system that was in force.

Beyond doubt it was accomplishing what it had been set up to do. If the outposts scattered along the littoral did not totally stamp out trade between the natives and the interlopers, they made such trade more difficult. The French, after being expelled from Pernambuco, sought other points along the coast. With time they could be removed from them as well. The Portuguese were producing offspring, and population grew, thanks to racial mixture. Trade and production could be counted on.

But the organism was being sapped by an essential flaw. Donataries began their businesses with their own resources, or they borrowed money. If things went well right from the start, their profits allowed them to proceed with greater efficacy. If not, as in the cases of Pero de Góis, Francisco Pereira, Antônio Cardoso, João de Barros, Aires da Cunha, and Fernando Álvares, they lost momentum. Otherwise, sickly captaincies, such as Ilhéus, Porto Seguro, Epírito Santo, Santo Amaro, and São Vicente, vegetated.

On top of this, since donataries were equal in power and the captaincies were like foreign states to one another, any concerted action was impossible. Crime spread with impunity. Piracy was the natural consequence. Duarte Coelho's letters poignantly demonstrate this sorry anarchy. And the anarchy among captaincies was intimately related to the anarchy within each one.[1] Authorities and more authorities, clear laws, restrictions, and prescriptions—but how could they be gotten to work? How could they be enforced? How was it that donataries could invest their resources in colonization when their funds weren't sufficient for the demands of the endeavor?

The remedy Dom João III preferred was to take possession of the captaincy left vacant by Coutinho's death. With backing from the Crown, it would be a more vigorous enterprise. It would have a central government strong enough to guarantee internal order and to establish concord among the different centers of population.

With no more ado than this, charters and codices were torn up because it seemed that what lay ahead were conflicts between manorial and hereditary lords. The situation promised to be a replay of the kings' struggles with powerful medieval vassals. The few protests from the interested parties went unattended. In 1549, without the total abolition of the feudal system, a new system was instituted.

It consisted of a capitão-mor,[2] or captain-major, in charge of civilian and military administration; a *provedor-mor*, who would be in charge of the treasury; and an *ouvidor-mor*, or chief justice. Their base of operations was Bahia. In other captaincies they had agents. When they visited a different captaincy, they had original jurisdiction and were to take notice of any new grievances. In their absence agents did their jobs. Excessive numbers of officials were placed in these three ministries or lived off meager sinecures.

In the company of 400 soldiers, 600 deportees, and many workers paid by the exchequer; Tomé de Sousa, the first governor of Brazil; along with Pero Borges, chief justice; and Antônio Cardoso de Barros, provedor-mor of the treasury; left Lisbon for Brazil in February 1549. They arrived in All Saints Bay at the end of March.

When they came ashore, they looked for a proper place for the city they had come to found. They would fortify it against attacks from land, and they would construct the buildings they needed most.

People came ashore as accommodations were being prepared. Larger caravelles sent to different points along the coast bartered regularly with the natives and brought back foodstuffs. The abundant supply of fish provided relief from the preserved (or most likely spoiled) goods brought from Portugal. From Cape Verde came some cattle that thrived admirably in the new environment. People were paid in kind, mainly tools and trifles, which they traded among themselves or with the natives.

With these people, the governor maintained order in the capital. The treasurer and chief justice eliminated many abuses in their continuous travels throughout the captaincies.

With this expedition came the first six Jesuits sent to this continent. They would have a tremendous effect on later developments. But at the time, they rounded out the colonial administration harmoniously, because, just like Tomé de Sousa or Pero Borges, Father Manuel de Nóbrega adhered to the collective sentiment. He worked for colonial unity, and, in the ardor of his 32 years, he considered All Saints' Bay too restricted for this unprecedented undertaking.

His efforts floundered in the indifference or hostility of other ecclesiastics. This is why he insisted with apostolic frankness and determination that the king should send a bishop to Bahia. Only a bishop would bring the sheep into the fold and keep the wolves out. An episcopate was formed. In June 1552, Dom Pedro Fernandes Sardinha, the first bishop of Salvador, had come to the diocese.

The old prelate engaged in constant battle with the second governor, Dom Duarte da Costa (1553–57). Their struggles were largely of an ordinary sort, but, given the tenor of relations between civil and ecclesiastic power, they were unavoidable. Salvador's society was divided down the middle. Passions were inflamed. Normally responsible people instigated hatred for one another. And the ignorant masses threw themselves into the struggle. Mere insinuations became matters of life and death. With changes in form, these conflicts were replayed during the centuries that followed. They only died out once modern constitutions eliminated the last trace of the medieval notion that two perfect societies could exist side by side.

The Jesuits were above and beyond these debates. They concentrated their efforts on the captaincy of São Vicente.

Crossing the Serra do Mar, on the shore of the Tietê River they established their first mission, which took the name of the Apostle to the Gentiles [Saint Paul]. It was founded on 25 January 1554.

They were attracted by the greater abundance of food on the plateau, the presence of Indians, who, owing to their gentle nature, were ripe for conversion. And, in addition to the locale's distance from Portuguese settlements, these men were guided by vague ideas of mingling with the Indians of Paraná and Paraguay. The name of São Paulo, heard then for the first time, would have powerful reverberations in the future.

The French, expelled from Pernambuco by Duarte Coelho and kept out of the center by the city of Salvador and the towns farther south, steered clear of the regularly visited areas and concentrated on Pero de Góis's captaincy and the neighboring lands belonging to Martim Afonso. There, along leagues of coastline, the faithful Tamoios ruled the land, and brazilwood abounded.

From privateering ships, adventurers who could speak língua geral made contact with the local populace. Some identified so well with the Indians that they were not offended when natives served them human flesh. This relationship, if it did not stop the progress of the Portuguese, it made life difficult for them. For some years the victory remained undecided. Had the opponents been a little more forceful, the final decision could have gone against Portugal.

It behooved the French to coordinate their efforts. They adopted a hybrid system. Part of the capital would be supplied by private citizens, and part would come from the king, who, however, would not be responsible for the endeavor. He would legitimize it only if the venture succeeded.

At the head of this expedition he placed Nicolas Durand de Villegaignon, who was famous for his bravery and knowledge. Sailing from Brest, Villegaignon reached his destination (the environs of present-day Rio de Janeiro) in November 1555.[3] He set up a post on an island in the bay. This splendid location allowed him to keep his distance from the Indians, whose friendship he relied on. Its lack of water made it less ideal for resisting the Portuguese, whose attacks might be long in coming, but would come. He built two formidable fortresses on the island. The name *Pay Colas* [Father (Ni)Colas] became loved and cherished by the Indians living in the area. More than once this outpost received immigrants from Europe.

Because of their having settled on a small, rocky, waterless island, the French garrison suffered, subject as it was to the whims of the Tamoios. Their chief's puritan austerity rankled the soldiers. The immigrants brought religious dissension to the island. The chief had to be severe, perhaps even cruel. Bad news and serious complaints reached the Old World and hindered the colony's support. Finally, possibly because he had become disillusioned with the colony's immediate future, or because he was convinced his presence would stir up the apathetic and inspire the outfitters in France, or because he wanted to participate in the more brilliant and glorious conflicts across the ocean, Villegaignon left French Antarctica (i.e. Guanabara Bay) in 1559.

He was succeeded by his nephew Bois de Comte, who did not improve the status quo. How could he improve matters? To succeed, the French should have come twenty years earlier, before the Portuguese had established roots there. It was already too late. When Mem de Sá and his fleet entered the bay in March 1560, they needed only three days of steady bombardment to lay waste to the castles.

The Portuguese victory was enhanced by two occurrences in the captaincies of Martim Afonso and Pero Lopes.

Mem de Sá moved the old town of Santo André, joining it to the Jesuit mission of Piratininga. Because of this, or for some other reason, the Tupiniquins rose up and attacked the village. The Jesuits' catechumens joined the Portuguese to fight against their relatives, who were beaten back and never returned. Martim Afonso Tibiriçá fought valiantly for the Portuguese, in July 1562.

During the following year, Nóbrega would carry out a plan that had finally come to term. He would make peace with the Tamoios, who, as they sailed by Bertioga, kept the people in São Vicente and Santo Amaro on edge. In the company of José de Anchieta, a young Jesuit who had come with Dom Duarte da Costa and who knew língua geral quite well, Nóbrega set sail for Iperoig, which is not far from present-day Ubatuba. After a few months of dramatic confrontations, during which both men's lives were on the line more than once, they attained their desired goal in September 1565.

With the backlands delivered from danger, and the northern shoreline under control, the people in São Vicente could help Eustácio de Sá. In 1564 he had been sent to conquer Rio, which, notwithstanding the recent victory, still lay in the hands of the natives and the overseas enemy.

With ships and people brought from Bahia, along with Indians taken in Espírito Santo, Eustácio de Sá founded the city of Saint Sebastian on 1 March 1565.

Contrary to Villegaignon's actions, he settled at the entrance to the bay, on the mainland, facing east. Along with building fortified hedgerows, he began to plant crops. He would not rely on supplies coming from other captaincies. Even so, his expedition suffered tremendous famine. The local Indians outdid themselves in setting traps and ambushes. The colony was attacked twice by French ships allied with the Tamoios at Cabo Frio. The young hero withstood these attacks for two years. If he made no headway worthy of mention, he at least weakened the strength of the allies. So when Mem de Sá, Eustácio de Sá's uncle, arrived with strong reinforcements, two battles, one at Ibiraguaçu-Mirim (Rio de Janeiro's Glória Hill?), another at Paranapecu Island (today Ilha do Governador), sufficed to make the area definitively Portuguese.

Eustácio de Sá succumbed to wounds received in combat, so his uncle the governor spent another year in the city. In 1567 and the following year, he moved the settlement farther into the bay, to the hill now known as *Morro do Castelo*, which he supplied with trenches, surrounded with walls, and to which he added buildings as befitted a royal city. This became the second Crown captaincy, even though in the charter awarded to Martim Afonso the property was his.

Around this time there were other wars in Espírito Santo, Porto Seguro, Ilhéus, and Bahia. The Indians had been subjugated from Camamu to Itapercuru—a distance of 40 leagues.

With the defeat of the natives at Paraguaçu and Ilhéus, the latter, a língua geral stronghold or *marca* [Abreu's italics], was destroyed, and the Tapuias, who had been crowded out, broke through. No one profited from their reappearance. "The Aimorés are fierce and robust men. They are always in the forest, where four of them suffice to destroy an entire army," whines one contemporary. This setback was only remedied in the following century.

These warring deeds are not all that Mem de Sá's government accomplished. The man was a statesman and an appellate judge at the *Casa da Suplicação*. Among all his accomplishments, his aid to Nóbrega's missionary work stands out.

Would Brazil's resources be squandered in miscegenation and servile occupations? Would the native population end up as little more than machines for bastard pleasure and unbearable work? If not in so many words, this was what colonists were doing to the native population with tenacious regularity. However, the Jesuits represented another facet of human nature. To them, natives appeared as rational as the rest of humanity and, therefore, educable. On the *tabula rasa* of their children's minds one could implant goodness in its entirety. Adults and old people were another matter. They could have their rough edges trimmed. They could be denied alcohol, the cause of so much chaos. They could be prohibited from their ritual eating of human flesh, which was so repugnant to the Western mind. In the interest of creating more stable families, they could have monogamy imposed on them as much as possible. To attain these ends it was necessary to shield these people from the colonists' violence. The Jesuits would have to show the natives real benefits if they were to cut down on their inveterate evil ways. Jesuits would need to be respected and obeyed. They would supervise natives' food, dress, health, and bodies and give form to their amorphous heathen souls. Such was Nóbrega's plan, which the Company of Jesus carried out during the centuries of its fertile and stormy presence in Brazil. He had already tried it in Piratininga. He could work more efficiently once he was shielded by Governor-General Mem de Sá.

The early missions around All Saints Bay were set up in a carefully chosen place. They were close to the sea so the Indians could support themselves by fishing. They were close to the forests so they could forage. The Indians lived in several villages under the rule of a single chief, a *meirinho*, or bailiff, whom the padres recognized as the most able to collaborate in their purifying endeavor. There was also a resident padre and a brother who supervised everything. A Jesuit of the time sums up life in the missions as follows:

> The padres teach some doctrine to everyone every day during the morning. They say a Mass for those who want to hear one before going off to their fields. Then the children go to school, where they learn to read and write, to count and other good customs pertinent to the Christian way of life. In the afternoon there is another, private session on doctrine, for those who take the Holy Sacrament. Every day the padres, along with some Indians authorized to accompany them, go and visit the sick. If they have special needs, they attend to them. They always administer the necessary sacraments. . . . Indians' punishment is meted out by the meirinhos appointed by the rulers. They are only punished when they commit an offense. The meirinho has them put in a stock for a day or two, as he deems fitting. The law has no chains or irons. . . . The padres have the Indians always tilling their fields and gathering their food so that, when it is necessary, the Indians, for their own salvation, can help the padres with the Portuguese. It is true that many Portuguese eat thanks to the Indian villages, which is to say that the padres of the Company are fathers to the Indians in both body and soul.[4]

Begun in 1558, work at the missions developed rapidly during the following years, mainly under the directorship of Luís da Grã. With the same rapidity it declined, owing especially to the mysterious and up to now unexplainable fact that primitive people are doomed to extinction when they come in contact with civilized beings. Nonetheless, this endeavor was not abandoned and continued with varying degrees of success up to the middle of the eighteenth century.

Around that time, in Pernambuco expansion toward its southern border on the São Francisco River was picking up speed. Between the years 1554 and 1560, before Duarte de Albuquerque Coelho came of age, his uncle, Jerônimo de Albuquerque, had opened up the Capibaribe lowlands. The young donatary and his brother Jorge, who had come to Brazil from Portugal, conquered the land around Cape São Agostinho and around Sarinhaém. At the cape, João Pais Barreto, the founder of a large family that is still in the area, started eight *engenhos*. After this there were wars in the backlands. Their pretext was to search for mines, but those wars were really started by a desire to capture slaves. Antônio de Gouveia played a major role in these wars. He was a cleric, an epileptic who suffered from hallucinations and who claimed to be on familiar terms with the devil. He could not sit still anywhere—he even escaped from the shackles of the Inquisition. He was considered to be, and considered himself to be, a necromancer. This migrating bird passed himself off as an expert in mining and is remembered in the mind of the folk as the *Golden Padre*. It is said that he was responsible for Duarte de Albuquerque Coelho's being arrested and sent to Portugal. Antônio de Salema came to Pernambuco to open an inquiry on this and other matters.

With Mem de Sá's death in March 1572, it seemed appropriate to divide Brazil's government into two parts headed by the royal cities of Salvador and São Sebastião.

Luís de Brito de Almeida attempted to go beyond Rio Real and annex Sergipe, which the Jesuits had been setting up for peaceful occupation in the form of missions. The colonists' greed and the wiles of some *mamalucos* wrecked their plans.

In Rio de Janeiro, Antnio Salema, aided by the capitão-mor of São Vicente, waged war on the Indians at Cabo Frio. He brought peace to the territory between São Sebastião [Rio] and Macaé, a distance of 30 leagues they figured at that time. Many Tamoios were killed, a considerable number was enslaved, and some were gathered into the Jesuits' villages. The ones who got away fled into the backlands. Furthermore, this time the French suffered a blow from which they never entirely recovered.

There were several expeditions in search of precious stones, principally in the area between Bahia and Espírito Santo. Sebastião Tourinho and others crossed the Serra do Espinhaço in search of emeralds. In São Vicente Brás Cubas was busy hunting for mines. These efforts produced no concrete results. More important was the disappearance of the Indians, which brought about an increase in the importation of Africans. A Jesuit in 1583 wrote the following:

> During the last 20 years, it seems beyond belief the number of people who have perished here in Bahia. Who could imagine that so many people would die, especially in so short a time? We counted some 40,000 souls assembled in the 14 villages the padres founded. There were more who came later on. But, if the three churches in operation now have a total of 3,500 parishioners, that would be a lot.

Six years ago a respected citizen of this city, with a clear conscience and as a member of the town council, declared that in the previous two years they counted 20,000 Indians who had come from the Arabó *Sertão* [backlands]. They went to work on the Portuguese enterprises. With all these (20,000 plus the 40,000 at the missions), that makes 60,000. During the last six years the Portuguese have been bringing in people. So-and-so brings 2,000. What's-his-name 3,000. Some bring more, some less. Let it be seen just how much this adds up to: 80,000 souls, more or less.

Now go take a look at Bahia's farms and sugar plantations. You will find them full of negroes from Guiné, but with very few natives. And if you ask about all the natives, people will say they died. This is a clear demonstration of God's punishment for all the insults made, and being made, to these Indians. The Portuguese go into the sertão and deceive these people. They say that if they go with them to the coast, life there will be just like it is in the backlands, but they will be neighbors with the Portuguese. The Indians, believing this is true, come away with them, and the Portuguese, lest the Indians change their minds, destroy their gardens. And thus they bring them. Once they get to the sea they divide them up. Some take the wives, some the husbands, some the children. They sell them all.[5]

Why did the colonists insist on setting up these farms, since their worthlessness should have been obvious at a glance?

They suffered from a shortcoming that can still be seen frequently in their descendants. They were unable to make a firm decision about any subject and then guide their behavior according to their decision. Add to this the fact that native slaves, with all their drawbacks, in an extraordinary manner aided those people who had come to start over in this land. And the first thing the Portuguese wanted were slaves so that they (the Portuguese) might make a living. According to Gandavo, when someone arrived he acquired two pairs of slaves, or maybe half a dozen. Even if colonists owned nothing else, they set up to support their families with honor. One slave fished. Another hunted. The others cultivated and attended their fields. In this way the colonists made no outlays to support their slaves or to support themselves.[6]

7

Frenchmen and Spaniards

In 1580 the Avis dynasty came to an end. Philip II of Spain, the grandson of Dom Manuel, supporting his claim with force, succeeded Dom Henrique and set the Portuguese throne under the Hapsburgs. Along with Portugal, all its possessions came under Spanish rule.

For Brazil the early consequences of this state of affairs were favorable. The colony's natural extremes were indicated by the Amazon and the River Plate. The populated parts of Brazil were separated from both rivers by enormous distances. Now, even though the distances remained the same, [colonization] efforts could be concentrated in one direction, instead of being dissipated toward the far reaches of the colony. The River Plate could wait, since it was partly settled. It was time to take possession of the Amazon, which was yet to be explored, but which several different nations had their eyes on. Thus, on the route to the Plate, work was reduced to mere consolidation, to tightening the web. Toward the Amazon, colonial expansion gained momentum. Giving preference, then, to chronological order in our look at the Amazon, we shall follow geographic order beginning at the opposite end of the colony.

Starting in the south, Cananéia was full of people from the São Vicente Captaincy. They also migrated to the area around Angra dos Reis. Through the intermountain plain [*baixada*] of Santa Cruz, where the Jesuits established a prominent undertaking, they maintained contact with São Sebastião [Rio]. The French went on making contact with the natives around Cabo Frio, but less frequently and with diminished profits.

Finally after beating the French in battle, Constantino Menelau blocked the port. Estêvão Gomes built a small fortress there. Plagued by smallpox, the Guaitacás approached the whites who might be able to help them. The Jesuit Domingos Rodrigues was an active agent in the reconciliation.

The very same Domingos Rodrigues, who later left the Company of Jesus, working in Ilhéus, and Álvaro Rodrigues Adorno, in Cachoeira, succeeded in pacifying the Aimorés. So it was that from Rio to Salvador the much feared coastal Tapuias temporarily ceased their devastation. They started anew, however, in the middle of the century.

The conquest of Sergipe, north of Bahia, was most remarkable. Ever since the last days of Mem de Sá's administration, this undertaking seemed easy, at least in the constant flow of messages asking the Jesuit fathers to come and bring the Good News with them. Along with the two Jesuits sent on this mission came some soldiers and mamalucos eager to capture slaves. They brought discord to the Tupinambás and destroyed the trust these Indians had in the Portuguese. The Indians' misgivings were confirmed in 1574 by Governor Luís de Brito de Almeida, who waged relentless war on them. He imprisoned some and ran others off. He devastated the area for the fun of it, so it seems, because the colonization of Sergipe stood still for nearly two decades.

At the end of 1589, Cristôvão de Barros, the interim governor after the death of Manuel Teles Barreto, attacked again, with better results. Part of his forces went by sea, part by land, and together they laid siege to the natives, who were defeated.

In pursuit of natives, a band of adventurers went all the way to the São Francisco River. In the vacated area Cristôvão de Barros cut out an enormous tract of land for his son. This award was a precedent for others, and in a short time there was no land left to dole out. This campaign also brought the French presence at Rio Real to an end.

Movement toward the São Francisco proceeded in Duarte Coelho's captaincy. Cattle ranches and cane fields spread through Alagoas territory. Among the settlers in this region Lins stands out. He was a German who would leave many descendants. João Pais, whom we have already mentioned, was also prominent. Moreover, the French had to abandon this territory.

In the early years of the seventeenth century, one could travel by land from Bahia to Pernambuco without encountering serious resistance from the natives, who had been vanquished or beaten back from the coastal area. The only obstacles to easy transit were the bigger rivers, which were the king's property, as we have seen. Smaller rivers could be forded. And that is how things stood during the following centuries. The river fords mark the inner reaches of coastal occupation.

Let us now examine the march to the Amazon.

For a long time the northern limit of Portuguese settlement was Itamaracá Island and the surrounding area. The Petiguares in the Serra maintained good relations with the colonists, who visited them peacefully in their villages. The ones on the beach remained friendly with the French, and had good dealings with them in Paraíba, where they were not bothered by the Portuguese. The latter were satisfied with their brief excursions farther north in search of amber, which abounded along the beaches all the way to Ceará. They also gathered brazilwood, which the Indians themselves brought from the interior.

In 1574, because of some fight involving an Indian woman in the backlands, people turned against those in Goiana, and war broke out. Two engenhos were attacked and burned, and with this easy victory the attackers became even more incensed. This war, which was frivolously begun, was to last 25 years.

Under the command of Luís de Brito, Ouvidor-Geral (chief magistrate) Fernão da Silva set out for Paraíba. His presence was enough to set the Indians to flight. He then wrought some edicts that had no effect. Frutuoso Barbosa, a wealthy man, offered his services to the capital if it would grant him certain favors. Both he and his "favors" arrived in Pernambuco in 1580, but he accomplished nothing because a storm blew him north to the Antilles and from there back to Europe. On his second attempt he did not have the courage to try to set up anything on land. He merely burned some French ships.

In 1583 Diogo Flores Valdez anchored at Bahia. He was on his way back from an unsuccessful attempt to reach the Straight of Magellan. He made the governor believe he was up to the task of conquering the Indians in Paraíba, and with the next favorable wind he set sail for Pernambuco along with a Spanish fleet and some Portuguese ships. In Recife they organized two expeditions: one by land, the other by sea. By sea, Diogo Flores arrived without incident at his destination, where he burned some French ships loaded with brazilwood. He founded a fort and left behind a Spanish garrison. The land expedition emerged victorious from several encounters and founded a settlement, the city of Filipéia, named by Frutuoso Barbosa in honor of the reigning dynasty. A Castilian named Castejón was left in charge of the fort, and Frutuoso Barbosa ran the city.

The civil leader and the military leader did not get along. Their discord separated the Portuguese from the Spaniards. The Petiguares, terrified by the first clashes, returned immediately in dense bands, more arrogant than before. They were guided by the French from the ships that had been burned. These Frenchmen were thirsty for vengeance, and well aware of the capital importance of the stakes at hand. They were fighting for territory that had been their exclusive domain for many years.

Castejón fought back bravely. He was never lacking for support, which the ouvidor-geral in Pernambuco, Martim Leitão, sent out. The ouvidor-geral himself went there in March 1586, accompanied by 500 white men and many Indians. But the Indians and the French got more and more daring and determined. Dispirited, Frutuoso Barbosa relinquished his rights and withdrew to Olinda. Castejón resisted until June. When he withdrew he set fire to the fort, broke its bell, sunk a ship, and dropped his cannonry into the sea. All his work had been dashed.

Years before, some adventurers from Pernambuco, who were making war along the São Francisco, were double-crossed by the Tabajaras. These old allies, faithful from the time of Duarte Coelho, killed them all and then fled from the ill-starred area. Going down one of the necks of the Borborema River, they headed for Paraíba to join their hereditary and irreconcilable foes, the língua geral-speaking Petiguares. Together they would wage war on the whites. Martim Leitão, when he left Olinda to help Castejón, recognized them and set up meetings, trying to bring them back into the fold. The Tabajaras were not about to be brought over and prepared themselves for battle. Their luck betrayed them, in spite of the bravery of two Tupiniquim chiefs: Braço de Peixe [Fish's Arm] and Assento de Pássaro [Bird's Perch].

This defeat reawoke the Tupinambás' ancestral hatred for the Tupiniquins, and they broke with their new allies, denouncing them as cowards, calling them traitors, and obliging them to go back whence they came. Martim Leitão found out about this and sent emissaries to Piragibá. To reestablish peace with them, he promised to forget their recent transgressions; he announced forthcoming aid; and he entreated them to stay where they were. Braço de Peixe gave in. With João Tavares (the registrar of orphans in Olinda) working as intermediary, the Tabajaras once more would fight alongside the Portuguese.

On August 5, the day of Our Lady of the Snow, João Tavares began anew the work that had been dashed by Castejón's defection. This endeavor was helped by Braço de Peixe, Assento de Pássaro, and their people, but it was constantly hampered by the Petiguares and the French.

Martim Leitão returned to Paraíba two more times. His always productive and prestigious deeds can be summed up in a few words: he burned ships; he burned brazilwood that had been cut; he burned villages; he ripped out crops; he rendered French supplies useless in Traição Bay, in the Serra de Copaoba, and in Tijucopapo.

In May 1587, Martim Leitão considered his mission accomplished and, after setting the foundation for a royal engenho, returned to Pernambuco. He was, however, mistaken. For more than ten years there were constant wars in the backlands and on the coast. The Portuguese fought French ships, some of which actually layed siege to the fortress at Cabedelo. They fought the Petiguares, who had acquired a daring and tenacity quite alien to their native character. Their ferocity was owed to the French, who had been marooned there by the burning of the ships that would have taken them home. We know nothing of the events during these wars. The chronicles only register the names of Pedro Lopes, Feliciano Coelho, Pedro Coelho, maybe Ambrósio Ferndandes Brandão, who might be the author of *Diálogos das Grandezas do Brasil*.[1] On the French side tradition remembers Rifault, whose deeds cannot be discerned because there are no documents.

So many tumultuous years and such desperate resistance made the need to occupy Rio Grande obvious. That was where the enemy retreated and regrouped. One time, 13 ships set out from Rio Grande to take Cabedelo, and the battle lasted from a Friday to a Monday. Another time, 20 French ships gathered there. Many French had taken Indian wives. Many Indian women had children with blond hair. Even today one can see vestiges of the lineage and persistence of these old rivals in the hair of the people living in that region and the neighboring backlands of Paraíba and Ceará.

The Rio Grande expedition had been conceived of under the government of Dom Francisco de Sousa. It was abundantly outfitted and directed from Pernambuco by Manuel de Mascarenhas Homem, the donatary's stand-in, and Alexandre de Moura, second in command. The expedition set out by land and by sea. The maritime division, headed by Manuel de Mascarenhas and joined by Jerônimo de Albuquerque, arrived at its destination without incident in January 1598. Part of the land division under the leadership of Feliciano Coelho, the capitão-mor of Paraíba, overcame the enemy, but it was dispersed by a smallpox epidemic. The plague attacked the enemy as well, which helped give Mascarenhas some relief, for he was being attacked once more in the fort he himself had built.

In March Feliciano Coelho, after gathering his troops, again set out for Rio Grande, where soldiers' numbers had been cut in half by the illness and by the retreat of the contingent from Pernambuco. With these reinforcements, Mascarenhas finished constructing the fort at Reis Magos and handed it over to Jerônimo de Albuquerque, who had been named its commander. In the shadow of this fort grew the city now known as Natal. On the way back Mascarenhas and Coelho went inland from the coast and devastated the Indians in the backlands once more.

In Jerônimo de Albuquerque's veins ran the Petiguar blood of his mother, Maria do Arco-Verde. He was not ashamed of this. Instead, in more than one tight spot, we can see him bragging about it. Thus, he must have liked the idea of bringing his relatives into the fold since they were in dire straits because of their many travails and their continuous persecution—plus their recent and forced abandonment by the French. After carefully instructing an Indian captive in what he should do to bring the Petiguares back to the Portugese, Albuquerque charged this leader and medicine man with such a mission. His humanitarian gesture was crowned with great success, especially thanks to the Indian women, who, according to a contemporary source, were annoyed with constantly having to bear the brunt of their tribes' moves, with having to flee through the forests, with having no permanent home, and even with not having the vegetables they used to plant. They threatened their husbands, saying they would go over to the whites because they would rather be their slaves than live with so much fear, constant warfare, and surprise attacks. By the order of Dom Francisco de Sousa, the peace was solemnly sworn in Paraíba on 15 June 1599. Friar Bernardino das Neves, the son of João Tavares (the registrar of orphans, whom we have mentioned) was the interpreter. This and later events kindled and nourished the Portuguese's friendship for Antônio Camarão, one of the Indian heroes in the struggle with Holland.

The conquest of Rio Grande had succeeded in removing the French from a huge stretch of territory and bringing the Indians to their senses. But, more important, this victory had shortened the distance to Maranhão and the Amazon. From the early days of Governor Diogo Botelho's administration, the notion of consummating the endeavor grew more and more compelling, and the Portuguese set out to reach the regions where nature's hand had determined the country's borders.

Pedro Coelho de Sousa, Frutuoso Barbosa's brother-in-law, took it upon himself to occupy Maranhão. He left Paraíba with a large following and landed at the Jaguaribe River in 1603. The Indians on those shores were at first stand-offish, but gave in to the interpreters' promises, so the entire untamed coast of Ceará was traversed in peace. Only at the Serra de Ibiapaba, which turned out to be a Tabajara retreat [*seminário*], did they meet resistance, which was instigated by the French. Pedro Coelho overcame the opposition and then headed down the mountains in search of the Punaré River, or the Parnaíba as it is called today. Because his men refused to go any farther, he had to turn back.

Up to that point all had gone well, but then things deteriorated. On his way back to the settlement, Pedro Coelho captured all the Indians he could among the Portugueses' old friends the Tabajaras and their new allies, the Petiguares. After having scattered them in Paraíba and Pernambuco, he returned to Ceará once more and found the state of affairs untenable. He was obliged to fall back. His woeful retreat was marked with bodies—victims of burning sands, hunger, and thirst.

In Fernão Cardim's territory [*provincialado*], under the governorship of Dom Diogo de Meneses, two Jesuits, Francisco Pinto and Luís Figueira, were commissioned to go to Maranhão. With the idea of setting them free, they took with them some of the Indians captured by Pedro Coelho and his followers. It required some doing to gain the natives' confidence, as it did to cross the Serra de Uruburetama and to get to Ibiapaba, where they were well-received in spite of everything. They were getting ready to push on when some Tapuias attacked the village they were staying in. Indians killed Francisco Pinto. Luís Figueira escaped and returned to Pernambuco, where, years later, he recorded this tragic odyssey in a letter that luckily has survived the ravages of time.

Neither Pedro Coelho's huge expedition armed for war nor the peaceful Jesuit mission had succeeded in taking a positive step in the expansions from east to west, which would have seemed doomed to indefinite delays were it not for Martim Soares Moreno's intervention. He had arrived from Portugal in 1602. His uncle, Diogo de Campos, a major, got him into Pedro Coelho's first expedition so he could learn the local language and become familiar with native ways. Soares Moreno was only 18 years old. He fulfilled and surpassed his uncle's expectations. So well did he get on with the natives that the Petiguar chief, Jacaúna, distinguished him from the crowd of thugs and treated him like a son. When he was named commander of the Reis Magos Fortress, he cultivated his relationship with Jacaúna, visiting his faithful friend more than once, always eager to dispel inequities and resentment. After some time Jacaúna let him take one of his sons to Bahia and introduce him to Governor Dom Diogo de Meneses. He also let Martim Soares and two soldiers set up camp among his people. Soares was able to establish a rudimentary fortress next to the minuscule Ceará River. There he resisted attacks from people not under Jacaúna's rule. And Soares, naked and in war paint as if he were an Indian brave, captured two foreign ships with Jacaúna's help. That place, which until then the French had considered an excellent source of fresh water, was avoided.

During the government of Gaspar de Sousa, plans were made to head farther north. Jerônimo de Albuquerque had been named capitão-mor for the conquest of Maranhão. Under Sousa's orders, Albuquerque left Pernambuco in the middle of 1613 with four ships. He was in command of 100 white men and many Indians. When he passed Ceará, he picked up Martim Soares Moreno according to plan and then sailed to Camocim, where he intended to set up a fort. Because Camocim did not seem right, he set up camp in Tartarugas Sound, at Jarerecuarcara, where he left 40 soldiers in a presidio. He had the ships follow the coast as best they could back to Pernambuco. With the remaining soldiers he returned to Pernambuco by land.

From Camocim he sent Martim Soares along with 20 soldiers to Maranhão. They were to gather information that would help carry out the conquest. Thanks to their launch's shallow draft, Soares sailed very close to the coast and was able to enter the mouth of the Preá River, and through inland waters he reached the bay now known as São José.

Jacaúna's name and his friendship helped Soares in this risky expedition. The Tupinambás received him with apparent affability, but were making plans to betray him, when one of them let Soares in on what was happening. For the past year there had been Frenchmen in the area. They had a fortress with twenty artillery pieces, soldiers, and people brought in by boat. They were under the command of Daniel de Latouche, the lord of Ravardière. Meanwhile, the French had been informed of the Portuguese' presence, and they set out in pursuit. Martim Soares escaped unharmed, along with his men and their Indian friend. The weather was less friendly, and it sent them north, to the coast of Venezuela, from where, passing through Santo Domingo, they ended up in Seville in April of the following year. Upon arrival Soares had news sent to Pernambuco. He also sent the pilot of the launch, Sebastião Martins, who had accompanied him on the peregrination, to Pernambuco. He arrived in the nick of time. Gaspar de Sousa was putting together a second and more powerful expedition for another conquest, and he was able to make use of Martins' information.

Once again Jerônimo de Albuquerque would be the capitão-mor. Diogo de Campos went as major and shared command. The governor recommended that they be cautious and suggested that they erect another fort in addition to the tiny one left there the year before. He also recommended that they plant some crops that would grow quickly. And he indicated that beginning at Tutóia it would be wise for part of the expedition to go by land and the other half to go by sea.

After getting some reinforcements at the fortress in Ceará, the expedition set sail again on 29 September 1614. Its next stop was Fort Rosário, which had tested its mettle against men on a French ship heading for Maranhão. After having praised the men to the hilt, they took from that fort 220 soldiers, 60 sailors, and 300 Indians with bows and arrows. Should they land at Tutóia? The pilots confessed total ignorance of that part of the coast. Martins was only familiar with the entrance to the Preá River. They set out for the Preá on October 12 and on the night of October 13 they tumbled around the bay in great confusion. "There were ships that touched and even slammed against the banks as they entered the harbor. So as not to frighten those who were following, they stopped and remained silent so not a word could be heard."[2]

Many of the men on this expedition were young, poorly disciplined, and impatient. They were eager to see how they would stand up against the French. They talked the capitão-mor into irresponsibly sailing up the Preá until they sighted the enemy. Before Soares Moreno's voyage, the entrance to the Preá River had been unknown to the French. After the voyage, they had set up a flimsy fort in Itapari. Ravardière had, however, concentrated on defending Saint Marcos Bay. People trusted its fortifications. Claude d'Abbeville, a Capuchin missionary proudly wrote:

> It is, thus, foolish to think that one could dislodge the French from that place since they are firmly set up there. And it is foolish to want someone to believe such a thing. Beyond demeaning their courage and making too little of their valor and generosity, that would be pure malice or foolhardiness. It would be as silly as having the blind describe colors. Those who have seen the location of that island and who know from experience the difficulties in reaching it would never accept such a proposition, which could only come from some timid soul.[3]

The attack from the Bay of São José, because of the fortuitous weakness of Martim Soares' launch, made this fierce talk sound foolish.

On October 26 the expedition reached the port that would later be called Guaxenduba. Two days later they began construction of Fort Santa Maria, on the mainland. On the adjacent island the appearance of some fires seemed to indicate the transmission of news. Some Indians, skittish in spite of Jerônimo de Albuquerque's solicitude, were consulted. They flatly denied that there were any French in the area. However, one of them, a native of Pernambuco, told them an attack was in the making. And on November 12, during the first quarter of the moon, the enemy fell upon the Portuguese ships and took three of them. This was followed by a more forceful attack on the nineteenth. The French brought ashore 200 infantrymen plus 2,000 Indians. La Ravadière, with 100 soldiers in reserve, stayed on board. This army had been brought by 57 ships (3 of which were those they had stolen earlier) and 50 canoes. They began to dig trenches, and, to gain some time, La Ravadière sent a threatening letter to Jerônimo de Albuquerque. Without answering the letter, the Portuguese began a desperate offensive. Diogo de Campos, Antônio de Albuquerque (son of the capitão-mor) and Jerônimo Fragoso advanced along the beach. From the interior came Jerônimo de Albuquerque, Francisco de Frias, and Manuel de Sousa de Sá.

Sousa de Sá writes that around 90 Frenchmen died on the spot—run-through by swords or by arrows from crossbows. Others drowned fleeing toward the ships—a total of 160. Nine were taken prisoner. The French had 46 canoes burned; they lost a total of 200 firearms (muskets and har-quebuses). The savages were reduced by 400, most of whom died by drowning. On the Portuguese side the losses were insignificant.

This defeat broke La Ravadière's spirit. Instead of immediately setting out to avenge it, he began an exchange of letters with Jerônimo de Albuquerque on the twenty-first. He started with harsh words, but gradually softened. The Portuguese were in a tight spot. The enemy fleet commanded the entrance to the bay. Help could only come from the Preá River, which would only accommodate ships with shallow drafts. In spite of everything, Albuquerque held his ground: "We are men who can get by on a handful of flour and snake meat, when we find it," he wrote back. He was seconded by a more diffuse Diogo de Campos:

> We are people who cannot swim the entire sea from here to Spain. And even though you might command the harbor, we hold the land we walk on, and our bodies shall remain on it until His Majesty, the king of Spain, our lord and master, whose all this is, orders something else.[4]

From this correspondence and from day-to-day goings-on, came the idea of a truce. If the two nations were friends and allies in the Old World, why were they at each other's throats in the New World? On the twenty-seventh they decided to suspend hostilities until the end of December 1615. The French would not come ashore, nor would the Portuguese go to the island. Both sides would avoid contact with Indians in the other's jurisdiction. Prisoners would be exchanged without ransom. The Portuguese would get free access to the sea. Reinforcements would not affect the armistice. The nation obliged to leave would have three months to prepare for departure. And two representatives from both sides would go to the courts of Madrid and Paris and find out from Their Most Christian and Catholic Majesties who should keep Maranhão.

After this, the capitão-mor sent Manuel de Sousa de Sá to Pernambuco on a caravelão. He took this news to the governor general. The *Regente*, which had fought with the contingent at Rosário, in Jarerecuarcara, left on December 16 carrying Du Prat and Gregório Fragoso as emissaries to France. On 4 January 1615 Diogo de Campos and Mathieu Maillart left for Portugal on a caravelle bought from Maillart for 500 cruzados. On March 3 they met with the viceroy, Dom Aleixo de Menezes. Major de Campos used the crossing to write *Jornada do Maranhão*.

The court's reception of the outcome of the expedition to Maranhão was icy. And its ill-will increased with the unexpected arrival of Manuel de Sousa de Sá, who had been sent from Pernambuco. He had been blown off course. Ocean currents carried him to the West Indies, from where he was escorted to Europe. Once the court heard Sousa de Sá's version of the story, which in essential points was different from Diogo de Campos's, a brigantine with munitions, gunpowder, and other necessities was readied and sent to Maranhão. By the beginning of June it had reached Ceará. It seems that Martim Soares was on board, without his uncle. Martim Soares was now a major. There were plans to punish Diogo de Campos, but a suggestion to send him away with Sousa de Sá and Gaspar de Sousa prevailed. Gaspar de Sousa had been ordered to carry out the original undertaking with greater zeal.

The governor had not been inattentive. In June he had sent out the old capitão-mor of Rio Grande, Francisco Caldeira de Castelo Branco, who headed a fleet made up of one brigantine, two caravelles, and one huge caravelão. Keeping clear of the Preá, he arrived at Santa Maria de Guaxenduba on July 1. In spite of the truce, La Ravadière was asked to leave the area. He balked for a while then agreed. But because of discord between the two Portuguese leaders, the French stayed on. Jerônimo de Albuquerque moved his contingent out to the island, where he built a fence and a fort, which he called São José. That is probably why the bay is now called São José.

Manuel de Sousa met the governor general in Pernambuco and gave him the letter and his orders. Without delay Gaspar de Sousa readied nine ships, five of which were big. To settle the land, he had more than 900 men, considerable armaments and money, plants and cattle.

He put Alexandre de Moura at the head of the expedition, which left Recife on October 5. On the seventeenth it approached the Preá. It did not take Moura long to realize that the Preá was not the right channel for his ships. He would have to sail outside it, checking the depth as he went, and facing head-on the Bay of São Marcos with its (according to d'Abbeville) terrible, unyielding forts. Furthermore, there was no time to lose. The Portuguese had splintered into two warring factions. Fort São José had been burned down. And Jerônimo de Albuquerque, the capitão-mor more in name than in fact, had been left with what little gunpowder and whatever arms he had managed to save from the fire.

They had decided to penetrate the entrance of São Marcos Bay on November 1. A smaller brigantine lead the way and the fleet assembled beyond the range of the enemy artillery. Jerônimo de Albuquerque marched overland with his troops. A post was outfitted with 8 pieces of artillery, 150 soldiers, and 200 archers. Another 100 men and 6 cannons would be stationed at the entrance to the harbor. On the third, La Ravadière was enjoined to surrender his colony and his fortress, with all existing artillery and supplies inside and outside the fort, as well as all ships, big and little, and with no indemnity whatsoever. Alexandre de Moura would be responsible for his transportation back to France, and the French would be obliged to leave once the ships arrived—provided they left some hostages. They were doing the French this favor because of the existing alliances between their lords the Catholic and Most Christian kings.

The fortress was surrendered. In two different ships, with no artillery, the French left for the fatherland while La Ravadière was taken with the victor to Pernambuco. Years later he showed up in Lisbon, where he petitioned the king for a pension, claiming he had done the Crown a service by abandoning his fortress and cannonry in Maranhão. Thus, the year 1615 would see the final defeat of the French after almost a century of resistance. They lost to Constantino Menelau in Cabo Frio and to the old capitão-mor of Pernambuco in Maranhão.

Alexandre de Moura had orders to expel the French from Pará and to reach the Amazon. Since there were no French in Pará and the Amazon had not been occupied, he sent in his place Francisco Caldeira de Castelo Branco, along with 150 men, 10 cannons, and 3 ships. In addition, by sending Castelo Branco north, he removed a particular thorn from his side. Castelo Branco took a French pilot with him, as well as the famous Charles Desvaux—"a man the capitão-mor must appreciate, with due caution." Antônio Vicente Cochado went as pilot.

They left on Christmas Day and headed 150 leagues up the coast, checking depths, anchoring every night, and making reconnaissance on land. They entered the harbor by Saparará Point and sailed among the islands. They were well received by the heathen, who favored them now that the French had been defeated. Many of the natives wore their hair long, and from a distance they looked like women. The explorers received some vague news that the English and Dutch had been in the area.

At a distance of 35 leagues from the sea, on the right bank of the Pará River, Francisco Caldeira de Castelo Branco founded a fortress, which he called Presepe [crèche].

The first step toward the occupation of the Amazon had been taken.

It is time for a quick overview of the country. Around 1618, the author of *Diálogos da Grandeza do Brasil* was writing his work, and Friar Vicente do Salvador was preparing to write his history book.[5]

The Portuguese settlements began almost on the equator, in Pará, and they went beyond the Tropics south to Cananéia. Between one captaincy and another there were huge, uninhabited stretches of land tens of leagues long. The population that spoke a European tongue was well under 100,000.

The lowest level of society was made up of slaves—natives, Africans, or Africans' descendants. There were fewer native slaves because of the original sparseness of their population, the great exoduses that distanced them from the coast, the constant epidemics that decimated them, and the not always useless impediments [missionaries erected] against their enslavement.

Above this landless, captive flock were the Portuguese or *Renóis* and their descendants. They too were landless, but they were free. They voted. They worked as sugar bosses and as skilled laborers, and lived off their salaries or from what they manufactured. These laborers generally knew more than one trade, because no one could live on one alone. They worked on plantations when their simple tools enabled them to, or when the plantation owners supplied the tools.

Among the rural landowners there were subsistence farmers and cattlemen. Cattle thrived only on the banks of the lower São Francisco River. Cattle ranching would only flourish later on, when it became independent from farming and invaded the fields and thickets of the interior. This hierarchy was crowned by the *senhor de engenho*, the plantation owner. Their *engenhos,* or mills, were run by water or by oxen and were served by carts or boats. In addition, they were situated next to the shore or farther inland. Not too far inland, however, because transportation conditions did not permit more than limited inland penetration. A royal sugar plantation needed huge fields of cane, abundant firewood, plenty of oxen or enough boats and boatmen, slaves, various apparatuses, grinders, copper kettles, molds, purging houses, and people trained in sugar manufacture. The raw material went through several stages before reaching the customer. Some plantations had a church and a chaplain who was paid better than the vicars. These chaplains were at times charged with teaching the rudiments of reading to the master's children. The opulent senhor de engenho sent his harvest directly to Portugal and in return he received fine cloth, wine, and wheat flour—in sum luxury items and things of pleasure.

Rich people's homes were, for practical purposes, autonomous economic systems. Petronius's declaration: *nec est quod putes illum quidquam emere, omnia domi nascuntur* which means "there is no reason to think that man lacks anything, everything is produced at home," could not be carried out literally, but up to a point that is how things were. Thread was spun and cloth was woven for the slaves' clothing. The family's clothes were made at home. Slaves were employed to furnish food: fresh or salt water fish, shellfish caught in the tidal swamps, or game. Because there were no butcher shops, small-scale raising of fowls, sheep, goats, and pigs served to feed surprise, last-minute dinner guests.

> Rich people's homes (even if it is at someone else's expense, since many are in debt for all they own) are stocked with all the essentials. They have slaves to hunt and fish for them. They have casks of wine and olive oil, which they buy in lots, and which cannot be purchased in town.

Commerce was carried out by sailors who came from Portugal with cargoes that they tried to sell quickly so they could return on the ship on which they arrived. Peddlers wandered through the backlands selling odds and ends. In business deals, barter or exchange of goods was the rule. The exchange of money was extremely rare. Moreover, since no one kept even approximate records of what they owned, most people were in debt.

Recently one economist has remarked that in primitive economies the goods made at home are never overproduced. If there is a surfeit of some product, it is stored, given away, or left to spoil. This explains Brazilians' hospitality, their Pantagruelesque feasts, and their gambling. What little money was in circulation was probably best spent on parades. Whatever was left over got spent on feasts of a religious or secular nature.

The absence of capital severely limited community life. There were no fountains or highways. If, thanks to some favorable turn of events, a fountain or highway was built, they wasted away for lack of care, or they simply fell apart. Because there was no money, taxes were taken to town, and the tax collector was paid in kind. Only the charity institutions [*casas de Misericórdia*] were to some extent solid organizations. Even the most prosperous capitals of captaincies were little more than one horse towns. Wealthy people had houses there, but they only came for holidays. These towns' permanent population consisted of government employees, ordinary workers, or low-life individuals.

Added to this was the colonists' natural disaffection for the land—which is easy to understand if we consider how these early settlers lived. They were overwhelmed by the virgin forests, bitten by insects, poisoned by snakes, attacked by wild animals, and threatened by Indians. They were defenseless against pirates, who would show up whenever they found out there was something worth stealing. Even if there had been an abundance of means, no one was inclined to work on behalf of future generations. People wanted to make their fortune as fast as possible and go back to Portugal to enjoy it. Gandavo tells us that those most accustomed to the country no longer wanted to leave. These people must have been Brazil's earliest promoters.

The different sectors of the population felt the same disaffection for one another as they felt for the land.

Examining the country's populace superficially, one discerns three irreducible races. Each one had come from a different continent, with nothing in support of their getting together. People of mixed background began to appear, and did not occasion sympathy or benevolence. Their appearances were unpredictable as far as skin color and blood lines were concerned. And, because racial mixture was so new and foreign, both skin color and background were measured and weighed with a precision we can no longer even comprehend today. We [Brazilians] have been exposed to this *fait accompli* from the cradle and are indifferent to skin color, whatever it may be, and to racial mixture of whatever proportions.

Disaffection among the three races and their intermingled offspring occurred within each group. *Ladino* [acculturated African] and Brazilian-born blacks or *crioulos* scorned the *boçais*, negroes who had not yet learned their masters' language. Indians who converted to Christianity, lived in

Christian communities, and wore clothes must have felt a profound separation between themselves and the wild Indians who were free and went around naked—even when they belonged to the same tribe. The *reinóis,* or native-born Portuguese, considered themselves far superior to the Portuguese or *mazombos* born in these distant and barbarian parts. And the mazombos felt and acknowledged their inferiority.

In sum, centrifugal, dispersing forces held forth in this social system. Scarcely were the differences noted that feelings of unity gave way to factionalism. Only very slowly and in the seventeenth century was this widespread notion of dispersion to diminish. In spite of all their obvious and irreducible differences, renóis and mozambos, boçais and ladinos, mamalucos and *caribocas* [Indian and white mixtures], mulattos, and *caboclos* [acculturated Indians] all felt closer to one another than they did to the Dutch invaders. That is why war broke out and continued unabated until its end, 30 years later. At São Vicente, in Rio, Bahia, everywhere, by different routes, they all arrived at the same conclusion.

Concerning how all these people were to be governed, a government proclamation of 1617 tells us the following: Public expenditures were to rise to fifty-four million, one hundred and thirty-eight thousand, two hundred and ninety-eight (54,138,298) reis, which would be divided among the church, the judiciary, the militia, and the ministry of finance.

The entire country constituted of only one diocese. The bishop officiated from his throne in Bahia. Next to him in the hierarchy were two administrators: one in Paraíba for the northern captaincies; another for the southern captaincies resided in Espírito Santo. Each captaincy formed a parish with a vicar and his assistant. There were, however, exceptions. São Vicente was made up of 4 parishes: Itanhaém, São Vicente, Santos, and São Paulo. Espírito Santo contained 2: Vitória and Espírito Santo. Bahia had 14: Vila-Velha, Santo Amaro, São Tiago, Peruaçu, Paripe, Matoim, Nossa Senhora do Socorro, Sergipe do Conde, Taparia, Passé, Pirajá, Cotegipe, Tamari, and Sergipe del Rei. Pernambuco was divided into 12 parishes: Olinda, São Pedro, Recife, São Lourenço, Igaraçu, Santo Antônio, Várzea, Moribeca, Santo Amaro, Pojuca, Serinhaém and Porto Calvo. Itamaracá consisted of 2: the island and Goiana. The government paid church salaries and furnished money for church expenses. In order to pay for this, the king, as Grand Master of the Ordem de Cristo, exacted a tithe.

There were Jesuit schools as well as Capuchine, Carmelite, and Benedictine monasteries in Bahia, Rio, Espírito Santo, and Pernambuco. They all received benefits of various sorts, in kind and in currency. Almost all the captaincies maintained houses of charity, to which the government contributed.

The judiciary was headed by the *Relação* or Court of Appeals, which, along with its staff of *desembargadores* and *ouvidores gerais* [judges], was located in Bahia. In the royal captaincies it seems that common judges presided in district courts, and these judges were contracted on a yearly basis. The judges in donataries' captaincies were ouvidores who often turned out to be the capitão-mor of the captaincy. The proclamation has little to say about them.

The ministry of finance was headed by a *provedor-mor*, who resided in the capital. Under him in rank were *provedores* [purveyors], scribes, suppliers, and customs officers.

The captaincies belonging to donataries were: São Vicente, Santo Amaro, Espírito Santo, Porto Seguro, Ilhéus, Pernambuco, and Itamaracá. Those beloning to the Crown were: Rio, Bahia, Sergipe, Paraíba, Rio Grande, Ceará, Maranhão, and Pará.

The governor-general, with his offices in Bahia, was in charge of civil and military administration. The militia consisted of paid soldiers and orderlies who formed a sort of national guard.

And now that we have seen how being under Spain's rule helped us rout the French and move rapidly toward the Amazon, let us examine the other side of the coin—the wars with the Dutch, which we also owe to Spain.

8

Fighting the Dutch

Relations between Portugal and the Low Countries had begun in the Middle Ages and were maintained throughout the period of discovery and colonization of Brazil. The Dutch and Flemish would travel to Lisbon to buy silks and exotic goods along the piers and waterfront. They marketed them to their vast clientele in northern and western Europe. This spared the Portuguese extra work and guaranteed them immediate profits. In addition to foreign exchange, the Portuguese obtained grains, salt fish, metal objects, nautical instruments, and fine cloth from their faithful customers.

This situation, which had been advantageous for both sides, was changed when the Spanish Monarchy laid claim to the entire peninsula, and Castile's enemies became enemies of Portugal. In 1585 Philip II ordered all Dutch vessels anchored in his ports to be confiscated and their crews to be imprisoned. He did the same in the years 1590, 1595, and 1599.

It would be hard to imagine a worse blow for a nation such as Holland, whose overseas trade supplied most of its wealth and whose independence had been paid for in blood. After all its heroic acts, would it have to bow to the lords of southern Europe? The Dutch devised the wildest of schemes to avoid these straits. They tried searching for another route to China and India in the northern seas. They tried transferring their commercial activity to the Mediterranean. They tried to take the Strait of Magellan. It all came to naught. They considered going around the Cape of Good Hope and getting their Oriental goods at the place of origin.

In 1595 some merchants in Amsterdam outfitted their first voyage to the Indian Ocean. It was a lengthy voyage, with little immediate profit, but its findings would turn out to be most fertile. It showed the Dutch the fragility of the Iberian Peninsula's grip on those distant regions. From Amsterdam three more expeditions would depart: one in May 1598, another in April 1599, and a third in December of the same year. From several provinces daring entrepreneurs came forth. Well-heeled companies were formed, and people were eager for spoils and adventures in the theater that was opening. Healthy emulation threatened to degenerate into pernicious rivalry. Sagacious men foresaw this danger. The Estates General intervened. And by granting concessions and privileges, they reconciled divergent ambitions and founded the Dutch East India Company in the beginning of 1602.

The 12-year truce signed in 1609 by the Low Countries and Spain was no hindrance to the adventurous career of the company. In the company's very few years of existence it forced itself on the native princes, it repelled the English, and it vanquished a mighty Luso-Hispanic trading post. It monopolized the spice trade. It paid enormous dividends. And it lent invaluable service to the government of the United Provinces.

With the armistice and its stability, the idea of a West Indies company came to fruition. Chartered on 3 June 1621, it would be similar to the East India Company as far as its aims and organization were concerned. It would have 7,100,000 florins in capital, and its original charter would last for 24 years. It would consist of five chambers representing stockholders in Amsterdam, Zealand, Maas, the Northern District, and Friesland. The 19 directors would alternate their meeting between Amsterdam and Middleburg. In Africa its theater of operations would include the territory from the tropic of Cancer to the Cape of Good Hope. In the New World it would operate between Newfoundland on the Atlantic to the Strait of Anian[?] in the Pacific.

The Estates General authorized the company to build forts in the designated regions. It could make treaties with the princes and native peoples. It could appoint officials and clerks. The Estates General offered subsidies in exchange for the right to a part of the company's profits. They furnished soldiers and warships according to the company's specifications. In sum, with the exception of the most blatant differences, the West Indies Company was a descendant of the donatary system begun by Dom João III.

The West Indies Company left evidence of its presence in African territory, along the coast of the United States, in the Antilles, in Brazil, and in Chile. We shall concern ourselves with its deeds in Brazil.

The company's creation was received coldly in Holland. As late as 1622, less than one fifth of the capital had been raised, and that fifth would only become available in 1624, once the company received extra advantages, among them the sole right to export Brazilian salt.

Beginning in 1623, the company started to put together an expeditionary force bound for Bahia. It would consist of 23 ships and 3 yachts with 500 cannons, and a crew totaling 1,600 sailors. In the last days of 1623 and the first part of 1624, they slowly gathered at São Vicente in Cape Verde. On 26 March 1624 they left, heading southwest. On May 4 they sighted the coast of Brazil, and on the eighth they were spotted from shore off of All Saints Bay.

Diogo de Mendonça Furtado governed both Salvador and the rest of Brazil. He had received news of imminent danger and had taken measures to protect the port.

He had plenty of courage and will, but he lacked everything else. Some of the fortresses were crumbling, others were not yet finished. The harbor was wide and easily entered at any time of day or night—by the largest of ships, and with no need of a [local] pilot. The garrison was small and not willing to fight. The populace was lukewarm in temperament and ready to take flight whenever some suspicious sail came into view. They could offer no real resistance. Dissension between the governor and the bishop had been on the rise, and was reflected, as usual, in the two popular factions that avidly followed the potentates' disagreements.

On May 9 the fleet entered the harbor and began the assault by land and by sea. At the entrance to the bay, Point Santo Antônio, 1,200 soldiers and 200 sailors came ashore. When they drew close to the colonial force posted there, the latter took to its heels in what seems to have been a panic. From the forts came a few cannon shots, and some ships seemed prepared to resist. When the enemy drew close, colonists resorted to fire, burning ships so the Dutch could not set their hands on the rich cargoes of sugar, brazilwood, tobacco, and hides. Even so, many cargoes were saved.

That night, the bishop, ecclesiastics, and all the residents who could, abandoned the city. At dawn, in addition to slaves and poor people, who had nothing to lose, only the governor and a few faithful followers were still in the deserted city. The invaders easily captured them and later on sent them all to Holland. The fugitives made out as best they could on nearby engenhos, in Indian villages, under trees, and on bare ground. One can well imagine the hardships and the difficulty with which this throng was sustained and managed. Even after they had gathered in a settlement and established some sort of rule of law, maintaining order was no simple feat.

The governor's post was vacant, and Matias de Albuquerque Coelho was in line to be the successor. However, he was over 100 leagues away, governing for his brother, the hereditary donatary of Pernambuco. They would lose time, precious time, were they to wait for official orders. For this reason Judge Antão de Mesquita was appointed interim capitão-mor. Shortly thereafter, for reasons that are still not understood, Bishop Dom Marcos Teixeira ended up as de facto governor.

There was only one thing to do given the colonists' resources—surround the invader inside Salvador and make it impossible for him to spread out and seek supplies and followers from the lower classes, who would be indifferent as far as masters were concerned, since slavery was slavery no matter who was boss. The lack of appropriate arms, the scarcity, and, finally, the total absence of gunpowder limited the colonists' operations to use of cold steel, arrows, hand-to-hand combat, and ambush. The 30 ambush parties, each of which consisted of a few dozen combatants, kept the enemy at bay by appearing suddenly and in a wide range of places. The many attacks, which were almost always successful, encouraged the colonists and bolstered their patriotic spirit.

Meanwhile, the news of the city's fall had made its way to Pernambuco. According to a contemporary of his, Matias de Albuquerque worked day and night. He refused to be carried around in a hammock, as was customary in Brazil. Instead, he went about on horseback or in boats. And in boats he did not sit down; he remained standing and took command himself. He had a prodigious memory and understood people, even those he met only once. He also recognized ships that had anchored only once in Recife. His feverish activity and indomitable energy will be evident in the narrative that follows.

Under his orders, Francisco Nunes Marinho left immediately with two big caravelles, gunpowder, firearms, and cannonry, as well as with 30 soldiers. He was beaten about by storms and landed at Sergipe with broken spars and masts. However, by the beginning of September he had joined up with the people at the settlement outside Salvador. Under his command the guerrillas advanced inland up to Itapagipe and, in the direction of the harbor, up to Point Santo Antônio. New and stronger trenches were dug. Two ships (one in Itapoã, the other at São Paulo Hill) patrolled the sea and warned Portuguese ships to avoid the port so as not to be taken prisoner as others had been.

At Pernambuco bits of aid arrived little by little, and Matias de Albuquerque added to them and sent them on without delay. Dom Francisco de Moura, the ex-governor of Cape Verde, had come with the title of capitão-mor of the *Recôncavo* [the area, including All Saints Bay, around the City of Salvador] and three caravelles. Thanks to Albuquerque, de Moura left Recife after a week's stay with an additional six large caravelles and 80,000 cruzados worth of fresh supplies. On December 3 the artillery in the encampment began to thunder, and the Dutch, surprised by the phenomenon, also learned that the bishop, a few days before he died, had been succeeded by Francisco Nunes Marinho, who now turned over his command to de Moura.

In the conquered city things were going badly for the Dutch. Johannes van Doorth, the company's governor, had been killed in an ambush. Albert Schout, his successor, attended to the fortifications, but at one of the parties and banquets he was always attending, he caught some disease that carried him off a few days later. His brother Willem Schout appeared incapable of commanding.

Still, the situation seemed likely to go on forever. With the company's fleet commanding the ocean, the stalemate could be broken by whoever got reinforcements first from across the sea. By a stroke of luck never to be repeated our side did. The Spanish Court, in general inattentive and inert, this time felt the weight of the blow. The king, or rather Olivares, his all-powerful minister, perceived [in Bahia's occupation] a future threat to Mexico and Peru. Royal letters written in the king's hand, parades, and novenas stirred up public furor. Spain and Portugal's noblemen enthusiastically enlisted in the crusade against the rebel heretics. Wealthy men and prelates made generous donations, chartered ships, and bankrolled companies. The Portuguese navy, as well as detachments or *armadas* of the ocean, the strait, the Bay of Biscay, the Four Villas, and Naples put together 52 warships. More than 12,000 armed soldiers set sail for the New World. The commander-in-chief of this expedition was Fradique de Toledo.

The fleet arrived at Bahia on Easter Saturday, 29 March 1625—on the same day the city's founder, Tomé de Sousa, had arrived 76 years earlier. Toledo's ships formed a half moon from Point Santo Antônio to Itapagipe sealing off the exit for the Dutch ships anchored in the bay.

The soldiers came ashore at Santo Antônio and immediately took up positions at São Bento, Palmeiras, Carmo, and other hills. The siege was on, by land and sea. The Dutch were obliged to surrender. On April 30 the capitulation was signed. On May 1 the gates were opened and the conquering army entered. On the twenty-sixth reinforcements from Holland showed up with 34 ships under the command of Boudewiyn Hendrikszoon. Both fleets avoided engaging in more battles, however. Then the Dutch went off to plunder other, weaker regions.

During the years that followed, the company sent out different ships that went to Brazil and to other places in Africa and America to sack and wreak havoc. Its greatest triumph was Pieter Heyn's capture of a Spanish flotilla off Cuba in September 1628. In one fell swoop he netted more than 14 million florins—twice the company's original capital. Its dividends rose to 50 percent. With its finances restored, the company prepared another expedition to Brazil. This time it chose to invade Pernambuco.

On 26 December 1629 a fleet of 52 powerfully outfitted ships, cutters, and yachts weighed anchor in São Vicente. They were carrying 3,680 sailors and 13,500 soldiers. On 3 February 1630 they sighted land. On the thirteenth they were at Olinda. The following day they attacked.

Matias de Albuquerque, the grandson of Duarte Coelho and brother of the fourth donatary, was in command. With news of the pending invasion he had left Lisbon on 12 August 1629. In one caravelle he brought 27 soldiers and some ammunition. He arrived in Recife on October 18 and threw himself into the desperate task at hand.

The fortresses, like those in Bahia, were in ruins. Even if Recife's harbor was not as accommodating as All Saints Bay, and even if it would not be hard to seal it off, it would still be easy for the Dutch to come ashore anywhere from Pau-Amarelo farther north to Candelária, south of Recife—a distance of seven leagues. Could one at least count on the sang-froid of the local population?

The enemy launched a three-pronged attack. The lion's share of the fleet, under the command of Admiral Loncq, set out for the harbor, but came to a standstill because it was blocked. Another sector headed directly for Olinda. With 3,000 men Colonel Diedrich van Weerdenburgh sailed toward the Tapado River, then for Pau-Amarelo farther north, where he came ashore the afternoon of February 15. The following morning he divided his forces into three columns and marched south. The locals' slight, sporadic resistance gave way to the mighty army and the vessels from which it had emerged. The ships sailed close to shore to support ground maneuvers.

At the town's entrance a few militia men nobly sacrificed themselves. The part of the fleet that had been sent the night before had taken the fortifications on the beach. By nightfall the Batavian standard fluttered over old Marim.

The residents abandoned the town and sought shelter in the forests and plantations. The invading army got drunk and began to pillage. Matias de Albuquerque had the ships and storehouses burned so they might at least wrench the fruit of their own bitterly sweat labor from the company's claws. Recife, lit up by the glare of fires, became a heap of ruins. It was still defended by two forts: one on the isthmus that links the town to Olinda, another in Recife itself. The general reinforced them with men and munitions, and more than one attack was repelled to the Portuguese's advantage. But on March 2 Fort São Jorge, old and only capable of withstanding Indian attacks, capitulated. Fort São Francisco followed suit. Only then did the Dutch navy enter the port.

Meanwhile, Matias de Albuquerque kept the enemy on edge. On his own he would never rout the Dutch, but he would not let them rest. He diminished their self-confidence, and their numbers. He interrupted their communication with forces on land. And he replaced the settlers' original foundering with a desire to fight back and a scorn for death. The Dutch conquest was a fact, but it would not be permanent.

On March 4 the general selected a high point near the Capibaribe River and even closer to Parnamirim Creek, about a league from Recife and from Olinda. There was good water and firewood in the area. He began his fortress with 20 people and four pieces of artillery. He called it Bom Jesus. Little by little people began to join them—adventurers, plantation owners (either alone or with their slaves), and acculturated Indians. Among the Indians came one individual whose brilliance became more and more apparent, Antônio Camarão. He was a 28-year-old Petiguar chief and the most faithful and valuable of allies. Ten days later this settlement was in the process of repelling an enemy assault and taking heavy losses. This is how things would be for the next five years.

How to tell the events of this unprecedented war? There was conflict on a daily basis, and some days there were more than one. Whether in search of workers or booty or just traveling from one place to another on the isthmus, Dutchmen fell into ambushes set up all over the place. Trenches were courageously wrested from the enemy; reinforcements were sent overland to distant places while ships raced them and often lost. Rivers were crossed at low tide to attack the heart of the enemy's fortifications. There was hunger, nakedness, little gunpowder, few doctors, and scanty medicine. And nobody noticed. Duarte de Albuquerque claimed that during the first two years the enemy was ensconced in Olinda and in

Recife, it had not, thanks to our general and his captains, captured as much as a single cow. He added that "All they had to eat was what Holland sent to them. One can rightly say that even though they had been ashore all that time, they were still at sea, since they had nothing to eat other than salt fish."

The reports sent to the Iberian Peninsula did not cause the uproar that the fall of Bahia had. Help came in small doses spaced far apart. And it was not always useful. The company controlled the sea, and it often captured the caravelles on their way to Pernambuco, or it forced them to sail inland where they would scuttle their cargoes or leave them far from where they were needed. The court's inertia was shrouded under a cape of profound Machiavellianism: the best way to fight the West Indies Company, according to those inscrutable schemers, was to make it spend itself into bankruptcy!

Only on 5 May 1631, was the famous Dom Antônio de Oquendo to leave Lisbon with a fleet of 20 ships. He carried reinforcements to Paraíba, Pernambuco, and Bahia. On his way back to Portugal, he was to convoy ships loaded with sugar. So as to allow the Dutch extra time to get ready, he headed first for Bahia. Once they learned of his coming, the Dutch sent a fleet commanded by Adrian Pater in the same direction.

Finally, on September 12, the two fleets met around the cays. Oquendo was on his way to Pernambuco. There were acts of bravery on both sides, and the Batavian captain went down with his flagship. The battle itself was a draw, because the West Indies Company retained its command of the sea. Oquendo was accompanied on this voyage by Duarte de Albuquerque, the donatary of Pernambuco and the admirable chronicler of this war—from the Dutch landing in Pau-Amarelo up to Nassau's attack on Bahia (1630–38). Count Bagnoli, João Vicente de San Felice, who had come with Dom Fradique de Toledo, was also on board. Both men stayed in Brazil. After this battle, the enemy, believing it could not defend Olinda, burned it to the ground and then gathered in Recife.

Up to this point all the efforts the company made to break through Matias de Albuquerque's iron ring had failed. It had only succeeded in setting up Fort Orange on Itamaracá Island. Now, however, luck began to run its way. On 20 April 1632 Domingos Fernandes Calabar joined the Dutch. Calabar was a mulatto born in Porto Calvo, where his mother and a few of his relatives lived. According to what one can glean from the few and unreliable sources that exist concerning this individual, Calabar was a smuggler. There is no other way to explain the robberies of the royal treasury he is accused of. How else can one explain the money he is said to have had? As a successful smuggler he had to be audacious, spirited, clever, and extremely knowledgeable about his surroundings. He was the only man who measured up to Matias de Albuquerque, and, because he had access to the sea, he was able to land decisive blows. What moved him to abandon his compatriots, we shall never know. It could have been ambition, or the hope of rising more quickly among the foreigners. Under new bosses his singular talents would make him indispensable. Or perhaps he was just dispirited and convinced that the invader was sure to win an easy victory.

Among the most notable deeds Calabar inspired are the attack on Iguaraçu, several incursions up the Formoso River, occupying Afogados, seriously threatening the settlement at Bom Jesus, raiding Alagoas, and capturing Itamaracá and Rio Grande. These last successes got the conquest of Paraíba underway. It would only be a matter of time now. At the end of February 1634 a fleet headed toward Paraíba, where fighting went on for two days. It was, however, a diversionary tactic. At the beginning of March, people realized the real target was Cape Santo Agostinho. At this port reinforcements from Bahia regularly came ashore, and local produce was sent out and traded abroad. The capture of Cape Santo Agostinho might not cut off overseas contact completely, but it would at least bring future resistance to a stand still.

The enemy divided its attack into three prongs: one with 13 ships, another with 11, and a third made up of launches carrying 1,000 men led by Calabar.

Owing to Calabar's familiarity with the locale, the Dutch entered the port and dug in on the spit. They received a violent attack, which began auspiciously for the colonists but which failed because the attackers panicked. One of our fortresses placed on a hill turned out to be of little use. Matias de Albuquerque was only able to send his guerrilla forces in. The attacks came one after another; the siege was unsurmountable. The Bom Jesus settlement received less attention. There would still be plenty of heroic deeds in that place, but Santo Agostinho demanded the general's courage and energy.

With the recently arrived reinforcements, the enemy set off for Paraíba under the command of Sigemundt von Schkoppe. Paraíba was under the governorship of Antônio de Albuquerque, the son of the conqueror of Maranhão and a worthy heir to his father's blood. However, even this man could not stop the enemy from coming ashore on December 4. Reinforcements from Pernambuco, who came by land, arrived too late. The forts fell one by one, and on Christmas Eve the city belonged to the company. Antônio de Albuquerque did not give up; he tried to found a settlement similar to Bom Jesus, but no one would join him. Those who refused to be ruled by foreigners retreated with Albuquerque to Pernambuco, where they joined up with Matias.

At the end of five years, from Rio Grande down to Recife, the enemy was in charge. Its only resistance came from Bom Jesus and Fort Nazaré, on Cape Santo Agostinho. From Paraíba Arciszewski marched overland to tighten the siege of Bom Jesus. Von Schkoppe left Recife for Guararapes to attack Nazaré. Matias de Albuquerque left Bom Jesus in the hands of soldiers he trusted and went to Serinhaém, where he would coordinate operations and send out reinforcements. By land and sea, on caravelles and rafts, and along the best defended roads, he helped his companions as long as he could. But resistance has its limits. Duarte de Albuquerque wrote:

> Finally their supply of food was totally exhausted. [And I am not speaking] of horse meat, which would have been a treat, but of leather, dogs, cats, and rats. And, whenever there was enough of that, there would be no gunpowder, or other munition. It is hardly strange, then, that they should have lost, not at all. What is strange is that in such a state Governor André Marin and his captains should have held out for three months and three days, as they did.

The surrender of Bom Jesus on June 3 was followed by the surrender of Fort Nazaré on 2 July 1635. "When our people came out, some of the soldiers dropped dead. It seems that only their immobility had kept them alive."

Before this happened, Bagnoli had retreated to Alagoas, and Matias de Albuquerque had joined him, with 200 front line soldiers, less than 100 guerrillas, and a few Indians. These few stalwart individuals began their exodus out of Serinhaém on the third.

> Sixty Indians set out along with their captains, Antônio de Cardoso and João de Almeida, both of whom were very brave and almost seemed brought up in those parts. Since they were so good at finding paths and forests, they led the way. They were followed by Captains Dom Fernando de la Riba Agüero, Afonso de Albuquerque, Dom Pedro Taveira Souto Mayor, Francisco Rabelo, Luiz de Magalhães, and Leonardo de Albuquerque.
>
> Behind them came the villagers who were evacuating, bringing with them 200 carts. Behind them were Captains Martim Ferreira, João de Magalhães, Dom Pedro Marinho, Manuel de Sousa e Abreu, Rodrigo Fernandes, Dom Gaspar de Valcáçar and Paulo Vernola. Capitão-mor An-

tônio Camarão and 80 of his followers armed with muskets and harquebuses made up the rear guard.[1]

They trusted Indians with the most dangerous positions. Do Nóbrega's efforts require more justification than this? The best route to their destination went close to Porto Calvo. To get by it Matias de Albuquerque would have to attack the settlement itself. He became adamant about attacking when he learned that Calabar had arrived in Porto Calvo with 200 reinforcements. Matias de Albuquerque sent the peaceful folk ahead. The battle began on July 12 and went on for several days. On the 19th the enemy offered its surrender. The attackers, not counting the Indians, were only 140 men. The enemy, besides Picard, the Dutch commander, and numerous officers, numbered 360. They were disarmed and then sent off to Álagoas in small contingents. This was done to avoid last minute changes of mind lest the enemy realize how small the colonists' forces were. Out of all the prisoners, Matias de Albuquerque selected Domingos Fernandes Calabar for royal justice. On the twenty-second Calabar was: "strangulatusque, jugulo defectionem expiavit, et dissectos artus infidelitatis ac miseriae suae testes ad spectaculum reliquit."[2]

For a long time the arrival of a new and stronger fleet carrying reinforcements from Spain had been in the offing. Matias de Albuquerque had left loyalists at various places on the coastline. He had charged them with giving sailors news from land and letting them know where best to come ashore. The fleet was to leave in March, then in May, but it only left on September 7 . Portuguese ships under the command of Dom Rodrigo Lobo and Spanish ships commanded by Don Lope de Hozes y Córdoba joined forces at Cape Verde and then set sail for Pernambuco.

On November 26 they sighted Olinda. Then outside Recife they spotted nine enemy ships on their way to Holland loaded with sugar, brazilwood, tobacco, cotton, and ginger. Each ship carried a crew of five or six men. They decided to attack, but the Spanish admiral, on the pretext that his ships' keels were too deep, gave a counter order. He did not even wait for news from land.

Seeing the fearsome fleet offshore, Von Schkoppe thought he was lost. But the winds were coming from the northeast, and the current was running south, so it was easy for Hozes y Córdoba to let his ships drift southward. At Cape Santo Agostinho a raftsman who had unfurled his sail managed to convey a message. They were to leave people at Serinhaém and to send a ship to pick up Matias de Albuquerque! The two fleets let themselves ride the wind and the current—at nightfall of the twenty-eighth they lowered anchors in Alagoas.

On board were two special individuals. One was Pedro da Silva, who had been named successor to Diogo Luís de Oliveira, the governor-general of Brazil. The other was Luis de Rojas y Borja, who would replace Matias de Albuquerque. The latter had been called back to the peninsula. Duarte de Albuquerque would continue as governor of his captaincy. Diogo Luís de Oliveira was to recapture Curaçao before returning.

Matias de Albuquerque gave Rojas y Borjas a complete account of the state of affairs. In sum, there still was hope. It was imperative that they head back up north then dislodge and expel the enemy. This advice sunk in. Don Luis set off for Pernambuco and on the way took Porto Calvo, which the enemy had reoccupied once our side headed south after executing Calabar. Would Oliveira be strong enough to follow Albuquerque's lead? Would he measure up to his heroic predecessor? At the battle of Mata Redonda on January 18, a musket ball in the leg knocked him off his horse, another in the chest took his life. He was 50 years old. Following the chain of command, Count Bagnoli became supreme commander. It is hard to judge this old warhorse fairly. Our historians have always treated him scornfully. They have called him names and denied him even the basic virtue of individual courage. One exception to this rule is Duarte de Albuquerque, who was always discreet and circumspect, but who, it seems, did not reveal all his thoughts. Concerning Bagnoli, if some line [in his favor] has been published regarding the period of Dutch occupation, it is lost in some obscure collection of writings, and we have no idea how he would defend himself from his accusers. Still, there is one honor that befalls him: he never gave up.

Bagnoli is famous for his use of fearless adventurers who met the enemy face to face. They took prisoners, slit people's throats, wasted cattle they could not carry off, and burned cane fields, stocks of sugar, brazilwood, and plantations. Their influence was felt as far as the Paraíban border. Matias de Albuquerque had struggled so as not to let the Dutch feel secure in their conquest. For a while Bagnoli planned to head north, and he lightly fortified the crossing point on the Una River, six leagues south of Serinhaém. He may have been encouraged to make this uncharacteristic move by Duarte de Albuquerque's presence. With this advance, the Dutch abandoned Paripuera and Barra Grande.

Once Bom Jesus and the fortress at Nazaré had been taken, the West Indies Company felt the time was right to appoint a governor-general, as its charter permitted.

It chose John Maurice, Count of Nassau-Siegen, a member of the Orange family. He was to be interim commander for a period of five years.

On 27 January 1637 Nassau landed at Pernambuco, where he was supposed to stay for the next eight years. With him, or immediately after his arrival, came numerous reinforcements. He set out at once to recapture Porto Calvo. At the same time 30 ships carrying 2,000 infantrymen under Arciszewski left Recife. On February 12 they anchored in Barra Grande, [to be met by] Nassau and von Schkoppe along with 3,000 soldiers and 500 Indians who crossed the Una River unhampered for Bagnoli had withdrawn his troops.

Together they gathered outside the town of Barra Grande on the seventeenth. On the eighteenth they engaged in a battle in which they got the best of our side. On the twentieth they sent launches carrying artillery and matériel up the Pedras River. Although their cannons came up against stalwart opposition, the Dutch blasted the walls of the fort at Porto Calvo and mixed dirt into the defenders' supplies. On March 5 the lack of victuals obliged the local commander, Miguel Giberton, to surrender.

On the night of February 18, after sending Alonso Ximénez and part of the army along the beach to escort those who wanted to retreat to Alagoas, Bagnoli set out overland for the same destination. On the twenty-fifth he reached the town of Madalena, where he thought it imprudent to tarry. On March 10 he set off once more, and on the seventeenth he approached the town of São Francisco, which the donatary had recently built on the left bank of the river halfway between the harbor and the falls. Duarte de Albuquerque advised him to dig in along the Piaguí River and to take on the enemy there, should it come by land. As had been the case with fortifications at the Una River crossing, Bagnoli paid Albuquerque no mind. In both cases the enemy crossed without as much as a stumble.

On the eighteenth Bagnoli had the Neapolitan and Castilian regiments cross the river into the captaincy of Sergipe. On the nineteenth, part of the Portuguese regiment went over. On the twenty-sixth the remainder crossed. And on the twenty-seventh the Dutch reached the encampment and found it empty. In the confusion many of the refugees were taken prisoner, while others escaped but lost all their belongings. On the site Bagnoli had abandoned, Nassau decided to build a fort, which he named Maurice—today it is the city of Penedo. Von Schkoppe was left in charge of building and commanding the fort. Nassau returned to Pernambuco.

On March 31 Bagnoli reached São Cristóvão. He ordered some of his followers to head for Alagoas, either above or below the fort. They were to do their customary deeds along the way. They also brought with them the news of an invasion of Sergipe being planned at Fort Maurice. The plan was to round up herds of cattle and exact revenge from those intrepid men who refused to leave the Dutch in peace with their new conquests. In fact, on November 17 von Schkoppe arrived at São Cristóvão, which had been abandoned. On December 25 he burned the city and withdrew to the other side of the river.

On November 14, having learned of the enemy's entering Sergipe, Bagnoli left for Bahia. This caused great sorrow and indignation among the Paraíban and Pernambucan emigrés, who had begun to plant in the area. On the twenty-fourth he reached Torre de García d'Avila, where he received orders from the governor-general to stay put. On December fifteenth, along with some followers, he set off for the city of Bahia for an audience with Pedro da Silva, the governor-general of the State of Brazil. Fearing that the Dutch would soon attack Brazil's capital, he wanted to make it known that he and his forces should gather at the old town of Pereira, where they could help the resistance.

Neither Pedro da Silva nor anyone else believed in the imminent danger. No one wanted the soldiers around. They had them stay at Torre, and, even though he felt offended, Bagnoli agreed to this. Shortly thereafter, however, his men brought news that Nassau was preparing an expedition to take Bahia. In spite of his agreement, Bagnoli marched toward Vila-Velha on 14 March 1638.

Prisoners taken by Sebastião do Souto and brought to the encampment on April 8 dispelled lingering doubts. On the sixteenth Nassau, at the head of a mighty fleet, entered All Saints Bay with 3,400 European soldiers and 1,000 Indians. They came ashore at Itapagipe.

During the days that followed, he took some forts, dug trenches, and built some walls. He also showered parts of the city with his artillery. What followed did not live up to the brilliant beginning. Bagnoli's troops and the city's garrison discarded their petty rivalries and fought back enthusiastically. The populace, at first confused and wary, ended up believing in their defenders' bravery and ability. Sailboats brought flour from Camamu without interruption. People brought in cattle from Itapircuru and Real. In repeated ambushes the defenders took prisoners who revealed all the enemy's plans. The defenders even carried out successful raids on the Dutch. On the night of May 25 and into the following day, John Maurice of Nassau ended six weeks of slaughter. Without the festivities he had promised and not as happy with things as he had wished he could be, he furtively set sail for Pernambuco.

News of the victory reached the Iberian Peninsula as preparations for a mighty rescue fleet were being made. The fleet would consist of 33 ships under the command of Dom Fernando Mascarenhas Count of Torre. It left Lisbon on September 7. After a debilitating delay in the pestilent climate of Cape Verde, it came within sight of Recife on 23 January 1639. Like the two preceding fleets, it did not dare attack. Instead, it continued toward Bahia. Thanks to that warning, and the grace period that the Portuguese admiral had allowed him, Nassau made full use of almost an entire year to improve Recife's fortifications. He organized a system of rapid communications, and he outfitted a squadron.

Only on November 19 did the rescuing fleet leave Bahia heading northward. It now consisted of 86 ships carrying nearly 12,000 men. Nassau found himself in the same situation Matias de Albuquerque had faced 12 years earlier, but he counted on a naval force that Albuquerque had lacked.

Count Torre could have come ashore around Santo Agostinho or Serinhaém, but he chose to take on Pau-Amarelo—which the watchful enemy prevented. Then the Dutch fleet showed up. Between Ponta Pedras, the easternmost point on the continent, and Canhaú, on the coast of Rio Grande, the contenders waged war on 12, 13, 14, and 17 January 1640. Only around 1,000 of our soldiers were able to make a beachhead on Touro Point, from where Luiz Barbalho, like a latter-day Xenophon wending his way through the enemy and through the backlands, heroically led his men back to Bahia. He had been beaten in his retreat by Count Torre, who had returned by sea with Bagnoli and with what remnants of his fleet he could salvage. Bagnoli died shortly thereafter. The rest of the fleet had been scattered to the winds.

The Dutch had suffered great losses. Some of their officers acted in a cowardly fashion and were executed. But they owed their victory to their arms, and, as never before, their hold on the land had been consolidated.

We can omit several Dutch sea maneuvers as well as numerous patriot raids that followed, because another turn of events demands our attention. On 1 December 1640 Portugal declared its independence from Spain; it proclaimed the Duke of Bragança king; and it proposed peace treaties with Spain's adversaries. On 12 June 1641 for European purposes it concluded an offensive and defensive alliance with Holland. For the colonies it proclaimed a 13-year truce, which should be valid for all the territory under the East India Company one year after the treaty was ratified. For the West Indies Company and its holdings, the treaty would go into effect once the news of its ratification had been officially communicated. This somewhat shady clause must have been suggested by the Portuguese, who hoped to improve their situation in the interstices. There is no other way to explain their delaying ratification until November 18. In February 1642 the Estates General ordered both companies to obey the treaty.

When the news of the events in Portugal arrived, Dom Jorge de Mascarenhas Marquis of Montalvão was in Bahia and governed as the first viceroy of Brazil. By foresight he put the small Spanish garrison out of commission. All the local magnates supported Portugal's independence and the Duke of Bragança's claim to the throne. And the rest of the country followed suit, even the captaincy of São Vicente, where there were many families of Castilian origin.

The viceroy had the news sent to John Maurice of Nassau, who received it happily and celebrated with festivals. The traditional enemy was the Spaniard. Anything that hurt Spain helped the United Provinces. Relations improved even more with the news of the treaty of June 12, even though its ratification was slow in coming. Count Nassau widened the company's domains, both in Maranhão and in Africa.

The last years of his administration can be told in a few words. Of his work as an administrator nothing survives. His palaces and gardens were consumed in the vortex of fire and blood during the years that followed. His artistic collections have enriched several European establishments and are being studied by Americanists. Thanks to his patronage, the books of Barlaeus, Piso, and Markgraf attained heights never before achieved by a Brazilian or a Portuguese work during colonial times. In spite of being written in Latin, the universal language of the time, even these books seem to have had scant readership in Brazil—so insignificant are their vestiges in our literature.[3]

The city of Mauricéia did not keep that name, but it has prospered and preserves Nassau's memory. Some aficionados of historical fantasy might interpret the Peddlers' War as vengeance, legacy, retaliation, or whatever on the part of Nassau. And having done that, they would not need any extra effort to turn Domingos Fernandes Calabar into a patriot and seer. Nassau's noble background pleased the colonials and made the other governors repulsive to them because the others were simple bourgeois, scarcely more than company clerks. Nassau himself warned his successors about this when he turned over his command.

Friar Manuel Calado, who knew and socialized with Nassau, describes him as a full-blooded nobleman who could understand injustice and remedy it. He loved feasts and wealth, was inclined to farces that were not always the most delicate in taste, admired the beauty of the Tropics, and was not overly concerned with returning to more civilized lands. As far as keeping his hands clean is concerned, he was less successful than Matias de Albuquerque. His collusion in contraband with Gaspar Dias Ferreira has been proven. And naturally, Dias Ferreira cheated him when their accounts were settled in Holland after the prince no longer governed.

Ten intensely tumultuous years followed Nassau's departure in May 1644.

Of those who had left with Matias de Albuquerque, some returned to their old properties and tried to reestablish their former wealth. The Dutch regime was severe, and extortion ruled the day. Even if Nassau were as just as they want to make him out to be, his arm was neither long enough nor strong enough to protect all the victims.

The invaders disarmed the rural population. They preferred to leave it vulnerable to the pitiless followers of Albuquerque rather than have to worry about an attempt at insurrection.

How could these people fight back?

The nucleus of resistance was being formed in Bahia.

Northern emigrés had been reduced to poverty. Bahians' plantations had been frequently devastated by the Dutch in their coastal operations. Both groups nurtured deep hatred for their antagonists. Expelled priests and friars who had been despoiled stirred up religious sentiment. Montalvão's successor, Antônio Teles da Silva, was such an ardent Catholic that he tried to found and finance at his own expense a Brazilian branch of the Holy Inquisition. Just as when he was in Goa, he could not abide heretics around him.

Under Nassau's administration the Catholic Church was tolerated, albeit in a limited and unstable fashion. After he left, Protestants and Jews constantly insulted the beliefs of the indigenous population. This is why the title Governor for Divine Liberty was the first one insurgent leaders assumed. Today we would call them Governors for Freedom of Conscience.

Any initiative against the Dutch would have to come from Bahia because it was the only source of armaments, officers, and warriors who could rally the timid Pernambucans. Nonetheless, they needed a Pernambucan chief so that the mission would not be lost before it took hold.

There was only one man in Pernambuco who could take this responsibility, if he wanted it. He was João Fernandes Vieira. Vieira was a native of the Island of Madeira and had come to Pernambuco at age 11. He had fought alongside Matias de Albuquerque and was taken prisoner at Bom

Jesus in June 1635. He went over to the Dutch side after the surrender and luck favored him. He became the richest man in the land. His countrymen respected him, and he helped and protected them in a liberal and generous fashion. He was also able to gain favor among the invaders. How he did this is explained in his will:

> They [the Dutch] also owe me more than 100,000 cruzados since, in the course of some eight or nine years, to avoid trouble and save my life from their tyrannical acts, I have regularly given bribes and gifts, as well as grandiose banquets, to all the governors and their ministers to keep them happy.[4]

At first glance no one seemed less appropriate for the role of hero and liberator. Nonetheless, Vidal de Negreiros, a Paraíban who had begun to distinguish himself under Matias de Albuquerque and who was an officer in the Bahia garrison, approached Vieira and found him positively disposed to the undertaking. Vidal noticed, however, the lack of munitions, armaments, and people versed in warfare. So that the uprising would not degenerate into a sterile protest and also to overcome the local people's limitations they needed time—as well as outside help. Everything was carried out with the greatest possible caution. In spite of all their safeguards, the Dutch got wind of the plot. It is actually surprising that it took them as long as it did to discover the plan, since the secret was on everybody's lips. The Dutch sent two emissaries to Antônio Teles to protest the Bahians who were fomenting revolution in the lands of Teles' new allies.

One of the emissaries, von Hoogstraten, promised to betray his bosses and turn over his command of the fort at Nazaré when the Portuguese demanded it.

When the Dutch sent their second emissary to Bahia, Camarão and his Indians, as well Henrique Dias and his blacks, had gone to Pernambuco. Vieira had invited them, and the governor had agreed to their going. Since the governor could not deny these men's absence, he told the agents of the West Indies Company to catch them and give them the punishment they deserved. And when Vieira's men began to make waves, Teles had two paid regiments sent north under the command of old Martim Soares Moreno and the fiery Vidal de Negreiros. Their official mission was to contain the rebels. The two field marshals landed near Serinhaém on 28 July 1645. On August 4 the Dutch fort there surrendered. On September 3 Hoogstraten turned over the fort at Pontal as he had promised.

One can take stock of the importance of Pontal by remembering that Matias de Albuquerque ceased operating out of Bom Jesus once Pontal had fallen to the Dutch. The rescue of Pernambuco began where its conquest had ended. The success of the Bahian regiments would have been greater if the Dutch had not destroyed Serrão de Paiva's flotilla that had brought troops to Serinhaém and if Salvador Correia had used his fleet, as he had been ordered to do, to attack Recife by land and by sea.

Since June, before the reinforcements from Bahia had arrived, Pernambuco's insurrection was out in the open. It had few people, no armaments, and no munitions. More than anything, Vieira had to try to avoid the enemy. Owing to the cautious measures he had taken early on and to the highly sophisticated system of spies who knew the lay of the land, Vieira was able to accomplish this. The first battle did not occur until August 3. It took place on Tabocas Mountain and our side won. Concerning those historians who criticize Vieira for his hesitations, his delays to allow Camarão and Henrique Dias to arrive, and his insistence on having reinforcements from Bahia, they should be reminded of one fact: at the Battle of Tabocas many people fought with fire-hardened sticks and sickles because they had no guns.

One of the spoils of victory was the supply of firearms and ammunition taken from fallen enemy soldiers. The fall of Casa Forte on August 16 spread the flames. When Serinhaém and Pontal surrendered to Martim Soares and André Vidal, an uprising began in the south, all the way to the São Francisco River. Things were as they had been in 1635. The Bahian forces, supposedly sent to pacify the insurgents, joined them without hesitation.

A settlement that they called Arraial Novo de Bom Jesus was erected on the right bank of the Capibaribe River. From this point they launched unending attacks on the people in Recife. One fortress on the continent, specifically Asseca's outfit, wreaked havoc on Recife. Von Schkoppe decided to use the same tactic with which he had cut off the settlement around Fort Nazaré and had obliged both the town and the fort to surrender. This time the plan backfired. The Battle of Guararapes (19 April 1648) was a complete disaster for the invaders, who left the battlefield strewn with corpses and wreckage. They gained one advantage. Asseca's devastating force came under their command and remained subordinate until the war's end.

A few days before the Battle of Guararapes, Francisco Barreto de Menezes had arrived from Portugal to take supreme command of the Pernambucans. The state of affairs Barreto de Menezes encountered is described by a historian, Rafael de Jesus, an emphatic admirer of Vieira's:

> Without arms or soldiers [Vieira] vanquished the enemy, who pursued him with soldiers and arms in the Battle of Tabocas. Once he joined forces with Field Marshal André Vidal de Negreiros, they gained the upper hand on the Dutch at the Dona Ana Pais plantation. They also took nine fortresses and other hideouts and strongholds. They captured nearly 80 artillery pieces of different calibers, most of them bronze. And they obtained enough arms, ammunition, and matériel to sustain them in open warfare for five straight years.[5]

The first Battle of Guararapes was followed by a second, on 19 February 1649. The Dutch, as before, came out the worse. And after this one, there were no more battles worthy of note, on sea or on land. In spite of the generous subsidies coming from the Estates General, the company was prostrate. In a short time the Estates General would be of no further help, because they were involved in a war with England. On the other hand, Portugal had organized a commercial company that set up operations on the coast of Pernambuco around December 1653. The patriots negotiated an agreement with the company, as the Bahians had with Dom Fradique de Toledo and his fleet years before. The Portuguese admiral came ashore on the Tapado River, at the very place Weerdenburgh first attempted to land. In Olinda he and the Pernambucan chiefs agreed on the plan of attack.

One by one the Dutch forts fell. On 26 January 1654 the Taborda capitulation was signed bringing this war to an end after 30 years of almost uninterrupted fighting.

The denouement had been predicted and set to print years before by Pierre Moreau, a native of Charolais in Burgundy. He had spent some time in Pernambuco among the Dutch. His words make clear some of the basic causes of the West Indies Company's ultimate failure.

In 1651, Moreau wrote:

> It does not seem likely that the Dutch can ever recover and regain what they had in Brazil. Even if their flotilla were to defeat the Portuguese flotilla, even if they received as many reinforcements as last time, they would only lose men and bankrupt their treasury—all to no avail. This is because the land they still hold, from Ceará to the city of Olinda, has been wasted and depopulated. The houses, settlements, villages, or towns, as well as the fruit-bearing regions, have been burnt to the ground, making them totally worthless. And even though they might hold onto the fortresses at Rio Grande and Paraíba, which besides Recife are the only ones still resisting, these forts are not good for much and cannot come to anyone's aid. Those

Dutch who set out to build some shacks and till the soil or those who wander any distance [away from the forts] are ambushed and killed by the knavish Portuguese corsairs, by the Tapuias, and by the untamed natives who pity no one.

The Portuguese have blocked off Recife on all sides by land: at Olinda, at Cape Santo Agostinho, and at the fortresses they have constructed all around Recife. Throughout the fertile and abundant surrounding area, they are in charge. They hold all the strongholds, ports, openings, and river crossings from Recife to beyond Rio de Janeiro and down to the southern end of Brazil. All the territory they possess has abundant population, with men ready for war. They can get by and live well on what the land produces. They have no need for European goods—which is the opposite for the Dutch, who, by the way, can only count on groups of soldiers they have bought rather than chosen from several nations. The soldiers are not suited to the local customs nor to the strange climate of the country. They do not know the lay of the land so they frequently get lost and ambushed. The Dutch cannot even be sure of their loyalty. On the other hand the majority of the Portuguese were born there. Some families go back four generations. They are thriving, united; they share similar customs and outlooks. They help one another. And they value and know every inch of the land and put it to good use. All they have to do is to wait for the enemy at river crossings and defeat them there.[6]

In other words, Holland and Olinda represented mercantilism and nationalism. National sentiment won. Europeans like Francisco Barreto, islanders like Vieira, Brazilian-born Portuguese like André Vidal, Indians like Camarão, blacks like Henrique Dias, *mamalucos*, mulattos, mixed people of all shades joined forces to fight for Divine Liberty.

Under external pressure they formed a bond. Superficial and imperfect though it was, it was still the beginning of a bond among diverse ethnic elements.

Having vanquished the Dutch, who had beaten the Spaniards, themselves for a time rulers of Portugal, the Pernambucan combatants became unto themselves a people, a heroic people. Testimony of official recognition confirmed their convictions. They were venerated by historians, such as Manuel Calado and Rafael de Jesus, whose works were published immediately. In those works and in a still unpublished work by Diogo Lopes de Santiago we can see the veterans as heirs to traditions that have been slightly altered over time. A document from 1703 sums up their feelings in the following terms:

Among all the nations of the globe the Portuguese are the ones who have assumed the most arduous undertakings and achieved the greatest triumphs. Their most heroic coat of arms has been the loyalty and intimate affection with which they not only venerate but also adore their native princes. And because of this it appears that in Pernambuco they stood out even more no matter how much they were oppressed, subjected, abandoned, out of favor, and deprived of human help. They rejected any accommodation with the Dutch, who knew how to bring souls into their fold through generosity. [Because the Dutch were there] so many years, favors might have helped the Portuguese. But they scorned it all in a sovereign impulse and attempted and achieved a most illustrious deed that warrants their immortal fame. They deserved this not just because they endured the entire war up to its bitter end with unvanquished suffering, but because they showed themselves to be even more generous by not asking for any special privileges for such relevant service. Indeed, they attained their goals but lost their wealth and ended up in poverty. And thus with no greater prize than receiving the glorious title of loyal vassals, most faithful to their king and most loving of their fatherland, which they recovered and restituted free from alien domination that had usurped it. These people, because of the price of so many lives and so much spilled blood, are a noble attribute to the royal Crown—especially because they also vouchsafed the Holy Cult which they had seen plagued by heresy for so many years.[7]

Once the early moments of enthusiasm were behind them, the reinóis tried to regain their superior and protective roles. At this point began the irreparable and irrepressible separation between the Pernambucans and Portuguese.

9

The Backlands

The Dutch invasion is little more than a minor episode in the occupation of Brazil's coastline. Settlement of Brazil's backlands is in all ways a more towering feat. It began at different times and at different places, but it finally became an inner current that was greater and more fertile than the tenuous thread of coastal population.

* * *

WE CAN BEGIN with the São Vicente Captaincy. The settling of Piratininga in 1530, at the edge of the backlands, is tantamount to a bloodless victory over the forest, which elsewhere cost several generations of struggle. The unique development of São Paulo stems from this advance.

The Tietê River ran nearby. One needed only to follow its course to reach the basin of the River Plate. And one easily traversed a gorge to reach the Paraíba River, which heads north between the Serra do Mar and the Mantiqueira Mountains. Southward lay vast open fields dotted with clumps of trees and even spotty forests. The forests were sometimes of decent size, but could not support southern expansion because they were so far from one another. To the east there was only a trail heading to the seashore. This trail was almost impassible and easy to block. And it was blocked more than once, leaving the backland populations independent from the authorities on the coast. Along that trail a handful of men could wipe out an army. And superhuman effort would be needed to open new pathways and to tame the rugged mountains, as well as to cut through massive vegetation and quell the natives' hostility.

At that latitude and altitude, a semi-European type of farming would have been possible. At least some if not all the grains and fruits typical of the Iberian Peninsula would grow there. People, however, vanished from the area. *Paulistas*, or inhabitants of São Paulo, became *bandeirantes*.

Bandeiras were groups of men or bandeirantes employed in capturing and enslaving indigenous heathens. The name for these expeditions [the word bandeira means flag, trans.] may come from a Tupiniquim custom that Anchieta mentions. The Tupiniquins would raise a flag to signal war. Bandeiras were under the command of supreme chiefs with ample power. They were lords of life and death over their subordinates. Below them marched people of graded statuses who financed the expedition or who supplied men.

An obligatory figure was the chaplain. Domingos Jorge Velho wrote in November 1629:

> My chaplain had gone somewhere when I was about to begin my campaign. I had him fetched. He refused to come. Out of necessity I fetched the enemy [priest]. Without him I had three white men die on me without confession, and that has hurt me more than anything else in my life. I ask him, for the love of God, send me a cleric if you have no friar. You cannot just go into the backlands and risk your life without a chaplain along.

Montoya mentions certain

> wolves dressed in sheep's clothing, tremendous hypocrites who flaunt the long rosaries they wear around their necks. While the others go around robbing and despoiling churches, tying up Indians, killing and hacking up children. These [people] go up to the [Spanish Jesuit] fathers and ask for confession . . . and while they are talking about all of this, they run [their fingers] quickly along the beads of their Rosary.[1]

Slaves worked as porters. Their cargo consisted of gunpowder, bullets, hatchets and other tools, rope to tie their captives, seeds from time to time, and sometimes salt and supplies. They carried few supplies. They regularly broke camp before dawn and they stopped before nightfall. The rest of the day they spent hunting, fishing, searching for wild honey, gathering heart-of-palm, and fruit. The meager crops the Indians planted provided bandeirantes with the necessary food supplements. One of the more effective means they used to subjugate Indians was to destroy their gardens.

Whenever they came upon a navigable river, they would make light canoes that could be easily run aground at the waterfalls, discarded in the lowlands, or towed on a rope from shore. On land they used the Indians' paths, or when those gave out, they followed brooks and streams, going from one side to the other, whichever was the better for traveling. Even today [this act] is remembered in place-names, such as Passa-Dois, Passa-Dez, Passa-Vinte, and Passa-Trinta [Second Crossing, tenth Crossing, etc.]. They wandered up and down the heights looking for ways to cross the mountains. Naturally they steered clear of the forests and preferred to travel along the crests. According to Montoya some bandeirantes spent so much time in the backlands that

> when they returned home, they found new children, by men who, believing them to have died, married their wives and brought with them the children they had sired in the hinterland.[2]

The Jesuits called the people in São Paulo mamalucos, that is, the offspring of Indian women. And they were right, because no white women ever reached those thickets.

There are insufficient documents for a history of the bandeiras, who were, by the way, always the same. Men outfitted with firearms attacked savages armed with bows and arrows. With the first attack many of the Indians died, and immediately thereafter the rest lost heart. The survivors were tied up, brought to town, and divided up according to the original terms of the expedition. Later on the Caiapós introduced a bit of novelty into this tragic monotony.

> Hoping to seal off any escape and burn us to death, they surround us with fire when they catch us in the fields. Some [of us] fight back by starting a backfire or yanking out the grass so the flames cannot get close. Others smear themselves with pitch, wrap themselves in leaves or cover themselves with charcoal. [They sometimes try to shield themselves] around green trees, or burnt ones.

The routes these expeditions traveled conform, more or less, to the following patterns. After the bandeirantes left the Tietê River behind, they reached the Paraíba do Sul River through the São Miguel Gorge. They traveled down the Paraíba to Cuapacaré, today's Lorena. From there they crossed the Mantiqueiras at approximately the same point that the Rio-Minas Railway crosses it today. Traveling the Parnaíba toward Jundiaí and Moji, they veered away from Urubupangá and reached Goiás. From Sorocaba the line of penetration led to the upper reaches of the eastern tributaries of the Paraná and Uruguay Rivers. Using the rivers that empty [into the Paraná] between the falls at Guiará and Urubupungá, they went from the Paraná River basin to that of the Paraguay and reached Cuiabá and Mato Grosso. As time went by, the Paraíba trail linked the high plateau of the Paraná River with that of the São Francisco and the Parnaíba. The Goiás and Mato Grosso trails linked the Amazon highlands to the inland sea using the Madeira, Tapajós, and Tocantins Rivers.

The bandeiras of the sixteenth century laid waste especially to the Tietê area, whose numerous Tupiniquins quickly disappeared. They also destroyed the upper Paraíba, which they called the Surubi River in Paratininga, according to Glimmer. With the passage of time, the radii of depopulation grew longer and longer, which is the essential and inseparable effect of these expeditions.

The Paulista movement toward the western backlands clashed with the Paraguayan movement toward the coast. Ciudad Real on the Piqueri River, next to the Sete Quedas falls area, and Vila Rica, on the Ivaí River, were founded during the second half of the sixteenth century, before Brazil came under Spanish rule. With these colonists the people from São Paulo established good relations, at the beginning. In their expeditions to hunt human beings, they were often allies and partners. In addition, an overland journey from Paraguay to the coast was easier by way of Piratininga than it was following the difficult trail blazed by Cabeza de Vaca. Both sides profited from mutual cooperation. Only later on did conflicts arise, and the two towns disappeared.

Around 1610 Spanish Jesuits from Asunción began some missions on the eastern bank of the Paraná River. They founded Loreto and San Ignacio on the Paranapanema. Then they stepped up their pace to found eleven more reductions [i.e., settlements] on the Tibagi, the Ivaí and the Corumbataí and the Iguaçu Rivers. Across the Uruguay River they set up another ten between the Ijuí and Ibicuí Rivers, as well as another six in the Tape area, on different tributaries of Lake Patos. From San Cristóbal and Jesús María, both located on the Pardo River, only a few leagues of land now separated them from the sea.

This grandiose catechism campaign was not just a simple translation of the basic prayers into língua geral to be mechanically and superficially repeated by the ignorant masses. One of the Jesuits who worked most diligently to spread the news was to say:

> We call Indian settlements reductions. Living in their old ways, in the
> forests, mountains, valleys, and in hidden gulches, these people [built vil-

lages] of only three to six households. [Their villages] were separated from one another by one, two, three, or more leagues. The padres' diligence has reduced [concentrated] them into large towns and brought them into political life so they can appreciate the cotton in which they dress themselves, because they normally go around naked, without covering what nature used to hide.[3]

It is hard to imagine a more tempting prize for slave hunters. Why venture off into bizarre territory with its strange, semihuman people speaking weird and incomprehensible languages, if nearby lived numerous villagers who had been initiated into the art of peace, conditioned to the yoke of authority, and indoctrinated in *Abanheen*, or língua geral?

From their beginning there were some raids on the reductions, but the Jesuits' energy and sang-froid, overcame the mamalucos, who, snarling and muttering threats, retreated. And to put their threats into practice they would need the connivance of the people at Asunción, which they obtained around the end of 1628. Luis Céspedes Xería, the governor of Paraguay, who had married into a family in Rio de Janeiro and who owned a plantation there, was instrumental in obtaining that connivance. He took a trip overland for his government and spent time in Loreto do Pirapó and San Ignacio de Ipaumbuçu, where he admired the churches: "which were most beautiful. I have seen none better in all the settlements I have visited in Chile and Perú." He also gave the bandeirantes a sign telling them they could advance.[4]

Santo Antônio, the first reduction to be invaded, rested on the right bank of the Ivaí. After it, they invaded reductions on the Tibagi River: San Miguel, Jesús María, San Pablo, and San Francisco Javier. It took less time for the others to be destroyed by the bandeirantes' devastating fury than it had taken idealistic inspiration to gather the settlements together. The only ones to survive were the reductions at Loreto and San Ignacio, on the Paranapanema River. The Jesuits decided to move them below the Sete Quedas area, between the Paraná and Uruguay Rivers. The story of their painful exodus brings tears to one's eyes even now. After devastating the missions at Guairá, the mamalucos moved on to those along the Uruguay and Tape rivers.

Montoya's description of their entrance into Jesús María on the Pardo River, near Lake Patos, sums up the techniques employed on these expeditions.

On the day of Saint Francis Xavier (3 December 1637), which was being celebrated by a mass and a sermon, 140 bandeirantes along with 150 Tupi Indians entered the settlement. They were well armed with muskets. They dressed from head to toe in *escupis*, a sort of vest padded with cotton that protected them from arrows as they fought. At the sound of a drum roll, with their flag raised, and without further ado the command was given. They attacked the church, firing their muskets. They fought for six hours, from eight in the morning until two in the afternoon.

The enemy, having seen the valor of the people under attack and realizing that their own dead were many, decided to burn the church where the Indians had taken refuge. Three times they set it on fire, and three times the fire was put out. The forth time the straw caught fire, and the people inside had to leave. They made an opening, and out they came, like a flock of sheep leaving the corral for a meadow. The bandeirantes used swords, machetes, and scimitars to cut off their heads, arms, and legs, as well as to run them through. They put their scimitars to the test by cutting children in two, breaking open their heads, and dismembering them.[5]

Do horrors such as these make it worth thanking the bandeirantes for taming this land and establishing it as part of Brazil?

We have little more than vague notions of the route the bandeirantes followed to Guairá, Uruguay, and Tape. Certainly Sorocaba, the last settlement, played an important part. Bandeirantes built canoes or rafts in the highlands and floated down the rivers. If one or another of these crafts drifted away, they served as a warning of imminent danger to the reductions, which means that not all expeditions were successful. To return, they trekked overland. There was no other way to bring back the gangs of prisoners, who walked shackled at the neck and tied to one another.

What fate awaited these people? Montoya tells us they were used to carry beef and pork down to the coast. They would, of course, carry salt on their way back. Others were sent to Rio, where there were people who made money off this piracy. Others ended up working on the head bandeirantes' ranches. In the backlands,

> in the settlements bandeirantes destroyed, the head man had the good-looking women, be they married, single, or savage, put in a room with him. He spent his nights with these women like a billy-goat in a corral of she-goats.[6]

The large number of people from the Jesuit reductions who were enslaved can be seen in the extent to which Carijós were found in places far removed from their original surroundings. (In São Paulo the name people used for Guarani Indians was Carijós.) These Indians, once they were tamed, were employed to conquer other Indians. They made up the bulk of the bandeirantes' forces, while the bandeirantes themselves acted mainly as leaders.

The events in the Tape region proved to be insoluble in Asunción, Rio, or Bahia. The missionaries hoped to be more successful across the sea, so they sent Antonio Ruiz de Montoya to Madrid and Francisco Días Taño to Rome. Días Taños brought back papal bulls and fulminating censures.[7] Ruiz de Montoya brought back the most precise and urgent orders for the colonial authorities. All were in vain. When the papal letters were made known in Rio, the population went berserk, and the bull was suspended. Their ire spread along the coast and increased as it extended inland. Defended by their unassailable isolation, the Paulistas expelled the Jesuits, who only returned years later, after having made extensive negotiations and concessions. Meanwhile, the *encomienda* or allotment system used in Spanish lands was established to manage the Indians. Some of the encomiendas ended up legally under Jesuit control.[8]

Montoya received permission to outfit the Indians with firearms and to teach them the art of warfare. Soon the bandeirantes lost their advantage. Defeated by the Jesuits, they sought easier prey, in the Maracaju Mountains, along the upper Paraguay River, among the Chiquito Indians, and finally among the marauding heathens whose language was inaccessible. These hunting grounds were not as lucrative, and the bandeira expeditions started to lose their original appeal and gradually disappeared. The reductions at Guairá and in the Tape region were never rebuilt. Along the Uruguay River seven towns were once more founded and later on incorporated into Brazil, as we shall see.

The Paulistas were of greater help in Bahia and north of the São Francisco River. Around the Paraguaçu River gathered some daring and brave tribes related to the Aimorés. They had been converted at the beginning of the century, but invaded the district of Capanema, slaughtered the farmers and cowhands at Aporá, and advanced up to Itapororocas. The Bahian expeditions sent out to fight them were of little use, so the idea occurred to someone to call to São Paulo for help. The call was answered by Domingos Barbosa Calheiros, who set sail from Santos. In Bahia he headed for Jacobinas, but was received by some peaceful Paiaiá Indians and accomplished nothing useful. He was accompanied in this journey by more than 200 white men, of whom few returned from the backlands.

With the failure of Calheiros' expedition, it is not surprising that the Tapuias continued their raids. Finally, on 4 March 1669, war was declared and Paulistas were invited to fight it. In August 1671 they arrived. The city council of Salvador had spent over 10,000 milreis to bring them. There were two leaders: Brás Rodrigues de Arzão and Estêvão Ribeiro Baião Parente. Cachoeira became their base of operations, and their operations went on for years. Brás Rodrigues withdrew after taking the village of Camisão, on the left bank of the Paraguaçu. Estêvão Ribeiro fought mainly on the right bank, where he took the village of Massaracá. In payment for his services, he was given the proprietorship of a town named for his son, João Amaro. After having been sold to some rich man in Bahia, the town vanished. The place-name is still remembered in the Bahian countryside.[9]

These maritime expeditions were followed by others coming overland. The first one may have been headed by Domingos de Freitas de Azevedo. All we know about it is that it was defeated along the São Francisco River. The overland approaches were facilitated by the abundance of forests along the upper reaches of the river, by its navigability on the plateau, and by canoes. There were Paulistas who built canoes and came down the river on them, then sold them in the falls area, where the scarcity of vegetation made such merchandise expensive. We know more about the overland expeditions of Domingos Jorge Velho, Matias Cardoso de Almeida, and Morais Navarro—all of whom were employed to fight the Paiacu, Janduí, and Icó Indians along the Açu and Jaguaribe Rivers. Domingos Jorge helped to thrash the Palmares settlement, a maroon community of blacks in the backlands of Pernambuco and Alagoas. This community had existed before the Dutch invasion and had made short work of the troops that had been sent out to destroy it.

The entire area between Cape Santo Agostinho and Porto Calvo was cleansed of troublesome elements.

Many of the Paulistas employed in the northern wars never went back to São Paulo. They preferred the life of a large landholder in the territory they had taken by force. In effect they went from being bandeirantes to being conquerors—that is, from depopulators to founders of stationary establishments. Even before the discovery of minerals, we know that along the banks of the Velhas and the São Francisco there were more than 100 families from São Paulo who raised cattle in the region.

We know too little about the family life of the rich and powerful bandeirantes in São Paulo to draw any conclusions. The following passage by Pedro Taques only partially fills this void, since it describes life after the discovery of the mines, which changed things drastically.

At the home of Guilherme Pompeu de Almeida, the feast of December 8 was celebrated on a yearly basis by a week-long feast of High Masses, with the Sacrament on display and sermons to several saints to whom he was especially devoted. The week concluded with an anniversary Mass for the souls in Purgatory, a Novena, a High Mass and a sermon to rouse the hearers' devotion. From São Paulo came the greater part of the nobility, along with the important leaders and the higher clergy from the four communities: the Jesuits, the Carmelites, the Benedictines, and the Franciscans. Dr. Guilherme Pompeu's home, thanks to its guests and their [high] status, was more like a large town or a court. To be aware of the grandeur with which guests were treated in the house of this Paulista hero, it is sufficient to know that without borrowing anything he had 100 beds made up, each with a canopy of its own, each with expensive Brittany sheets, each adorned with embroidery, and each with a silver basin underneath it. At the entrance to Araçariguama (his ranch) he had a portico. Between it and the buildings lay a level field some 500 paces wide. It was all walled in, and the open space was the patio for the Conceição Chapel or Church.

The guests' livery remained at the gate. The guests themselves dismounted there and took off their spurs and other riding gear. Everything was turned over to the livery, to the slaves, who, for this political undertaking, Dr. Pompeu kept strictly disciplined.

The guest, or however many guests there were, came in, and, no matter how long they stayed, be it a week or a month, none of them heard a thing about their slaves, horses, or riding gear. However, whenever any of the guests, be they 1, 15, or many leaving at the same time; they all found the horse on which they had come, the same adornments, the same spurs, and all the gear ready for them at the gate. All this happened without producing the slightest confusion among the livery, who had been trained to perform these tasks. The horses were kept in stables, where they were given good rations of grass and corn, which is what horses are fed in Brazil, especially in São Paulo. This attention to detail was just one of the many things that amazed the guests, who observed that, among the multitude of people who on a daily basis arrived to visit and regale Dr. Guilherme Pompeu de Almeida for days on end, no one ever lost or missed a thing. There was never a record of someone's gear being replaced by someone else's. Dr. Guilherme Pompeu's table was so generous and the delicacies were set out with such attention that, if a meal had been finished and a few hours later more guests arrived, their banquet left nothing to be desired.

For this reason the larder was always well stocked. Wheat was so abundant in this house that bread was made on a daily basis, which meant that the following day one did not serve bread left over from the previous day. The wine was outstanding. It came from a well-cultivated vineyard. And even though it was consumed in quantity, there was some left over every year.[10]

Life of the common folk bore little resemblance to such splendor. The majority of them lived off *canjica*, corn meal mush. They got along without salt, because there was not enough to go around.

The Paulistas were not content with going from being bandeirantes to being conquerors. There was always some mining going on around Iguape and Paranaguá. Beginning in 1670, and in even greater numbers, they threw themselves into prospecting, once the Portuguese monarch appealed to their sense of pride. Before the great diaspora which was brought about by the discovery of gold, the population was concentrated along the banks of the Tietê and the Paraíba Rivers. The towns of Mogi das Cruzes, Parnaíba, Itu, and Sorocaba were situated along the former; and Jacareí, Taubaté, and Guaratinguetá, along the latter. All these settlements antedate the discoveries. The density of population was probably greatest along the Paraíba, because its valley was narrowed on the right by the Serra do Mar and on the left by the Serra da Mantiqueira, and this made people live close to one another. Nonetheless, an abundance of towns does not necessarily imply a tremendous population. On the lands of the donataries the founding of towns must have been facilitated by the owners' pride in being able to add the title of lord of several of these towns to their names and their being able to name clerks and other officials for these towns.[11]

By this time, Piratininga was no longer the only way onto the plateau. Other groupings of coastal and backlands towns arose: Parati and Taubaté, São Vicente, Santos, São Paulo, Moji, and perhaps Jacareí; which, at least later on, obtained a direct line to the coast. Other towns included Iguape, Paranaguá, São Francisco and Curitiba. Curitiba was destined to play a leading role in the region, but it attracted few people. It struggled along until it became a distribution center, largely of pack animals that were brought up from the south.

An anonymous writer described the Paulista of the 1690s:

> Your Majesty could make good use of the Paulistas by honoring them and granting them concessions. Awards and interest will make men take great risks. And these are the sort of men who will venture all through the backlands. They are always tramping through it, with no more sustenance than forest game: animals, snakes, lizards, wild fruit, and roots of several different trees. They do not mind spending years on end in the backlands, used as they are to its way of life. And even if these Paulistas, owing to some fracases among one another, might seem unruly, no one can deny it was they who wrested from the wild heathens all the backlands we now possess. Those heathens are responsible for laying waste to the towns of Cairu, Boipeba, Camamu, Jaguaribe, Maragogipe, and Peruaçu during the ad-

ministration of Governor Afonso Furtado de Mendonça. And, no earlier governor was able to do this [defeat the heathen?] no matter how hard he tried.

Also, one cannot deny that they conquered the maroon communities in Pernambuco. Likewise, let no one think that without the Paulistas and their bands of Indians will we be able to conquer those wild heathens on the warpath in Ceará, Rio Grande do Norte, as well as in the backlands of Paraíba and Pernambuco. This is because wild heathens hiding out in the mountains, cliffs, forest, and scrub can only be caught by tame heathens and no one else. So Your Majesty should make use of the Paulistas to conquer your lands.[12]

* * *

ALEXANDRE DE MOURA made Jerônimo de Albuquerque capitão-mor of Maranhão. He put Martin Soares in charge of the subordinate captaincy of Cumá. Under the leadership of Francisco Caldeira de Castelo Branco, Pará would remain independent so as to avoid further friction among the recent rivals. Bento Maciel Parente was appointed as a *capitão de entradas,* or invading captain. He was a reinol who had been raised in Pernambuco. He had fought in the Paraíba and Rio Grande wars; he had gone on the saltpeter expedition in Bahia; and he had accompanied Dom Francisco de Sousa to São Vicente. In the south he had spent three years on bandeira and mining expeditions, and another three years as a sergeant major in five southern towns.

According to the unimpeachable opinion of Gaspar de Sousa, Jerônimo de Albuquerque lacked some of the qualities of good governorship. He has received many accusations, which, if true, are serious. He seems to have disregarded some of Alexandre de Moura's instructions. And he proved to be more given to bellicose bluster than to peacemaking. He died in February 1618, leaving his office to his son, Antônio de Albuquerque. He was advised by Bento Maciel and Diogo da Costa Machado. The 22-year-old youth scorned the limits his father had put on his authority. When the governor-general arrested Bento Maciel, he made Machado young Albuquerque's adviser. Albuquerque chose to return to Portugal. His command was taken over by Machado, who handed it over in May 1622 to Antônio Muniz Barreiros, who commanded until 1626.

Through this first decade, Bento Maciel made several forays up the Mearim and Pindaré Rivers. He copied the bandeirantes' policies and actions and built a fort on the Itapicuru River well above the harbor. Francisco de Azevedo made other incursions and was the first to penetrate the

Turi and Gurupi backlands. The natives at Cumá rose up right after Martim Soares, suffering from long-term illnesses, left for Portugal. Soares' successor was Matias de Albuquerque, Antônio's brother. Under him the Indians laid waste to almost the entire Portuguese garrison, and their uprising spread and approached Point Saparará. The Indians suffered terrible losses. The Jesuits Manuel Gomes and Diogo Nunes, convinced of the uselessness of their efforts on the Indians' behalf, set off for the West Indies. Friar Cristóvão de Lisboa, the head of the Capuchines, witnessed disregard for explicit laws and censures.

During Diogo da Costa Machado's administration, several hundred people from the Azores arrived at São Luís. They had been brought as settlers, but found nothing set up for them and endured great deprivation and suffering. Immigration, begun with beguiling hopes, never regained the original energy it had received from the propaganda in Simão Estaço da Silveira's book.

In an endeavor to create new sugar mills, the governor general contracted Antônio Barreiros to build two or three. The appointment of Barreiros's son as capitão-mor of Maranhão was supposed to help carry the deal off. Bento Maciel built one sugar mill. The land was well suited for sugar cane. The Indians pressed into service through the Spanish encomienda system, which Bento Maciel had brought in, would supply the labor. The big problem was transport. Pernambuco, the biggest market in the country, was nearby, but one could only sail there during the part of the year when the winds blew in that direction. Land journeys during the rainy season, which were necessary to avoid the storms Pedro Coelho experienced when he tried to colonize Ceará, were only good for transporting slaves. And that is what they were used for. During that period one individual speaks of the "great quantity of *patacões* [silver coins] people in Maranhão acquired sending slaves to Pernambuco."

Besides sugar cane, people planted cotton and tobacco. Cotton cloth and thread served as mediums of exchange. Ships left for Portugal in August or September.

The difficulties in seaboard communication between Maranhão and the rest of Brazil favored setting up Maranhão as an independent state. It was so ordered in 1621. Its territory began in present-day Ceará around São Roque and went up the coast to the as yet undefined northern border of Pará. Francisco Coelho de Carvalho, the first governor of Maranhão, landed in Pernambuco during the time of the Dutch invasion. Matias de Albuquerque retained him there. Later, using several pretexts, Carvalho stayed on. He only reached São Luís in 1626. With him he brought

Manuel de Sousa de Sá, the capitão-mor of Pará, which had been declared a dependency of the state of Maranhão.

In the captaincy of Pará, Francisco Caldeira de Castelo Branco was amicably received by the natives, but he seized the first opportunity to make war on them. The abundance of waterways must have inspired him to adapt a medieval form of torture that probably seemed novel and grisly to those primitive children of nature. He ordered criminals tied to several canoes after which the boatmen rowed in different directions until the victims' limbs were pulled from their bodies. His quarrelsome personality, which he had revealed to some Frenchmen, did not endear him to his fellow Portuguese either. They got fed up and overthrew him, clasped him in irons, and in November 1618 put Baltasar Rodrigues in charge of the colony. Not even these measures quelled the Indians' rage. The Cumá movement joined the one in Pará. Help was sought from Pernambuco, and it arrived, commanded by Jerônimo Fragoso. Fragoso had been named capitão-mor by Dom Luís de Sousa, the governor-general. He immediately carried out an order to arrest Castelo Branco, Rodrigues, and the other leaders of the revolt. Castelo Branco died in Limoeiro prison, in Lisbon.

Bento Maciel had gone to Pernambuco after the problems with Antônio de Albuquerque. He returned with people he had recruited in the two neighboring captaincies and went back to his old ways with greater fury. From Tapuitapera up to Amazon territory, he wreaked such havoc that Jerônimo Fragoso intimated that he should back off. However, Bento Maciel paid no attention to Fragoso's suggestion because, since he had been made commander of war by the governor-general, he was not subordinate to the capitão-mor of Pará. Fragoso died shortly thereafter. There were several pretenders to his position. Finally, Bento Maciel was nominated. He began an overland route to Maranhão, perhaps by traveling on the Capim and Pindaré Rivers, which was tried later on. He governed for four years, until the arrival of Manuel de Sousa de Sá in 1627.

When Francisco Caldeira arrived, he had been informed of voyages the English and Dutch had made up the Amazon, as well as of the forts they had built. The same year that Belém was founded Pedro Teixeira captured a Dutch vessel whose artillery was used to reinforce Presepe's. The English concentrated on the mouth of the Amazon, and their westernmost establishment was on the Caraji River. The Dutch went as far as the Xingu River. Several different expeditions, especially those under Pedro Teixeira, Pedro da Costa Favela, Feliciano Coelho, and Jácome Raimundo de Noronha captured ships, took many prisoners, and razed all the forts, one by one. Concerning the attack on the English fortress known as Fort Philip, Noronha boasts of having captured four pieces of heavy artillery, *roqueiras* or "shot canons," and many weapons. He claims to have killed 83 foreigners, taken 13 prisoners, and destroyed their native allies. The natives "were so terrified that never again would they make peace with foreigners."[13]

The absence of friendly Indian suppliers of tobacco, cotton, and arnoto fruit (known as *urutu* in the Cariba language), as well as other raw materials, would suffice to dissuade the interlopers from further ventures. The fortress at Gurupá would make matters even more difficult for them. It was built at the edge of the Amazon delta, on the site of a former Dutch fort and was an excellent post for observing movement on the left bank of the river. It was a modern fort and an invaluable complement to Fort Presepe, on the right bank. The last Dutch establishment in the region, as far as we know, was at Maiacaré, adjacent to Cape Norte. It fell to Sebastião de Lucena in 1646. The English had been gone for years. Portugal's sovereignty was now firmly implanted from Cape Norte to Point Saparará, and the entire lower Amazon had been swept clean of foreigners.

During Francisco Coelho's time the State of Maranhão was divided into several hereditary captaincies. Tapuitapera and Cametá were awarded to the governor's son and to his brother. Álvaro de Sousa received Caeté or Gurupi. Álvaro was the son of Gaspar de Sousa, who had distinguished himself in the conquest of Maranhão. The government in Portugal awarded him the territory between the Parnaíba and Pindaré Rivers in Maranhão, as well as the land from Maracanã to the Tocantins in Pará. Later Bento Maciel received the Cape Norte Captaincy, which was bordered by the Vicente Pinzón or Oiapoque, the Amazon, and the Paru Rivers. Antônio de Sousa de Macedo received the captaincy of Marajó Island.

Penetration of the Amazon was slow. On the northern shore, the goal had been simply to drive out the interlopers. On the south side, the village of Maturu was the settlement farthest to the west. It was on the right bank of the Xingu River, which was also known as the Parnaíba. At this point the poison arrows of the Tapajó Indians brought inland expeditions to a standstill. They had begun in 1637 with the arrival of two lay Franciscans who had come from the foothills of the Andes. Jácome de Noronha, who with a bit of heavy-handedness had assumed the leadership after Francisco Coelho de Carvalho's death, decided to make contact with the Spanish colonies across the Andes. Pedro Teixeira was put at the head of this mission and on 17 October 1637 left the Amazon behind. On 15 August 1638 he reached the Paiamino River, a tributary of the Napo, from where he continued on to Quito. After receiving orders from the viceroy of Perú, he headed back and arrived in Pará on 12 December 1639. On his way back, on 16 March 1639, in a harbor on the Aguarico, he took possession of the land extending eastward to the coast for the Portuguese Crown. Bento Maciel, now governor of Maranhão, rewarded this and other services his companion in arms had performed over a score of years by granting him an encomienda of 300 Indian households. It was to be valid for three generations.

The old warrior had no idea of the approaching danger. In 1637, Gideon Morris, a Dutchman taken prisoner during a battle on the Amazon and who had remained a prisoner for eight years, had succeeded in returning to Holland, where he busied himself trying to get the Zealand chamber to conquer Maranhão. If they could take it, he alleged, it would put under Dutch rule over 400 leagues of seacoast occupied by only 1,400 Portuguese and 40,000 Indians. These Indians had been pacified more through fear than through any love for the Portuguese, who were scattered everywhere in the territory. Their soldiers were unhappy and rebellious owing to poor leadership and no pay. Their forts were hard to defend. Moreover, the Indians would think of the Dutch as their liberators. The West Indies Company would take possession of fine stands of sugar cane, tobacco, cotton, oranges, indigo, dyes, oils, balms, ginger, gums, and several types of first-class wood. It could sell slaves to Pernambuco "as the Portuguese had done before war began in that captaincy, and which had been their most profitable activity."

As Morris detailed these ideas in Middelburg, something happened in the colony to help the Dutch endeavor. Responding to repeated appeals for help from the Indians in Ceará, the company sent an expedition that landed at Mocuripe. After valiant but futile resistance on the part of the Portuguese garrison, the Dutch took possession of the fort Martin Soares Moreno had founded. Now there was a point of support for the supposedly profitable expedition. Gideon Morris was named commander of Ceará, where he discovered the Ipanema salt deposits, which seemed to set the stage for his advance.

As soon as he learned of Pedro Teixeira's expedition, Morris felt his plans and aspirations were confirmed. Along with all the advantages he had already presented, to the conquest of Maranhão Morris proposed adding that of the surrounding area and those of the Viceroyalty of Perú, which, he again insisted, would constitute a masterstroke against the

Spaniards. He was not understood. Nassau and the high-ranking authorities were more interested in taking Buenos Aires and Chile. They sought a distant target when there was one close at hand. Later on they heeded his call, and in November 1641 a Dutch squadron arrived in São Marcos Bay.

Owing to the indecisive policies of Dom João IV, no one knew exactly what to do. They were not at war, because in Europe Portugal and Holland had entered into an alliance where they would defend one another and attack each other's enemies. But the colonies were not at peace because the treaty had not been ratified. Bento Maciel gave up without a fight because he had been deceived, or was decrepit or terrified. Once again the company widened its domain. Morris, who took part in the operation, was upset with Nassau's role. Why, after having taken the island, did they not attack Pará immediately? Why didn't they expel the wealthy Portuguese and keep the poorest ones as overseers? Where, in all of Brazil, was it possible for a Portuguese on his own to export 100 crates of sugar, only four months after having lost his land? This is what Inácio do Rêgo, the chief provider, had done. He had also gone off to the Indies. What use was it to conquer Maranhão without also taking the Amazon?

While they were in control of Pernambuco, the Dutch had to deal with rampant greed and venality in the region. Meanwhile the population [in Maranhão] remained quiet and even seemed unwilling to react, if it had not been for Antônio Muniz Barreiro, the old capitão-mor, and two Jesuits: Benedito Amadeu and Lobo do Couto. Lobo do Couto along with a coadjutor had arrived in Brazil in 1624. These Jesuit rebel chiefs were motivated by religious considerations. The Dutch were heretics and the Catholic faith was in danger. The movement began in Itapicuru, which was liberated in a few days. Then they attacked the island, where the Dutch put up greater resistance. Reinforcements came from Pernambuco for the Dutch, and the Portuguese got help from Pará. However their shortage of arms and ammunition obliged them to retreat back to Tapuitapera, on the mainland. Later, when supplies had arrived from Bahia, they once again began their liberating endeavor. Teixeira de Melo succeeded Barreiros, who had died from wounds in battle. He received the distinction of liberating São Luís in 1643. Maranhão's example was followed in Ceará, where the Indians massacred the Dutch, who nonetheless came back and stayed until 1654. It also made an impression in Pernambuco, giving heart to still muddled patriotic longings and setting an example.

During the years that followed, the most noteworthy occurrence was the introduction of Jesuits into the region. Alexandre de Moura was accompanied by two of them, who abandoned him once they realized the futility of any efforts to defend the Indians. Luís Figueira, who had come with Antônio Barreiros, succeeded in quelling the colonists' misgivings about the Jesuits and their intentions by limiting and hiding some of their activities. Some time later he withdrew to Europe. Lobo do Couto, even though he had been isolated and therefore powerless, succeeded in gaining sympathy for his cause in the heat of the reconquest that he inspired. Figueira, who since 1638 had been planning an overseas expedition, finally departed. He left Portugal with many partners and with Pedro de Albuquerque, who had been named Bento Maciel's successor. Because the Dutch were still in command of São Luís, they headed for Pará. In June 1643 near Sol Bay Figueira and the bulk of his party drowned or were killed by Indians. The survivors, once they were able to, made their way to Maranhão, where they were not much use and where they were slaughtered by the savages at Itapecuru. By 1649 there was not a single Jesuit father in the entire state.

Meanwhile, Father Antônio Vieira, a favorite of Dom João IV's and one of the greatest writers in Portuguese, was on the move. As a student of Fernão Cardim, he had heard the story of the early Jesuit missions. One of the first aspirations of this ambitious soul was to become a missionary. He had been sent to Portugal when news of its independence reached Brazil. On Jesuit or Crown business he had spent ten years on European soil. He prevailed in sacred courts, worked on thorny diplomatic negotiations, and dreamed up financial associations, such as the Companhia de Comércio, which was so useful in the Pernambucan war of liberation. He was influential on Crown councils, where he opined and defended his and (mainly) other people's ideas using his abundant stock of expressions, his subtle ratiocination, his Byzantine arguments, and a panoply of truly admirable [verbal] distinctions. Finally, all this pomp and circumstance seemed vacuous to him, and he was overtaken by longing for his youth and for his adopted homeland. He wanted to do missionary work in Maranhão.

In September 1652 an advance party of nine missionaries departed, with father Francisco Veloso in command. Two of them went on to Pará, where they set up a mission. After the first wave of missionaries, Father Vieira, along with three other Jesuits, set sail from the Tagus. On 16 January 1653, they anchored in the harbor at São Luís. Finally someone had arrived to defend the Indians. But why tell this story? As far as the Indians were concerned, there were only two rational policies. One could either let them be taken prisoner, as was the case, or one could put a total ban on slavery. Neither policy was followed by the government or by the Jesuits themselves. This meant that Jesuits would have to contend with greedy colonists, with venal rulers, with simoniacal priests and friars, with incoherent lawmakers, and with unstable legislation. They traveled through the backlands and up the rivers. They crossed the ocean. They preached caustic sermons, coped with seditious leaflets, expulsions, and rebukes. Life was a series of tragic or burlesque ups and downs. A look at the State's functioning in 1662 is even more interesting than these cliff-hangers. Vieira dissects it in a memorable passage, which shows signs of life even in the pallid résumé I shall offer.[14]

The foundations rested on blood. With blood they gathered and constructed the edifice. Now the rocks come apart, separate, and crumble. The land goes barren. There is not enough manioc growing to keep people alive. The stands of lumber and the tobacco fields are far away. Fish and game have grown scarce. Settlements are far from one another, and just to row [from one to another] consumes the Indians' strength. There are no butcher shops, cattle pastures [*ribeiras*], gardens, nor are there stores selling ordinary foodstuffs. One cannot even buy a pound of sugar—and they grow it here. In Pará, where all the roads are waterways, there are no canoes for rent. If a man wants bread, he needs a farm. If he wants meat, he needs a hunter. If it is fish he wants, he needs a fisherman. If he wants clean clothes, a washerwoman. And if he wants to go to Mass or wherever, he needs canoes and oarsmen. People of greater means have seamstresses, spinners, lacemakers, looms, and other manufacturing instruments and tradespeople—which means that each family is a sort of republic.

The early settlers were poor folk. Some were soldiers who had left Pernambuco. They were so poorly paid that only a few of them had shoes and stockings to wear. Others were noble but impoverished Azoreans, who, owing to scarcity on the islands, had to emigrate. Still others were ragged and forlorn soldiers who had been captured by the Dutch during the wars, then abandoned on the shore. Finally, some were deportees.

The number of friars is disproportionate, considering the population. Pará has 80 households and four convents. The owners of these houses pay for Masses, offices, and burials. To finance their celebrations, they are obliged to contribute great sums of money to a good number of brotherhoods. Whether they want to or not, they hear sermons preached from pulpits. And what they can manage to scrape together in a year is not enough to pay for this involuntary devotion. The Jesuits are the only ones who do not weigh on the colonists, and that is because the income they receive from the royal treasury spares them from destitution. The state's exports decline in value, and they are scarcely worth the price one pays to ship them. On the other hand, everything from Europe costs a fortune. Idleness, sloth, and ostentation are the order of the day. Alcoholism is rampant. In the city of Pará alone, people spend 15,000 cruzados per year on the local firewater—not to mention what they spend on the brandy from Portugal. The governors and treasury officers are first in line to pay themselves and leave little for the vicars and soldiers. They save the best jobs for their servants. They arrest people, try them, recruit soldiers, and handle imports and exports.

Finally, the Indians, because of their weak constitutions and the idle ease and liberty in which they are raised, are not capable of withstanding the work they are obliged to perform for any length of time. The Portuguese send them mainly to the cane fields, sugar mills, and tobacco fields—where they constantly die. And because the entire wealth of colonists is based on their slaves, it is commonplace for people who at one point thought of themselves as extremely rich and well off to fall into abject poverty. A person's assets are not his lands, but the products he extracts from them, and the only instruments for their extraction are the Indians. We have Antônio Vieira to thank for this vivid description of our primitive economy.

With the exception of Bartolomeu Barreiros de Ataíde's expedition to the Ouro River, that is, to the territory Pedro Teixeira had claimed for the Portuguese Crown, and João Betancourt Muniz' expedition against the Anibá Indians on the Jari River, the Portuguese had kept to the right shore of the Amazon River. In 1663 Antônio Arnau Vilela explored the left shore and met an untimely end when he ventured up the Urubu River. Pedro da Costa Favela sought to avenge his death. He killed 700 Indians, he took another 400 Guaneena and Caboquena Indians prisoner, and he burned 300 villages. After these expeditions others followed, attracted by the dense Indian population. In a short time they began to visit the Rio Negro and finally the Branco. The fort on a Rio Negro harbor, near present day Manaus, was soon founded. It became the point of departure for further inward movement.

In 1693 the territories in which each order could set up missions were determined. The Jesuits were to work on the southern shore of the Amazon; the Franciscans between Cape Norte and the Urubu River; and the Carmelites were sent to the Rio Negro.

Meanwhile, the Spanish Jesuits in their catechistic ardor worked their way down the Solimões River, just as those in Paraguay had worked the Paranapanema, Ivaí, Iguaçu, and Uruguay Rivers. Samuel Fritz, a native of Bohemia who was doing missionary work around the Juruá River or farther east, had brought several tribes speaking their own languages, as well as some who spoke língua geral (the Cambebas and the Omagoas) into the flock. For reasons of health he went to Pará, where, under various pretexts, he was detained for nearly two years. On his return, in spite of their excuses, the Portuguese provided him with an escort back to his reductions. Once he arrived, the commanding officer protested, saying that all the land up to the Napo River belonged to Portugal. While the apostle of the Maina Indians was on his way to Lima to warn the viceroy of the impending usurpation, people in Pará and Lisbon were considering extending the Portuguese domain in that direction—indeed they had been talking about it since 1695. The viceroy of Perú did nothing. And the problem of succession in Spain gave the Portuguese the opportunity to expand. Inácio Corrêa de Oliveira expelled the Spanish Jesuits from the Solimões River. Thus the war between the two kingdoms produced in the north the same effect that their union had in Guairá, Uruguay, and Tape. Carmelite friars joined these, as well as later expeditions. They were worthy counterparts of the Capuchine friars who joined the bandeirantes in the south. On these missions the invaders learned uses for rubber.

Portuguese incursions up the Amazon's right-bank tributaries went on, too. In 1669 Gonçalo Pires and Manuel Brandão discovered clove, cinnamon, and Brazil nuts [*castanhas*] along the Tocantins. In 1716 João de Barros Guerra defeated the Torá Indians on the Madeira River. In 1720 an expedition set off against the Juína Indians on the Juruá River. In 1724 Francisco de Melo Palheta went up the Madeira River and reached the Spanish villages. With the discovery of mines in the interior, people tried to reach them on the Amazon's southern tributaries. More than one of these attempts was successful, so Maranhão demanded that the mines at São Félix and Natividade should be under its authority, since they were located on the Tocantins River. From the third decade of the eighteenth century miners from Goiás and Mato Grosso had traveled down the Amazon. Of all these voyages the one with the most fertile consequences was Manuel Félix de Lima's. In 1742 he traveled down the Sararé, the Guaporé, the Mamoré, and the Madeira to reach Maranhão. When the governor of Mato Grosso set up his capital on the shore of the Guaporé, it was the logical consequence of Lima's having found this route, which over time became the one most traveled.

Little by little the population increased. However, frequent epidemics of a few months' duration could destroy the work of years. As evidence of better times, it is sufficient to cite Antônio de Albuquerque Coelho's founding of a royal fishery on Marajó Island in 1692, as well as the development of cattle farms on that island beginning in the early years of the eighteenth century. At Easter time in 1726 a butcher shop began operations in Belém. When La Condamine visited Belém in 1743, the local currency was cacao beans. Starting in May 1749, gold, silver, and copper coins began to circulate.

In 1751, Pará, still subordinate to Maranhão, had nine parishes and six small parish churches. It had 7 fortresses, 24 sugar mills, 42 distilleries, and 63 Indian mission villages. The government undertook many measures to foment agriculture, but they were only successful in the area around Belém. Coffee, brought from Cayenne by Francisco de Melo Palheta, seemed to wake the population from its lethargy. The experiment did not last long. People preferred to gather wild products, such as clove, cinnamon, cacao, and parsley. They were more valuable and nature provided them.

The years after 1661, when Antônio Vieira returned to Europe, are marked by chaotic legislation concerning Indian villages, spiritual and temporal jurisdiction over Indians, their transportation from the interior to the coast, their salaries, and their enslavement. In 1680 a law was passed prohibiting enslavement of Indians. This was the only sensible and just solution, had there been enough honest and industrious people to enforce such a law.[15]

A commercial association was created to mitigate colonists' complaints. It would have the right to sell basic supplies to the colonists; it would buy everything the state produced; and it would bring in slaves from Africa. Africans were believed to be stronger and better suited for heavy agricultural toil.

This did not upset people in Pará because their somewhat different concerns were protected by their distance from Maranhão, where the news caused a great uproar. The Jesuits were expelled, the capitão-mor was put in prison, solicitors were sent to the court to plead for the king's pardon. Manuel Bequimão [Beckman], a Portuguese national of Germanic background and the leader of the mob, took the reins of government. Not withstanding its auspicious beginning, his movement stagnated. It was not even joined by the adjacent Tapuitapera Captaincy. And many of the movement's early participants began to slink away.

Cases like this occur over and over again in Brazilian history. Triumphs are obtained as a result of the enemy's laxity or cowardliness rather than because of the ability or strength of the attacker. Then, after the cheaply purchased victory, people realize that their accomplishment has consequences, and they start wondering what these consequences might be. Bequimão was not exempt from this intellectual sloth. When Gomes Freire de Andrada, who had been named governor of the state, appeared in the harbor accompanied by an armed contingent to back his command, it suddenly occurred to Bequimão that he could stop the governor from coming ashore. Bequimão had foreseen nothing, and he had not prepared for this eventuality. Now it was too late. There was no opposition to the governor's takeover.

There was still the hope that the governor had brought a pardon from the king, but he had not. The trial began immediately. Manuel Bequimão, Jorge de Sampaio, and Deiró were sentenced to die. Deiró was executed in effigy, the others climbed the scaffold. The governor, who stood out among governors for his generosity and benevolence, went easy on the mass of followers. After taking counsel, the governor abolished the company and the royal monopoly. The Indian question went on as usual, with gains, losses, and surprises.

During Gomes Freire's government, the primary concern was finding a means of communicating with the rest of Brazil without having to rely on the seasonal winds or on fording the rivers along the seacoast.

A few years earlier, after having defeated the Tremembé Indians and having cleared a beach route to Ceará, Vital Maciel Parente, the son of the old prisoner of the Dutch, sailed many leagues up the Parnaíba and recognized that it flowed from south to north. This realization must have been the source of the notion that the Parnaíba or Paraguaçu River was close to or part of the São Francisco River. Thus, the matter became clear: Bahia was the objective and the Parnaíba was the route to follow.

João Velho do Vale was charged with confirming this hypothesis, and he succeeded. He actually recorded the discovery and later on, in Portugal, gave the manuscript to Gomes Freire. This important book has been mislaid or lost, to the detriment of Brazil's history and ethnography—if one can judge from the references to it in Friar Domingos Teixeira's biography of Gomes Freire.

> After he benefited the country by writing an extensive report in which he gave an exact account of his travels through the backland areas, their rivers, and the people living there (complete with latitudes), João Velho do Vale, more worn out by his efforts than by his age, died. His ashes rest in a humble grave in the city of São Salvador, where he came to the end of his labors with more honor than profit.[16]

Vale went on two expeditions. On the first one he reached the Ibiapaba mountain range, where he blazed three trails. On the second, which of course began in the mountains, he reached Bahia, which suggests an extremely eastward trajectory, perhaps along the banks of the Poti River as well as on others flowing away from the São Francisco: the Cabrobó, Ibó, and Jeremoabo.[17]

It is impossible to say if this or the other trail is the one referred to in a letter written in July 1694 by Antônio de Albuquerque, a successor of Gomes Freire's. This letter was delivered in Bahia on 19 April 1695, to Governor General Dom João de Lencastro.[18] Two days later Sergeant Major Francisco dos Santos, along with four soldiers and 20 Indians, approached the same city with a letter from Albuquerque dated 15 December 1694. To repay Albuquerque's courtesy and to see if he could shorten his trip, the governor general dispatched André Lopes to Maranhão. He carried a letter dated 21 May 1695 to Albuquerque. André Lopes reached São Luís in November, but he had to wait for Albuquerque's return, for he had gone to Pará. With an answer dated 15 March 1696, Lopes was back in Bahia on September 22.

The most difficult part of the journey was in Maranhão. On the Piauí and Canindé Rivers, on the flood plains of the Ceará River, on both sides of the São Francisco, cattle ranches abounded, and there must have been numerous routes of communication. With cattle from this region, people came to the Pastos Bons area of the *sertão* or backlands. For some time people in Pastos Bons dealt exclusively with Bahia, as did the people in Pernambuco who lived upstream from Paulo Afonso.

Later, Father Malagrida took his Catholic mission to the Codó River. His successor, João Ferreira, founded Aldeias Altas, which is today known as Caxias. Once people were aware of the short distance between the Itapecuru and Parnaíba Rivers, the Parnaíba became the preferred route. By 1747 Dom Manuel da Cruz used it when church headquarters had been transferred from Maranhão to Mariana.

Maranhão began to wither beginning with or even before Gomes Freire's government. This is partly because agriculture was neglected in favor of forest produce similar to that in Pará. Sugar plantations gave way to clove, cinnamon, and Brazil nuts.

In 1703 one witness wrote:

> They erected nearly 50 sugar mills, which functioned as long as clove and cacao went undiscovered. And their discovery was the ruin of all those men. It caused them to let the increased production of sugar and tobacco fall into idleness. The mill owners have a terribly difficult time working

things out with their farmers, for whom cultivating sugar cane is also impractical. All of them say [gathering wild fruit] is easier. The [mill owners] complain that when they fail to plant cane they suffer, and when they planted it they lived well. However there is nothing to be done. The farmers are right to complain about such injustice. The mill owners are tyrants of their own making. This lack of unity between mill owners and cane growers may stop the building of more mills. And the mill and plantation owners are also wrong to want to manufacture everything they use: firewood, ashes, oil, flour, planks, and canoes. By busying themselves in this activity, people on sugar plantations have no time to make sugar.

To this quotation Antônio de Albuquerque would add that since people were consigned to the backlands, they became pathologically dependent on the heathen, whom they seek and lust after because they have no alternative, and they do not even attempt a different solution to their problems.

In 1751 the captaincy had eight parishes, five sugar mills, 203 cattle ranches, 44 of which were in Pastos Bons, with 35 in Aldeias Altas.

The issues surrounding the borders with Spanish colonies, which were no less important than the growing importance of Pará itself, were the reasons why Lisbon made Maranhão subordinate to Pará and why it moved the state's capital to the Amazon basin. Within a short time, however, and thanks to the cultivation of cotton and rice, as well as the introduction of African slaves and the help from a new commercial enterprise, a new era of relative prosperity began. But it was still less impressive than the immense natural resources in the area.

*   *   *

SUGAR PLANTATIONS, tobacco fields, and truck gardens were confined to an area defined by the cost of transporting their produce. Beyond a certain radius, fields lay forever fallow. Backland royal properties would bring no profit to their owner. Given the primitive state of Brazil's economy, this pattern could have persisted, but it finally became obvious that agriculture would only be profitable near the coast or on the short, navigable stretches along rivers without rapids or falls. The earlier chroniclers complain that their contemporaries spent their time scratching the coastal sand like crabs rather than working their way inland. This would be easy in São Paulo, where the inhumane hunt for slaves attracted people and kept them busy. It was also easy in Amazonia, where mighty, freeflowing rivers were everywhere, and where precious crops could be harvested without planting. In other parts of the interior the problem could be solved in a different fashion.

And bovine cattle were the solution to the problem.

Livestock did not need to be raised near the shore. Just like the bandeirantes' victims, cattle could carry themselves over great distances. Indeed, it was easier to transport cattle. Cattle grew well in areas unsuited for cultivating sugar cane, whether their unsuitability came from poor soil or whether it came from a scarcity of forests without which the engenho's furnaces would not work. Cattle raising did not require many cowhands nor special skills, and this was a strong argument for it in a thinly populated land. It almost made capital unnecessary, since cattle were both stable and in circulation at the same time. They constantly increased their numbers. They were a dependable and better source of food than shellfish, fish, and other land and sea animals people ate along the coast. All they cost was salt, and the many salt marshes in the backlands furnished plenty of that.

Cattle ranching first developed in the area around the city of Salvador. The conquest of Sergipe extended it to the right bank of the São Francisco. On the other bank a similar, albeit slower and weaker, movement had spread from Pernambuco. When the war with the Dutch broke out, the banks of the lower part of that river were swarming with cattle. And that was why John Maurice of Nassau brought the area under the domain of the West Indies Company and why the patriots of Divine Liberty defended it so resolutely.

Cattle followed the course of the São Francisco. The largest town, Bahia (Salvador), attracted all the cattle from the southern side. And cattle reached Salvador by a route running parallel to the beach and fording the rivers where they could.

Later, as ranching spread farther inland, other routes became necessary. One of the oldest routes went along the Itapecuru through Pombal and through Jeremoabo on the Vazabarris. It met the São Francisco above the falls region and attracted cattle from the north side of the river. This area, by all rights part of Pernambuco, became a de facto part of Bahia. It was populated by Bahians. Like the São Francisco flatlands, this area narrows where the Parnaíba achieves its greatest length, after the great bend in the São Francisco. In this narrow area, passage from one river to the other was achieved, and people from Bahia met up with people from Maranhão. The Terra Nova and Brígida streams facilitated travel to Ceará. The road to Piauí ran along the Pontal and through the Dois Irmãos Mountains. Not even the Parnaíba could contain the invading wave. Pastos Bons was settled by Bahians, and, until the middle of the eighteenth century, people there did business exclusively with Bahia.

The concern known as the Casa da Torre, which was founded by García d'Ávila (who was himself a protegé of Tomé de Sousa), owned 260 leagues of land along a public highway on the Pernambucan side of the São Francisco. It also possessed 80 leagues of land along a road between the Parnaíba and the São Francisco. It had acquired this land with the pens, ink, and paper it used to request grants of land. Since it did not possess enough cattle to range over this tremendous area, at the turn of the eighteenth century it leased plots of land generally one league in length and charged 10 réis per year. One of those lessees, Domingos Afonso (nicknamed Sertão), set off from one of his "mansions" on the bank of the São Francisco. (In those parts people used the word *sobrado* or "stately house" for anything vaguely resembling a building.) Domingo Afonso founded many important ranches on the Piauí and Canindé Rivers. When he died he left them all to the Jesuits. These ranches were eventually confiscated, once the government expelled the Jesuits from Brazil.

On the Pernambucan side of the São Francisco, there were still many Indian tribes, most of whom belonged the Cariri nation. Some, like the Pimenteiras, belonged to the Caribas nation. Others, e.g., the Amoipiras, were even of Tupi stock. Ranchers went to war against these tribes either because they would not give up their lands peacefully or because they would use the cattle without the ranchers' permission. These conflicts [with the natives] were less bloody than the ones of old. Cattle raising did not require as many hands as farming did. It did not demand the same amount of work. Nor did it seem as repellent as farming did to the Indians. In addition, there was plenty of empty land for the Indians to occupy. Still, many of the Indians were enslaved. Some fled to mission villages. And others sought protection from powerful individuals whose struggles they joined and whose hates they served.

The Indians in the Pajeú region put up considerable resistance, but when Dom João de Lencastro governed, he had Manuel de Araújo de Carvalho attack them. At the same time, Teodósio de Oliveira Ledo was making his way inland from Paraíba. Thanks to these two men, the Pajeú, Piancó, and Piranhas regions were pacified. In those areas some people began to contact Pernambuco and to send their cattle there. Pajeú, in spite of its proximity, had no dealings with Pernambuco until the nineteenth century. Before that it was under the influence of Bahia.

In step with the spread of cattle inland, new passages and roads were being traveled, e.g., Jacobinas Road and the Juazeiro Passage, through which a railway was to go. As Cachoeira grew and as tobacco planting spread, an important branch road toward the lower Paraguaçu River was opened.

On the Bahian side of the São Francisco, cattle were raised in similar quantities, albeit on mountainous terrain. Numerous Indians lived in the coastal and river forests and were given to raiding. Bandeiras under Arzão, Estêvão Parente, and other people weakened but did not stamp out native resistance, and years later there was still fighting going on in the headwaters of the Contas, Pardo, and other rivers. The most important landowner of this area was Antônio Guedes de Brito, who owned 160 leagues of land between Morro do Chapéu [Hat Hill] and the Velhas River. Worthy of mention as well are João Peixoto Viegas, who took possession of the land around the Upper Paraguaçu. Matias Cardoso and Antônio Gonçalves Figueira were conquistadors from São Paulo who set themselves up in places to favor contact with their native region. The roads of this region came together first along the left bank of the São Francisco then ran toward the Parnaíba flatlands. Only later on was the Paraguaçu sought in its upper reaches and then followed to Cachoeira, which is near the harbor.

The first settlers in the sertão lived in dire straits. They were not grantees. They were instead agents and slaves. They had abundant meat and milk, but nothing else. In the beginning they had no manioc flour, which is the only food the folk really trust. They judged the land to be unfit to grow manioc, not because the soil was poor, but because during most of the year it did not rain. The only corn they ate was fresh corn, for it was hard to grind corn in that region where there were no water mills [*monjolos*]. The wildest fruit and the least tasty types of honey were ravenously devoured. One can sum up those backlanders' facts of life by saying that they lived in the age of leather. The doors to their huts were made of leather, as were their sleeping and parturition beds (which lay on the hard ground). Their rope was made of leather, as were water bags, pouches and saddlebags, suitcases, feed bags for horses, harnesses, knife sheaths, packs and bundles, clothes for riding through the brush, handbarrows for curing leather or refining salt. When they built reservoirs, fill dirt was pulled on pieces of leather by oxen who left hoofprints on the ground owing to their weight. Snuff was ground in leather.

Once ranch land was acquired, the first task was to get the cattle used to its new diet. This took time and many people. Afterward, everything was up to the cowhand. He was the one who roped and branded the calves. He cured their sores; burned the appropriate fields on alternate seasons; hunted jaguars, snakes, and bats; knew the clumps of trees from which the cattle would eat their fill; and he dug water holes and made drinking troughs. In fulfillment of his duty, one observer writes, a cowboy rarely slept anywhere but outdoors. Or at least by dawn he was no longer at home. This was especially the case during the winter, which, in addition to its greater rains and thunderstorms, is the time when most calves are born. The cowhand visited the clumps of trees and checked the cattle before they dispersed at the break of day, as is their habit. He marked the cows about to give birth. He kept close watch on them so that when they gave birth they wouldn't hide their calves, who would grow up wild or be killed by botflies.

After four of five years of service, the cowhand began to be paid. He received one out of every four calves. This was how he started his own ranch. From the beginning of the eighteenth century, grants of land were limited to three leagues and separated from each other by a league of open range. According to the anonymous author of the admirable *Roteiro do Maranhão a Goiás*,[19] the backlanders in Bahia, Pernambuco, and Ceará were so favorably disposed to cattle ranching that they tried every means to become ranchers. Their greatest aim in life was to be called a cattleman [*vaqueiro*]. Cattleman, breeder, or rancher were honorific titles for these people.

The cowhands who went on cattle drives sought the great centers of population: Recife and Salvador, the capitals of Pernambuco and Bahia.

Concerning those who went to Bahia, André João Antonil, a scrambling of the name João Antônio Andreoni, a worthy Jesuit, wrote:

> The herds of cattle that ordinarily come to Bahia consist of 100, 150, 200, and 300 head. Almost on a weekly basis some of the largest herds reach Capoame, which is eight leagues away from Salvador. At Capoame they are fattened and sold. During some periods of the year, herds arrive on a daily basis. They are driven by whites, mulattos, blacks, and Indians who make a living driving cattle. Some days they ride in front of the herd and sing, and the cattle follow behind. Other days they follow the cattle and prod the animals along keeping them on the trail and keeping them from going off into the mountains. Each day they travel some four, five, or six leagues. Each day's travel is determined by the availability of pastures that can accommodate them. However, when there is no water, they keep going for 15 to 20 leagues at a stretch, day and night, with little rest until they find a suitable place to stop. When they cross certain rivers, one of the cowhands puts a set of horns on his head and goes into the water to show the steers how they are to ford the river.[20]

No matter how well these drives were managed, a few steers would stray. Others became too weak to travel on. Counting on strays and stragglers, people settled along these routes and bought weakened cattle cheaply. Later on they would sell them in good shape. In addition, they grew some crops and sold the surplus to the travelers. Some of the settlers, thanks to their knowledge of the region, improved the roads and shortened the routes. They built reservoirs, planted sugar cane, which provided one of the backlanders' delights: *rapadura*, i.e., blocks of unrefined cane sugar. Along the São Francisco River, from Salitre to São Romão, they discovered extensive salt deposits. This salt, once refined, proved excellent. Because of these circumstances, a relatively dense population arose along the cattle routes. It was only equaled by the one that came about once the mines were discovered around Rio de Janeiro.

With the advent of cattle raising, trips through the backlands were no longer frightening. Around 1690, there were reasons to undertake such travels. A writer who understood the situation reports the extremely elevated price of foreign goods. He also mentions the depreciation of native fruit, the decreasing fertility of the soil owing to its depletion, the limits imposed on tobacco planting, which was "a product made by blacks, by whites, by freedmen, by slaves, by rich, and by poor. Everyone, no matter what their station in life was, ate and wore clothes thanks to tobacco." He also mentions the excesses in salt commerce, the magistrates' despotism, the difficulty in collecting debts, and the abnormal growth of mortmain, or institutional ownership of land.

From the ranches, lands, farms, and properties owned by the Church, His Majesty receives no tribute, subsidies, even tithes, charities, hospitals, sees, mother churches, or any other type of church. Nor do Church properties provide for religious fraternities or brotherhoods. Poor orphans and widows receive no alms. These lands are only useful to the church and to no one else.... Every year many properties, ranches, and land fall into the church's hands. They are bought, abandoned by their owners, left to the church, or they are acquired by court actions that last 60, 70, 80, 90, and 100 years. This land, under the power of secular vassals, was subject to tithes, tributes, and other payments. Once the church gets them they become immediately exempt. And the worst part is that whatever assessments, tribute, subsidies, or other taxes they paid now fall on the poverty-stricken secular population.[21]

Once the terrors of backland travel were dispelled, some more resolute individuals brought their families to live temporarily or permanently on their ranches. However it was, life improved. There were substantial, spacious houses with welcoming front porches, corrals whose walls could be walked upon, mills [*bolandeiras*] for grinding manioc, modest looms for making hammocks or rough cloth, reservoirs, sugar processors [*engenhocas*] for making rapadura, chapels and even chaplains, and prize horses. African blacks were brought in not so much to work, but, as time passed, as signs of wealth. They demonstrated ranchers' good fortune and magnificence.

If the deeper backlands were dominated by Bahia, the outer ones fell to Pernambuco. In this area, beginning at Borborema all the way to Ceará, people from Pernambuco and Bahia came together. The road that left the bank of the Aracaru River crossed the Jaguaribe Road, headed toward the upper Piranhas River, and went through Pombal, Patos, and Campina Grande then split toward the Paraíba and Capibaribe Rivers. It benefited all who lived in the region. Also in the upper Piranhas area, the Bahian and Pernambucan movements met up, as I have said.

On the expanse of land where bovine cattle grazed, the marvelous Father Antonil-Andreoni gives us positive data:

> The Bahian sertão goes up the coast 80 leagues to the harbor on the São Francisco. It goes up the river to the port they call Água Grande. Salvador is 115 leagues away from said port. It is 130 leagues from Santunse; Rodelas is 80 leagues inland; Jacobinas 90; Tucano 50. . . . The Bahian corrals are built on the banks of rivers: the São Francisco, the Velhas, the Rãs, the Verde, the Parnamirim, the Jacuípe, the Ipojuca, the Inhambupe, the Itapicuru, the Real, the Vazabarris, the Sergipe, and others. According to the information gathered from several people who know the backlands, there are over 500 corrals.
>
> And even though there might be many corrals within Bahia, in Pernambuco there are many more. Pernambuco's sertão, beginning at the city of Olinda, extends 80 leagues south along the coast to the São Francisco. From the São Francisco harbor to the Iguaçu, one travels 200 leagues. The distance from Olinda westward to Piagui (Nossa Senhora da Vitória Parish) is 160 leagues. From Olinda northward the sertão extends another 80 leagues to the Ceará-Mirim River, and from there to the Açu, 35 leagues, and to the Ceará Grande River, 80. From Olinda to this area there is a distance of almost 200 leagues.
>
> There must be more than 800 corrals in this region, and all of them send cattle to Recife, Olinda, and their surrounding towns. They supply draft oxen for all the sugar mills between the São Francisco and the Rio Grande. Except for those I have mentioned, from Piagui to the Iguaçu and Paranaguá harbors and the Preto River, almost all the cattle go to Bahia,

because there is a better road through the Jacobinas, and they go that way free of trouble.

It is believed that there are a half million head of cattle in Bahia and another 800,000 in Pernambuco. Still, more cattle from Pernambuco are consumed in Bahia than in Pernambuco.[22]

For a long time this war was waged on its own terms, with no one representing order or organization. Everyone was Catholic, and the church required people to take the sacraments. So any vicar, or [perhaps] a more spirited, zealous, or covetous one would set off from time to time to hear the confessions of the far-flung sheep. After the installation of the archbishopric at Salvador, enormous parishes were created in the sertão. They extended for 80 leagues, 100 leagues, and even more. In those areas the half-civil, half-ecclesiastic tax or tithe was charged. The tithe collectors who got the job, after performing it once, chose to leave tax-collecting to someone else—to a rancher or some person in the backlands who, in the name of the tax collector, would travel from ranch to ranch and collect the tithed calves, since payment was made in kind. After a few years (in most contracts three or four), the agent would settle accounts. Just as cowhands did, tax collectors received a quarter of the cattle they collected for their work .

The royal charter of 20 January 1699[23] was the first attempt at imposing order on that amorphous mass. It set up judgeships in those backland parishes, and the judges would be similar to the *vintena* judges, who were selected from the most powerful people in the land.[24] Each parish would have a capitão-mor and a militia corporal to guard and help the judges. These judges met the same resistance other colonial magistrates [*juízes de fora*] had. A prisoner's possessions were sequestered until the final sentencing. Pecuniary punishment must have been preferred, owing to the difficulty in carrying out corporal punishment. Justices of the peace and magistrates were obliged to make triennial visits. If any of these orders was carried out and if in the overseas archives there might exist some accounts of their visits, no other document could be as helpful as these records would be for our study and research on life in the sertão.

The capitães-mores were famous for being violent, arbitrary, and cruel. However, they were not omnipotent, and, whether it was great or small, they always encountered some opposition. There was a natural respect for property. "Thief" was and is still today the most insulting epithet. Human life was not held in the same regard. Matters of land, family quarrels, even involuntary slights, sometimes mere trifles beyond outsiders' comprehension were settled by blood baths. To our disgrace, these encounters did not occur out in the open. The murderous shot hit its target from behind a tree, through a door or window left open in a careless moment, or in some barren or sinister place along a highway. At times these shots marked the beginning of a long string of murders and vendettas. Given the primitive state of the economy, it was not expensive to gather a few thugs and crooks and flout authority and the law. There were only two ways to hold one's own against these robber barons: a man could be cagey or he might form alliances with his neighbors.

In addition to the pride cattlemen felt from being rich, from being far away from effective law enforcers, and from acting with impunity; there was another, wide-ranging effect of cattle ranching. It was ranchers who discovered the mines. Beginning in 1618, the author of *Diálogos das Grandezas do Brasil* maintained that the problem was not one of finding metals, they existed beyond a doubt simply because the Orient is more noble than the Occident, and therefore Brazil is richer than Perú. The real problem was how to feed the miners. He laid out the following plan:

> The first thing that should be done before working the mines, once we know that they are worth working, is to establish a source of supplies around the mining sites. Once there are sufficient supplies, then it will be time to begin mining. It is now being done backwards. People have set off to mine for gold, but, because the mines are far back in the sertão, they leave with the necessary supplies packed, and when the supplies run out, they return, abandoning the work they began. And this, I believe, is the real reason mines have been unprofitable.[25]

The plan was based on reality, and even though Fernão Dias Pais never read the *Diálogos* because they were only recently published, he followed the author's plan in his renowned emerald expedition. And the old tactic would suffice as long as miners were limited to bands of greater or lesser numbers, and cultivated foods could be supplemented by fish and game. But after the hubbub brought on by the early discoveries, miners needed less chancy resources. Having bovine cattle in great quantities became absolutely necessary.

And this cattle could not be sent from São Paulo. In March 1700 Pedro Taques de Almeida wrote to Dom João de Lencastro and confessed:

> From this town one can send no cattle. Even if we send just 20 head, people will die. There is no meat for sale now. While a steer normally costs two milreis, the *mineiros* [people from the Minas Gerais area] are offering eight, because of what they can get for them at the mines. The price [for

meat] was, up to now, 50 pieces of eight and when it was scarce it went as high as 100.[26]

Livestock could only come from the São Francisco River basin. A document written shortly after 1705 says:

> By the aforementioned river and the road along it come the cattle that feed the great numbers of people at the mines. Things are such that from nowhere else can so many cattle come. They simply do not exist in the backlands of São Paulo or Rio de Janeiro. The horses they ride on, the salt extracted from the land around the São Francisco, the manioc flour, and all the other things they need for daily life and sustenance come from that region.
>
> From its sea harbor adjacent to the town of Penedo, equidistant 80 leagues from Bahia and Pernambuco, on either side, whether under Pernambucan or Bahian jurisdiction, the São Francisco River (which forms the border between the two) has many settlements along its banks. Some are quite close to the river, others farther away. This is the case for over 600 leagues, up to where the Velhas River joins the São Francisco and forms a harbor. The last cattle ranches on either bank of the river are found at this point. From the São Francisco's outlet up to here, no stretch of land is so desolate that it is necessary for travelers to set up camp and sleep, because they can always stay at cattlemen's houses, where they are normally well received.[27]

Thus, just like in the upper reaches of the Paraíba do Sul River, but in much more grandiose proportions, the São Francisco also brought people together.

In view of this, one might expect many towns in these populous regions. However that would be totally wrong. Towns were only founded in the eighteenth century, which is one more indication of the difference between the royal captaincies and those established by donataries, as far as the founding of towns was concerned.

The backland councils were no different from those on the littoral—which means they had the right to petition; they could tax local goods; they produced ordinary judges; and above all else they were nothing more than administrative entities.

From the chairs of the town council of Icó, Ceará, in 1738, we have ordinances pertaining to the planting of cassava for manioc flour and to the planting of *carrapateira* for the production of castor oil. Laws were passed prohibiting the shipment of manioc flour because of its high prices [elsewhere]. There were laws regulating how much tailors, shoemakers, and other tradesmen should charge, even laws pertaining to the death of parakeets.

There is nothing to confirm the putative omnipotence of these town councils. João Francisco Lisboa "discovered" it and others have perpetuated it because they were too lazy to check the sources.

Earlier, Cristóvão Jacques and Martim Afonso had given in to the lure of the mines. João de Barros and his partners expected to find mines in their captaincies. Duarte Coelho counted on finding mines along the São Francisco and did not search for them in person because he was not allowed to. In Porto Seguro within 40 years of Pedro Álvares's arrival, people talked of gold. Luís de Melo da Silva set off for the Amazon to search for mines.

Tomé de Sousa put together an expedition that crossed the Espinhaço mountain range. Under his successors, subsequent explorers came back with precious stones, especially emeralds. In the perspicacious mind of Gabriel Soares, there appeared such abundant and conclusive proof of mineral wealth that he abandoned his prosperous sugar plantation at Jeriquiriçá and spent years petitioning the courts in Lisbon and Madrid to allow him to serve his fatherland by finding its hidden resources.

In the last chapter of his monumental *Tratado* he writes:

> Concerning the metals that the world most appreciates, and which we have neglected up to now, saving them for the moral and the end of this story, when we should have spoken of them first, for this land of Bahia has as much gold and silver as one can imagine. It can supply Spain with greater loads on a yearly basis than all the metal that came from the West Indies, if it pleases Your Majesty.[28]

Soares' attempt at finding this precious metal belied his assertions, but perpetuated his name. The tradition of grand expeditions into the backlands and inexhaustible silver mines is ascribed to him. Melchior Dias, a relative of Soares, offered to produce the white metal in quantities equal to the amount of iron in Biscay. After many enticements, his bluff was called, and he took the governor-general of Brazil and some miners to the Itabaiana Mountains. His experiments with quicksilver produced nothing but a smoke screen, according to one eyewitness. In spite of everything, no one doubted Melchior's hidden treasures and the existence of silver riches. As late as the last quarter of the seventeenth century people still expected, hoped, and searched for silver.

Sharing Gabriel Soares' beliefs, Dom Francisco de Sousa ruled the land from Espírito Santo to the emerald fields and from São Vicente to

Sabarabuçu. When his substitute arrived, he set off for Madrid, where in 1608 he obtained a partition of Brazil into two jurisdictions. He received the southern portion and the exclusive superintendency of all the mines in the colony. He lost his life searching for mines in São Paulo. His hope did not die, however. It spread to other people.

With his death, Dom Francisco's task was passed on to Salvador Correia and some of his descendants. For four generations they searched for gold, silver, and emeralds in widely scattered directions. Salvador Neto finally became skeptical about discovering precious metals. He was the first to be convinced that there was no silver to be found. On 3 May 1677, before the Overseas Council, Neto maintained:

> In his [clearest] conscience he declares that 40 leagues from the sea, from Itabaiana south, there are no silver deposits. He has traveled and studied all this terrain and has carried out tests to discover silver, and [has concluded] that this land is different from that around Potosí.[29]

He could speak about Potosí with authority. He had gone all the way to the Andes.

Why did this belief spread and hang on so tenaciously? Why did people believe in the structural identity of western and eastern America? As Salvador says about Melchior Dias, why did people mistake mica for silver? Why did people believe that the East was more noble than the West, and that the East could not lack anything that abounded in the West? In a document from the year 1610, one can read: "There is a good philosophical reason why this region must have more and better mines than Perú. It is farther east and more suited for the creation of metals." The name, River Plate [Silver River], which the early explorers gave that estuary, and the confusing information the natives offered, must have had some influence.

Meanwhile, gold, which was not sought, or which was sought with less resolve, was found in small quantities in the captaincy of São Vicente. Ever since Mem de Sá's time, people such as Brás Cubas, the finance purveyor, and Luís Martins, a miner who had come from Portugal, had found some nuggets.

Others had been equally successful. If one can believe the traditional stories, great riches were discovered. Afonso Sardinha, it was said, had left behind 80,000 cruzados worth of gold dust. There is probably some exaggeration in this sum, or at least some fools' gold in his pile. If gold existed in such abundance, people would have come in droves and the Paulistas would not have gone on being bandeirantes.

Antonil-Andreoni seems to be closer to the truth when he speaks of these early mining sites:

> From a high hillock known as Jaraguá, three leagues from São Paulo, quantities of gold ranging from eighths of an ounce to pounds have been extracted. In Parnaíba, also adjacent to the town of that name in the Ibituruna Mountains, people have found minuscule quantities of gold. Over many years and in great amounts, gold has been mined in Paranaguá and Curitiba. At first it came out measured in *oitavas* [eighths of an ounce], then in pounds that eventually added up to a few *arrobas* [one arroba equals approximately 15 kilograms]. To collect that much required considerable labor, which meant that mining gold did not pay well.[30]

The tastes for prospecting and for the practice of panning for gold were greater than the pounds and eighths, or oitavas, that people accumulated. And the ensuing familiarity [with mining] was beneficial to later developments elsewhere.

After having seen all the hopes and expectations of mining come to naught, or next to naught, the King decided to change his tactics. He had the most flattering letters sent to the important people in São Paulo. In these letters, he left the matter of prospecting up to them.

His appeal to their pride made the Paulistas enthusiastic. At that time a king was almost God, and to receive a royal letter was an honor almost divine. Out of the blue, numerous bandeiras were outfitted and then sent out in the most diverse directions. It was immediately obvious that if Brazil contained any mineral wealth, the minerals would not spend much more time under ground.

The most famous of these bandeirantes, who had now become a miner owing to the king's request, was Fernão Dias Pais. He was advanced in years, he ran some villages populated by Guanãan Indians, and he lived in a big house typical of the primitive economy of his era. In spite of all this, he enlisted in the crusade. He spent 10 years on the endeavor, and, when he died in the thickets along the Doce River, he knew for sure that he had discovered the emeralds that had been beyond reach for centuries.[31]

His death came shortly before the beginning of the phenomenal discoveries. Garcia Rodrigues Pais was his son. His son-in-law was Manuel da Borba Gato. Both men were major figures in these events.

The name Minas Gerais [general mines] denotes the plenitude, the omnipresence of wealth. Their first discoverer is impossible to determine, so conflicting are the stories. But they were discovered shortly after 1690.

According to Antonil-Adreoni, a mulatto from Curitiba found some iron-colored nuggets in Tripuí Creek.[32] He sold them for half a *pataca* per oitava in Taubaté to Miguel de Sousa. In Rio the nuggets were recognized to be pure gold. This was the first discovery.

After this discovery came another, by Antônio Dias, half a league from Ouro Preto; then a little farther away another one by João de Faria followed, then another by Bueno, and another by Bento Rodrigues. There was gold in Carmo Stream and in the Ibupiranga, both of which were near Ouro Preto and Mariana. Part of the upper Rio Doce basin was excavated, justifying the name Minas Gerais, which was applied first to this region.

Other mining centers lay along the Mortes River near São João and São José de El-Rei, on the way to São Paulo. Those on the Velhas River, heading for Bahia, were discovered by Manuel da Borba Gato. Another center was Caeté. The upper Rio Doce, the Espinhaço cordillera, and the Frio Mountains were and are mining regions. More mines were discovered in Pitangui, Paracatu, and elsewhere. They belong to the second wave of discoveries and need not be enumerated.

One of the early roads left São Paulo, followed the Parnaíba, crossed the Mantiqueira Mountains, cut across the Rio Grande and then split either toward the Velhas or the Doce, depending on one's destination. Another left Cachoeira in Bahia, and headed up the Paraguaçu. Or, if one took a different route, one crossed the São Francisco, traveled along its banks for a greater or lesser distance, up to the Velhas, which it bordered. The road from Rio went overland or by sea to Parati. On the old Guaianá Trail it crossed the Facão Mountains near the present-day city of Cunha. In Taubaté it met up with the São Paulo Road. Later on, two roads met at Pindamonhagaba.

Artur de Sá, the first official to visit these newly discovered mines, contracted Garcia Rodrigues Pais to open a more direct line of communication with the City of Saint Sebastian [Rio de Janeiro], which was the true southern capital. The son of Fernão Dias performed the task brilliantly. Near the present-day city of Barbacena the roads to the Mortes, Velhas, and Doce Rivers came together. The road to Rio began at this point. It crossed the Mantiqueiras, headed toward the Paraibuna River, which it followed up to where that river joins the Paraíba. It reached Guanabara Bay by going over the Órgãos Mountains and passing through Cabaru, Marcos da Costa, Couto, and Pilar. The section between the Paraíba River and the bay was linked by another road, thanks to Bernardo Soares de Proença. Part of the way it followed the route the railway now runs connecting Petrópolis with Entre-Rios. Partway it followed the Inhomirim River.

A decade after the first discoveries, an ox cost 100 oitavas, a bundle of 60 ears of corn, 30 oitavas, an *alqueire* [13.8 liters] of manioc flour, 40 oitavas, a chicken, 3 or 4 oitavas, a cask of brandy (small enough that a single slave can carry), 100 oitavas, a cask of wine (also born by a single slave) 200 oitavas, and a cask of olive oil cost two pounds (a pound was worth 128 oitavas).[33]

According to Antonil-Andreoni

The early miners' suffering for lack of food is beyond belief. Many ended up dying with an ear of corn clutched in their hands and nothing else to eat. However, no sooner had people seen the amount of gold that was being extracted and the sums of money people were willing to pay for goods in the mining regions than inns were set up, and merchants began to send to the mines the best goods that arrived from Portugal and elsewhere. They sent both foodstuffs and fancy, pompous articles of clothing, in addition to the thousands of novelties [*burgiarias*] from France that also ended up there. And since there was no money in the mining area, other than gold dust, the lowest price anything cost was an oitava.

By selling things to eat, brandy, and other beverages, many people quickly accumulated great amounts of gold. Since the blacks and Indians hide some oitavas for themselves as they work along the streams, and on holidays and during the late afternoon they pan for gold on their own, most of this gold is spent on food and drink. Without realizing it, they make these vendors rich, just like slow rain on a field. The field gets watered without getting drenched, and it ends up being very fertile. And for this reason even men of great assets have deigned to invest in concerns such as this to make their fortune: they have black cooks, mulatto women making sweets, native-born blacks running taverns. All of these people are engaged in this most profitable type of mining, and they bring in from the ports all sorts of things likely to appeal to eager buyers.[34]

The mines at Cuiabá were found by chance. Pascoal Moreira Cabral and his companions were searching for Indians when they found the first gold nuggets in 1719. They were so abundant that they could be gathered by hand, or with pointed sticks. Gold was extracted from the ground like whey from milk, as Eschwege so picturesquely put it. Bandeirantes inadvertently turned into miners. Disorder in the Minas Gerais region taught these men a lesson, and they did not experience the same terrible upheavals that made the Mortes River, i.e., the "River of Death," so sadly famous.

Once the news of this uniquely easy mining reached the centers of population, people were aroused and, without further ado, threw themselves into the terrible journey. They began on the Tietê River near the Itu; they followed the Paraná up to the Sete Quedas falls area; then set off toward the Mbotetéu and its harbor on the Paraguay River. Finally they headed up the Paraguay toward the São Lourenço and the Cuiabá Rivers. Many expeditions went awry. People died of exhaustion and lack of food, or were eaten by animals. Of those who eluded death in the rapids or over falls, many lost the cloth they had brought with them to sell. The cloth they saved became rotten, because the canoes were not covered. And after so much danger, they found the blackest of misery in Cuiabá.

Some facts told by Barbosa de Sá, a witness and chronicler of that period, demonstrate how bad things really were.

Only in 1721 did the first mining tools arrive. There were no fishermen, and if someone happened to catch a *dourado* [a fresh water fish that can weigh up to 20 kilograms], it could be sold for seven or eight oitavas. Many people appeared to be ravaged and affected by dropsy. Everybody's legs and bellies were swollen; their skin was the color of death. Dirt looked good to eat, and many ate it. The first pigs and chickens arrived in 1723. In 1725 someone paid half a pound of gold for a flask of salt. Corn, before it sprouted, was eaten by mice. If it sprouted, it was fallen upon by grasshoppers. If the corn actually grew ears, the ears had no kernals. If there were ears of corn with kernals on them, they had to be picked fresh so the birds would not eat the grain. There were so many rats that a pair of cats was sold for a pound of gold. Their kittens were worth 20 to 30 oitavas. In 1729, because there was no cloth, shirts were made out of sheets that were coming apart. These shirts sold for 12 oitavas each. A *vara* [43.3 inches] of domestic cotton cloth went for three or four oitavas. And there was no salt, even for baptisms.

The situation improved very slowly. In 1725 navigation was begun along the Pardo, Coxim, and Taquari Rivers, and this made the journey easier, especially after some fields were planted and some cattle were brought in, as well as ox carts to carry the canoes over the Camapuã Portage between the Paraguay and the Paraná.

In 1728 sugar cane was planted.

Soon they began to grind the cane in the little grinders we call *escaroçadores* [hullers]. They distilled [the juice] in stills made from metal bowls and produced cane brandy, which they sold for five or six oitavas. A rack of bottles [*frasqueira*] cost 48 oitavas. At this point people began to recuperate from their illnesses. Men regained their natural color, they no longer looked like corpses. The signs of dropsy and swollen legs and bellies began to wane, as did the deaths among slaves, which up to then had been the norm—every day piles of them were buried.[35]

Until then people concentrated around Cuiabá. In 1734 they crossed the mountains and in the Parecis region found more mines. Huge forests in that region gave it the name Mato Grosso, or "Dense Forest." In 1736 an overland route from Cuiabá to the Paraguay River was discovered. Mining extended up the Guaporé River. People in that area, which was even more remote than Cuiabá, suffered the same deprivations. There was a silver lining, however. They soon discovered nearby Indian villages run by Spanish Jesuits. The first to visit these reductions were well received and obtained some cattle. The idea arose that they might begin to trade with these people, and soon other adventurers made more than one expedition, all of which failed to yield the expected fruit. The villages had strict orders not to do business with the Portuguese. They were also informed that the reductions lay in the Madeira River basin.

A few years earlier, Francisco de Melo Palheta had left Pará and reached the Marmoré villages. Inspired by this feat, Manuel Félix de Lima in 1742 set off on the Guaporé River and ended up in Belém, at the mouth of the Amazon. Later, João de Sousa de Azevedo began a journey on the Arinos River, traveled to the Tapajós, and returned along the Madeira. In spite of the navigational difficulties, which even today have not been vanquished, trips from river to river were repeated and the northeast backlands became linked to the Amazon flood plains.

Another overland link with São Paulo had been established so as to avoid wild Indians. Beginning at the São Lourenço River harbor, the Paiaguá and Cuaicuru Indians would harass people going to Cuiabá or coming back from there. They appeared all of a sudden in a myriad of canoes. And since they knew every inch of those swamps, they chose the best places to attack and easily eluded anyone who pursued them. It is said that the Spanish in Asunción encouraged this activity, and that may be so, because no one wants miners and bandeirantes as neighbors. At any rate, whatever gold these Indians captured could be sold in Paraguay and was a sufficient stimulus for their raiding parties.

The first raid occurred in 1725. Diogo de Sousa along with many others traveling on the Xané River had just entered the São Lourenço delta and was met by heathens. Six hundred people were killed. Only one white man and a black man escaped. The Paiaguás carried off 20 canoes as their trophies and spoils. There were similar attacks in the years to come.

Sometimes they were closer to Taquari, sometimes farther away. After passing the Camapuã plantations and the Pardo River, one had to pass by Taquari. During one of the retaliatory expeditions against these barbarians, someone got the idea of opening a road to Goiás. People contributed 3,000 oitavas to this endeavor. It was built by Antônio Pinto de Azevedo, who returned to Cuiabá in September 1737, bringing the first horses and cattle to the area.

The discoveries in Cuiabá are reminiscent of those of Bartolomeu Bueno da Silva, who, 40 years earlier, traveling through the backland with his father, the first Anhangüera or "daredevil," had seen Guaiá Indians wearing gold nuggets as jewelry. He reasoned that those parts must be full of gold because it had attracted the natives' attention. He believed he could go back there again; he offered to do it; and once his offer was accepted, he left São Paulo in 1722.

He had believed too strongly in his memory. For over three years he wandered aimlessly in all directions, ending up at the headwaters of the Araguaia River. One part of his expedition went down the Tocantins and reached Pará. Another part perished in an encounter with Indians. Still another died of hunger after having eaten their dogs and some of their horses. A member of the second Anhangüera's expedition reports the following:

> I preached 35 sermons on the same theme. I encouraged them not to lose hope, assuring them that just ahead lay rivers full of fish, fields with many deer in them, forests full of game, honey, and tropical fruit [*guarirobas*]. "When?" the poor wretches would ask. "Any day now," I would answer. And finally God allowed us to find some food, and all was well. People stopped dying, and no one else died. Woe to all of them, had I not been their preacher.[36]

Finally, on 21 October 1725 Bartomomeu Bueno arrived triumphantly in São Paulo. He assured people there were riches equal to those in Cuiabá, and, even better, the air around them was not as pestilent. The rivers he traveled along with his partner Bartolomeu Pais de Abreu (father of the distinguished historian Pedro Taques) give one an approximate idea of their itinerary, which, in part, the Mogiana Railway now follows. They traveled the Atibaia, Jaguari, Moji, Sapucaí, Pardo Grande, Velhas, Parnaíba, Corumbá, Meia-Ponte and Pasmados Rivers.

The first mining community was formed along the Vermelho River, a tributary of the Araguaia. But here, as elsewhere, there were deposits all around, and the prospectors spread out.

In 1733 Domingos Rodrigues do Prado discovered the Crixá mines, Manuel Dias da Silva the Santa Cruz mines, and Calhamare the Antas mines. The same year Manuel Rodrigues Tomar discovered the São Félix mines. In 1736 he discovered more in Cachoeira, Santa Rita, and Moquém. In 1737 Francisco de Albuquerque Cavalcante discovered the ones that bear his name today. Amaro Leite discovered his in 1739. Arraias was discovered in 1740 thanks to Francisco Lopes; Pilar, in 1740 thanks to João de Godói Pinto da Silveira; and Santa Luzia, thanks to Antônio Bueno de Azeredo. These dates are approximations. They vary according to different chroniclers.

Goiás's location made it easy for that region to maintain contact with the Amazon flood plain and the Parnaíba, São Francisco, and Paraná flatlands. Its relatively late historical debut and its (relative) proximity to populated areas spared it many of the deprivations people suffered in Minas Gerais and Mato Grosso. The first road to São Paulo was soon not the only one. In spite of repeated arbitrary prohibitions, other trails were opened, and cattle and adventurers flooded in from Minas Gerais, Bahia, Pernambuco, Piauí, and Maranhão. We have already seen how a few years later supplies for the people in Cuiabá were shipped from this area.

Many expeditions set out in search of particularly abundant deposits that had been described by soothsayers in mysterious treasure maps [*roteiros*]. [One mining area was] called Martírios [martyrdom] because the rock formations around it resembled the instruments of Christ's Passion. One on the Rico River was called Araez. Eschwege actually saw some of these treasure maps, which families have jealously guarded. He claims that three brothers or three sisters, as well as the Trinity, could represent three rivers or mountain ranges. On many of them one finds a lever leaning against a *gameleira* tree, or a stream next to a cedar, or a tin plate left in a grotto. These were held to be secret but sure signs of treasure. Martírios, if it in fact exists, has yet to be discovered.

To these three gold producing captaincies one should add Bahia, which was no less rich. Jacobinas and (especially) the Contas River justified all of old Gabriel Soares' hopes. But Lisbon prohibited mining in these areas because it considered them too near the coast and susceptible to pirates. Even though appearances were maintained, the prohibition was not long respected. This explains the somewhat clandestine nature of mining in Bahia, which in turn makes more specific data about it impossible to come by. Later on, the prohibition was lifted, but Bahia went on being primarily an agricultural and pastoral region rather than a mining one. It was overwhelmed by the splendor of Goiás.

The Laws of the Kingdom (*Ordenações do Reino*) registered the mines as royal property. An almost century-long experiment made the difficulty of exploiting them perfectly clear. So the idea of permitting mining to go on while reserving a fifth, or *quinto*, of the proceeds for the Crown was incorporated into the 1603 statutes. The author of this idea may have been Dom Francisco de Sousa. As long as gold was a matter of oitavas and pounds, the royal percentage was, in a manner of speaking, left up to the scruples of individual miners. With the discovery of extensive riches in Cataguases, what had been more or less a theoretical principle, became the axis of the entire colonial mechanism.

During the original chaos, the only authority was the superintendent, or *guarda-mor*, who measured out parcels of land and gave the king a portion of it, which he auctioned off to the highest bidder. Ad hoc purveyors collected the quinto, or it was levied on gold at points through which the gold had to pass: Taubaté if it were destined for São Paulo, Parati on the way to Rio. Along the São Francisco, collection was more difficult, because beginning at the village of Matias Cardoso, near present-day Januária, many roads spread out toward the north and toward the east. Many canoes floated down the river, and many preferred this means of transportation, because it was safer and cheaper. Levying the quinto on gold was still a major problem when Garcia Pais set up communications directly with Guanabara Bay (Rio de Janeiro). Even so, the amount collected was considerable.

A new era began with the arrival of Antônio de Albuquerque in 1711. Towns were founded and municipalities, set up. Albuquerque called for councils and important people to determine the best means of guaranteeing the Crown's interests. It seemed reasonable to charge a head tax or *capitação* on every pan or sluice used in mining. The town councils preferred to charge duties on all dry goods, liquids, and slaves brought in. Duguay-Trouin's invasion called the governor out of Rio. Everything was halted. And the old system of levies and collections continued to operate.

Brás Baltasar da Silveira, the next governor, accepted the offer made by the town councils of Vila-Rica [present-day Ouro Preto], Sabará, and Carmo. They would give, on an annual basis, 30 arrobas (450 kilograms) of gold. To aid in collection, Dom Brás gave them a share of the duties charged on goods brought in. This arrangement lasted for five years, and during that time the government in Lisbon never seemed satisfied.

From 1718 to 1722, town councils relinquished their share of import duties and promised to pay 25 arrobas per annum. The Court became even more exacting, however, as far as the capitação on operations was concerned. It set up foundries where all the gold dust would be brought and melted into ingots, from which the royal quinto would be taken. In opposition to this system, the municipalities offered to pay 37 arrobas, and this is what they did, until 1725.

From 1725 to 1750, sometimes operations were taxed, other times the foundry system was in effect. The foundry system was established definitively at the beginning of the reign of José I. Town councils supplied another 100 arrobas every year. If there was gold left over, it could be used for the following year's payment. If the following year also produced a surplus, the first year's surplus became Crown property. Whenever a deficit occurred and could not be made up in the manner described, an apportionment system was used. Each municipality would be taxed proportionately so as to furnish an average of 100 arrobas per township. The wealthiest council of all, Vila-Rica's, had among its exclusive resources the control over weights and measures, house furnishings, income from butcher shops and from the jail. Added up it did not come to 5,000 milreis per year. What this means is that the high-minded imperial capital delegated the responsibility for the hated capitação to other people.

It would be beyond our scope to detail the system of surveillance imposed on people in Minas Gerais, as well as on people in parts of Bahia, Goiás, and Mato Grosso that were not too far away or too sparsely populated [to be controlled]. It was against the law to open new trails, to open new mills, to carry gold dust or gold coins. People could not be goldsmiths. They paid many taxes. They were besought for specific, short-term donations and later these "donations" were demanded over much longer periods of time. The brazenness of changing the terms of an original agreement would seem strange, except in cases such as these, where in an impenetrable part of the world we are confronted with a tactless, clumsy administration and with listless individuals.

For example: When news got out in 1730 that there were diamonds to be mined, Dom Lourenço de Almeida, the governor of Minas Gerais, put a head tax of 5 milreis on each slave employed in mining. The following year he had the mines evacuated. He expelled freed blacks and all mulattos from the entire Serro district. He limited mining to a specific zone, where people paid a minimum tax of 60 milreis per year, which he finally deigned to reduce to 20 milreis. He prohibited any sales outside of town, while in town people could only do business during daylight hours. In 1734 the capitação was raised to 40 milreis. Then, all of a sudden, mining was prohibited. No inhabitant was allowed to have a pan, a pick, a spike, or any other mining implement. As time passed, control became even more tyrannical, so that the Portuguese Crown became master of the diamond market for the entire world.

The amount of gold produced in Brazil cannot be determined with any precision. Taking considerable data into account, Calógeras estimates that Goiás and Mato Grosso, from the time mining began to 1770, produced 9,000 arrobas.[37] From 1770 to 1822 another 2,500 arrobas were produced. It produced a grand total of 190,000 kilograms. São Paulo, Bahia, and Ceará together must have produced another 75,000 to 80,000 kilograms. The total production from these parts of Brazil reached 270,000 kilograms during the colonial period, which lasted until 1822.

For Minas Gerais the amount of gold produced until 1725 is estimated to be 7,500 arrobas. For the next 11 years it was 6,500 arrobas; 12,000, from 1736 to 1751; 18,000, from 1752 to 1787; 3,500, from 1788 to 1801; and 3,500, from 1801 to 1820. Until 1820 the total amount extracted from Minas Gerais must have been around 51,500 arrobas, in other words, 772,500 kilograms.

The quintos were only one part of the taxation system: in addition there were tithes, import duties, and fees for using rivers.

Tithes were set up in 1704. In Teixeira Coelho's time they brought in more than 60,000 milreis every year. For the six year-period running from 1 August 1777 to 31 December 1783, the tithe contract was auctioned off for 388,000 milreis.[38]

Entrance or import duties were paid at the customs houses along the new road: in the Mantiqueira Mountains; at Sete Lagoas; on the Itajubá, Jaguara, Ouro-Fino, and Jacuí, Jequitibá, Zabelê and on the Pardo Rivers; on streams, such as the Areia, Nazaré, Olhos d'Água, São Luís, Santo Antônio, Santa Isabel, Pé do Morro, Rebelo, Inhacica, Caeté-Mirim, Galheiro, Bom-Jardim, Simão Vieira, Jequitinhonha, and the Itacambira. A tax was levied on slaves coming in for the first time, on heads of bovine cattle, as well as on horses and mules, and on dry or liquid goods. The term liquid goods [*molhados*] denoted things to eat, iron, steel, gunpowder, and anything else that could not be worn. The income from import duties for the year 1776 was more than 140,000 milreis.

One paid to travel on the following rivers: the Sapucaí, Verde, Mortes, Grande, Paraupela, Velhas, Urucuia, Baependi, Pará, São Francisco, and Jequitinhonha. People working in law enforcement and in public finance made donations and paid quotas [*terças*] and more duties.

Owing to the constant use of the tax apportionment system, or *derrama*, the first signs of decay in mining operations arose. Scholars have explained this decay by emphasizing the many alternative ways of shipping the gold out. Teixeira Coelho, who spent 11 years working on important jobs in Minas Gerais, left behind a precious document on that captaincy. He suggests other causes for its decay: miners' poverty, the scarcity of blacks, monopolies on slaves, excessive duties paid, dishonest allocations of concessions from superintendents, lawsuits over matters of land and mineral water, bad mining techniques, lawsuits concerning miners' rights known as *trintadas*, division of assets through inheritance, etc.

All of this had significant influence on the decay of mining, as Eschwege has pointed out. But all these ills are based on two main causes: the opening of the mining area to all, without restrictions, and the lack of inspection of their operations and the absence of any mining laws suitable for this country. The local miners used only the metal they could extract mechanically, and in a most imperfect manner at that. Thus, beginning at the mining site, then going to the foundry, and then ending at the mint, it would be no exaggeration to say that half the supply of gold was lost because of ignorance.[39]

Disenchanted with the search for gold, people looked for other means of getting by. They raised cattle, grew grain, planted sugar cane, tobacco, and cotton. Over time this production grew to such an extent that it brought about a special transport industry run by the honorable *tropeiros* or "muleteers" of yore.

Several attempts were made to create a direct route through the forest to the sea. The most successful was begun around 1766 and went from the upper Doce River to the Pomba River. The presence of milkwort in the region facilitated trade with Indians there. Indians from the Coroado and Coropoto tribes gathered this medicinal herb, whose use, according to a legend Martius discovered, was taught to them by an animal. He writes that:

> [t]hese children of nature have guaranteed us that they learned to use this emetic root from an *irara*, which is a type of marten that will chew this root and herb to induce vomiting if it drinks too much polluted or saline water from streams and pools. Still, this may well be one of the many baseless stories that the Portuguese uncritically accepted from the Indians.[40]

Thus penetration into or "exterioration" from the scrublands became quick. Around 1780 Miguel Henriques, known as *Mão de Luva* [Single Glove], used this route to get to the Cantagalo Mines. Later on, people planted coffee in that district, and the coffee was transported down the Paraíba or through Aparecida, Serra do Capim, Paquequer. It was sent to the port of Majé on the road built by Baron Aiuruoca. Still later it was sent on the Pedro II Railway and on the Leopoldina Line.

*   *   *

FACTORS THAT CHANGED the colonists' outlooks included their triumphs in wars with foreigners, bandeirantes' feats within and beyond the country's borders, the abundance of cattle that brought life to the immense backlands, the copious amounts of wealth sent to Portugal, the many fortunes, and a growth in the population. The discovery of gold completed their transformation. Mazombos would not and could not go on thinking of themselves as inferior to those born across the sea. They were no longer the humble, bashful people of the early seventeenth century. Because of their service to the Crown, because of their wealth and the magnificence of their native land, they considered themselves among the most worthy subjects of the Portuguese Crown.

The sons of Portugal were not quick in acknowledging this transformation. Gregório de Matos was a Bahian who graduated from the University of Coimbra and does not seem to have been especially fond of his countrymen. By the second half of the seventeenth century he was cracking the satirical whip on the reinóis. He depicted the Portuguese coming to Brazil because they had been deported as criminals, because they had fled from their fathers, or because they had nothing to eat. They got off the boat barefoot, dressed in rags, and were flat broke. Their only collateral were lice and jeers. They lived miserable lives as sneakthieves; they socked money away; they married well; and they ended up government officials! There was no lack of mordant responses and digs at the Portuguese from other quarters.

This friction and ill will between the Portuguese and the Brazilians brought forth the first public violence in the gold fields. It was the so-called *Emboaba* War. ("Emboaba" was a word used for Portuguese in língua geral.) As far as the events about to be related are concerned, this designation is less than exact. In those thickets so far removed from the littoral, there must have been few Portuguese. It is probable, indeed likely, that the Portuguese were in the minority in these struggles. But this moniker, besides being an insult, provided a solution to the dilemma of what to call the enemy. Most of the "emboabas" were people from the banks of the São Francisco, and many had come from São Paulo, or were descendants of Paulistas. On one side of the river these people were Bahians, on the other, Pernambucans. According to Rocha Pita, people who had left their original territory were known as emboabas.

The Paulistas showed deep scorn for emboabas. According to the chronicler of these events, they addressed them with the *vós*, second person pronoun, which they also used with slaves. During the time the

Paulistas predominated in the area between the Mantiqueira and the Espinhaço Mountains, which was during the early decades of unrestrainable anarchy, they committed tremendous excesses, which only subsided after the use of force. One day Manuel Nunes Viana protested when he witnessed an act of violence on a poor devil. Nunes Viana was a powerful emboaba. He had a ranch on the banks of the Carinhanha. He had fought against the heathen in the wars along the São Francisco and had earned the title of field marshal. For these reasons he was promoted to leader of the oppressed. The Paulistas, in turn, felt they were being despoiled owing to the presence of so many outsiders. Antônio Rodrigues da Costa, a member of the Overseas Council, reminds us that the Paulistas went on hating the renóis because they considered them usurpers of those wealthy mines, which the Paulistas believed belonged to them and only them, owing to their good luck or their hard work. A conflict was inevitable between the despoiled and the oppressed.

The death of unimportant people was not a matter of great concern, but one day outsiders killed José Pardo, a powerful Paulista. His fellow Paulistas began to arm themselves so that in January of the following year, 1709, they could finish off the emboabas. The emboabas, impassioned now that they had chosen a prestigious leader, anticipated this threat and set out to meet the enemy and to fight. The force from São Paulo had set up camp carelessly along the Mortes River. It retreated to a clump of trees with the arrival of the crowd that had been rounded up at the Velhas and upper Doce Rivers. From the tops of trees the Paulistas dispatched well placed bullets, but they could not last long in that clump of trees. They had been surrounded, and could not escape. Besides this they had no food. The news got out that the emboabas would settle for disarming their adversaries, who, trusting this vague promise, put themselves at the emboabas' mercy and promised to turn over their weapons. Bento do Amaral Gurgel, a corporal in the attacking forces, an instinctively bloody native of Rio de Janeiro, was not to be trusted.[41] Once the Paulistas were disarmed, "he wreaked such havoc on those wretches and left that field so covered with corpses and wounded men that he gave that place the infamous name of Treason Forest."[42]

Feeling empowered by that victory, the emboabas proclaimed Manuel Nunes Viana governor of the mining region. Nunes Viana, unaware of Bento do Amaral's treacherous cruelty, which was carried out far away and without Viana's permission, was up to the job. He went from being the head of a faction to the head of a government. He appointed judges, government officials, and created jobs and charters. He standardized mining concessions. He levied the quintos owed to the royal exchequer, exacted duty on imported livestock and goods, and suppressed the reigning anarchy. Of course he was somewhat heavy-handed, it would have been difficult not to be, but his work was beneficial, and in the days that followed one can see a cooling off of the wide-spread barbarism. In addition, Viana was a somewhat cultured individual. He liked to read *Cidade de Deus* and works of that ilk. At his expense he had Nuno Marques Pereira's *Peregrino da América* printed. This book was one of our eighteenth-century forebears' favorites, to which its numerous printings can attest.

The news of the events along the Mortes River brought Fernando de Lencastro, the governor of Rio, to the mining region. People were still too agitated to acknowledge his authority, even if they admitted that Lencastro might be impartial. And even if he was impartial, they were still suspicious of him. At Congonhas, near Ouro Preto, Nunes Viana, surrounded by cavalry and foot soldiers, confronted Lencastro. The governor was intimidated and turned tail and headed for the capital. It is said that the emboaba chief met him in secret, assured him of his loyalty, and promised to bow to legal authority once his followers calmed down. The story seems correct, because later on Antônio de Albuquerque showed up with two captains, two adjutants, and ten soldiers. Albuquerque was Dom Fernando's successor, and Nunes Viana voluntarily turned over command to him and retired to his ranches on the Pernambucan side of the São Francisco.

From an unexpected quarter a new storm was brewing. The Paulistas who survived the massacre at Treason Forest were received back home with scorn, even by their own wives,

> who put on airs of classic wives [*Pantasiléas, Semíramis,* and *Zenóbias*] and cursed them for having left the mines with their tails between their legs and without avenging their wrongs. They goaded them into returning and redeeming themselves by wiping out the foreigners.[43]

These ardent words echoed throughout the land. Piratininga turned into a warrior camp. Numerous volunteers thirsty for vengeance gathered around Amador Bueno da Veiga and set off across the Mantiqueiras. They maintained a slow pace, and were met by Antônio de Albuquerque, who was looking for an outcome as happy as the one with the emboabas. He was, however, mistaken. The Paulistas' slow march was not owed to second thoughts or fear, and they met the governor head-on. Albuquerque, fearful of being captured by those stormy subjects, turned and headed for Rio on the old Parati Road. From Rio he sent an emissary out on the Garcia Pais Road to warn the emboabas of the impending danger.

Thus the emboabas had time to arm and fortify themselves before Amador Bueno and his 1,300 soldiers arrived. They immediately began to fight, and the battle lasted several days. Some Paulistas, daunted by the emboabas' resistance, considered lifting their siege. Some emboabas, seeing how many had died on their side, considered surrendering. On both sides, however, there was too much hate for a more humane solution to prevail.

Finally, when the emboabas could no longer hold the opposition and were preparing a desperate maneuver, the Paulistas mysteriously withdrew. There may have been a rumor afoot that numerous reinforcements were on their way from the Velhas River and Ouro Preto. This did not make them feel their cause was lost. They tried (or pretended to try) to prepare another, stronger expedition in order to begin the fight anew, but Dom João V intervened with what to those rudimentary minds appeared to be his godlike royal prestige.

> The sovereign understood that generous souls can be brought in with a bit of tenderness, so he sent them a portrait of himself, by way of the new governor. This was to make them understand that he was paying them a royal visit, not in person, but with this picture. And by doing that, he was putting them under his royal wing.[44]

With this singular present the Paulistas were satisfied. They forgot their past grievances and laid down their arms.

After the Emboaba War, there were still some fracases in Minas Gerais. One, in 1720, was put down with considerable force. The quarrels were no longer inspired by nativistic feelings, which means that the charge of despoilment was purely local, as was the importance of the charge.

Barely were the gold fields pacified when a similar phenomenon arose in the captaincy of Pernambuco.

Once the Dutch were expelled, the governor set up his residence in Olinda, which is where the first bishop established his See in 1688. The old nobility rebuilt the houses that had been destroyed. They occupied them only during festival time because they spent most of the year on their plantations. Recife, thanks to its superior harbor, continued to prosper and acquired many more permanent residents. Merchants and other people who had come to get rich quick and enjoy their fortunes across the sea preferred to live in Recife. Those living in Olinda looked down their noses at the inhabitants of Recife. They called them peddlers and were always ruffled by their debts to the peddlers. Some complained of usury and extortion, others of bad debts and ill will.

After they had made their fortune, some people in Recife wanted to have a role in the government, to wear ceremonial robes, and to have posts in the militia. They achieved this despite great protest from the nobility, who felt these privileges were theirs exclusively. In 1703 Recife not only produced voters, it elected a councilman. This exacerbated bad feelings. Olinda used its dual advantage as a civil and ecclesiastic capital and took every opportunity to humiliate its rival. From that time on the "peddlers" began to work towards obtaining the title of *vila* or "township" for Recife, which would make it autonomous within the municipality. As long as Pedro II was on the throne of Portugal, the memory of the 24 years of war with the Dutch was alive, and the nobility's opposition to Recife continued to prevail. Dom João V gave in to the other side a few years after having ascended the throne.

The king's decision offended Olinda's pride, but it might not have led to violence if someone else had been chosen to carry out his order. Sebastião de Castro Caldas, the former governor of Rio and of Paraíba, had become governor of Pernambuco. He was a flippant, sarcastic Portuguese, who disdained his subordinates and constantly sided with fellow renóis. On 15 February 1719 he erected the pillory of the new vila, which was called São Sebastião in his honor.[45] On 3 March he erected a second one, with greater solemnity, because he had not been satisfied by the first ceremony. The setting of Recife's boundaries, the jurisdiction of ordinary judges, and the different tradesmen's spheres put the head magistrate [ouvidor] and other judges out of sorts with the governor. Someone started a rumor that they planned to depose him, as they had deposed Jerônimo de Mendonça Furtado. Whether or not it was true or false, under this pretext the governor began to arrest important people. He was threatening others when at four in the afternoon on October 17 he was gunned down in the middle of the street. This dénouement was long overdue. A few years earlier someone had written: "it seems that in Pernambuco more people have been killed by muskets after its restoration than during the war."

No one arrested the three pawns who shot him, nor has anyone discovered who put them up to it. Caldas had been slightly wounded. He prohibited anyone within ten leagues of Recife from bearing arms, and he had more people arrested. His supervision of all activity, plus the scant medical care he received, gave the agitators reason to claim that the governor's wound had been faked and that Caldas himself had planned the whole affair. They pointed to his prohibition of bearing arms as proof of his willingness to turn the land over to the French, who had recently attacked Rio. This made the populace grow even more tumultuous. Caldas lost all self control and sent several detachments to the inland parishes to arrest more people. The people took up arms. Some of the troops were surrounded, some of them capitulated, some joined the rebels, and numerous waves of common folk set off for Recife.

On November 5 news of the uprising reached Recife. The next day Caldas attempted to negotiate with the rebels, who turned a deaf ear. On the seventh a smack carrying some of Caldas' most hated supporters set sail for Bahia.

The rebels had been recruited mainly in Santo Antão, São Lourenço, Jaboatão, Varge, and Muribeca. Some of them had been angered by the governor's presumed treason, others by their hatred for the "peddlers". Part of their plan was to sack Recife. They were dissuaded from this endeavor by some clergymen, both laymen and priests. At the entrance to the new township there was some violence, but of small import. The tempest ended without the destruction that the people had feared. The pillory was torn down, the election annulled, cannonballs put out of commission, peddler officers lost their insignias. Now and then a particular debtor would liquidate his debts in a summary fashion. Still, there was more farce and insult than violence and vengeance.

With Sebastião de Castro Caldas's retreat the governorship had been vacated. The bishop of the diocese was next in line to succeed him. But some of the insurgents opposed his leadership. Bernardo Vieira de Melo, a sergeant major, and one of the corporals in the Palmares War, proposed that they proclaim themselves a republic, as Venice had done. Or propose that they seek the protection of some Christian power. November 10 is today a state holiday in Pernambuco; it commemorates this far sighted gesture. What notions of republics must this man have had? What could he know of their adaptability to such backward lands, whose people were so unused to political and administrative practices? What must he have understood about the delicate and complex organism that was the Venetian Constitution? Until the end of time no one will ever know. He had heard, perhaps, of the Venetians' aristocratic character, and his naïveté had led him to put the Olinda nobility on the same plane as the cultured patricians of the floating city. As a protectorate, under what Christian nation would Recife be led? Whichever led it, the arrangement would meet the same end as the Dutch invasion had. And this was proven by the present movement, which had triumphed owing mainly to the widespread belief that the expelled governor had schemed with the French. Besides, these allegations could all be false, the product of rancorous adversaries bent on making the sins of the vanquished seem worse. It all ended with the recognition of the legitimacy of the successor in the chain of command. This was his Most Illustrious Majesty Dom Manuel.

Dom Manuel Álvares da Costa had arrived from Portugal at the beginning of the year. His relations with the representative of civil power had been on the cool side. Normally heads of the two perfect societies had cordial relations with one another. When he learned of the wound Caldas had suffered, he paid him a visit, at which time he also said goodbye, because he was leaving for Paraíba. On the way there, José Inácio Arouche, according to a plan set up beforehand, joined his party. Arouche was the former chief magistrate who had been out of sorts with the governor owing to the latter's determination of Recife's city limits. Arouche, in spite of being a Portuguese, was also hated by the governor and by the peddlers. Sebastião de Castro had linked Arouche to the murder plot as well as to original conspirators. He ordered him captured, and when Arouche was not found at home, he had him hunted down, wherever he was. This was not hard to do, because Arouche was not one to keep things quiet.

On the morning of October 20, the church at Tapirema, where the bishop had spent the night, was surrounded by a platoon of soldiers ordered to take Arouche prisoner. Dom Manuel wrote to Sebastião de Castro protesting against this lack of regard for his authority and the unmerited ill will. Dom Manuel said he would be responsible for the hunted man. The governor responded by sending more troops, as well as a bitter accusation against the former judge and orders to bring him in dead or alive.

> If this lawyer is innocent, I have the means to pay him for whatever injury [he has suffered,] and I will pay with my own head if perchance I deserve to be punished. . . . This lawyer has remained in Pernambuco thanks to sins of the land or sins of mine. He has not only made my work as governor difficult, but he has also put Your Grace at odds with your flock, as is publicly and notoriously [known]. Everyone acknowledges your titles and virtues, and they attribute [all the problems] we have seen and experienced to his counsel and [desire] for vengeance.[46]

Arouche got away because some local priests helped him and took him to Paraíba on back roads.

Dom Manuel returned to Olinda on November 10. On the fifteenth he took possession of the government. Immediately, in order to calm the people who, from the São Francisco River to Paraíba, were up in arms, Dom Manuel pardoned their rebellion and the shot fired at Caldas. He wrote: "I am confident in the grandeur of our lord the king, may God be with him, that he should support [my decision]."[47]

A few months of apparent calm went by. The nobility celebrated its victory noisily, considering the matter closed. Only in June of the following year did people begin to talk of using the fortresses to stop the new governor from returning, if he did not come back with the expected pardon, or letting him come ashore only under certain conditions.

Meanwhile, the peddlers' inertia hid some very intense underground goings-on. The parishes between Cape Santo Agostinho and the São Francisco River were cleverly wooed away from Olinda's side. And cooperation was obtained from the capitão-mor of Paraíba, from the field marshal of the Henriques regiment, from the governor of the Indians, and from the commander of the fortress at Tamandaré. Little by little, so as not to attract attention, supplies were gathered in sufficient quantities to help the peddlers withstand a siege. Even the troops in Recife, who up to the last minute had been loyal to Sebastião de Castro, were won over. This was how they told the story in Olinda.

It is hard to explain how everything was kept secret up until the decisive moment. One does not know who was more astonishing: the wily peddlers or the blind nobles. In fact the story told by the peddlers seems more truthful. They maintained that nothing had been foreseen or planned. Things just happened all of a sudden. Up to the beginning of the twentieth century, only spur of the moment movements triumphed in Brazil. No movement has been based on extended plotting or great feats of cerebration.

Soldiers of the regiment in Recife and those of Bernardo Vieira de Melo got into a fracas over some prostitutes. The sergeant major sided with his men and demanded that the others be punished. They begged for clemency, but they found him to be out of sorts and implacable, so they took to the streets. They shot their guns, shouted "Long live the king" and "Death to the traitors." They arrested Vieira de Melo and put him in jail. Valenzuela Ortiz was a former judge, who, on an interim basis, substituted at the bench for Arouche. Both he and the bishop witnessed and approved Vieira's arrest. As if under a magic spell, the people from Recife occupied the fortresses. All this happened on 18 June 1711. On the following day the bishop sent communiqués to the rural parishes, which calmed them down. If in fact there had been a plan, it worked perfectly. In one fell swoop the fortresses were garrisoned with friendly staff. The most determined head of the enemy group had been immobilized. And the legality of everything was vouched for by the presence and approval of the spiritual and civil leader of the captaincy, as well as by his chief magistrate. Three days later the bishop and his judge left Recife for Olinda, where the unexpected turn of events had caused great upheaval.

Dom Manuel was a virtuous and lettered gentleman, but he was easily swayed. He was both prudent and violent at the same time—drawn in one direction by his conscience and then in the opposite direction by his counselors and their intrigues. It was not hard to convince him that the peddlers had tried to arrest him; that the fortresses were cloaking the blackest of horrors; and that he could not and should not permit any lack of respect for royal majesty, for which he was responsible. He sent several communiqués intimating that people in Recife should abandon the fortresses, forget the land fortifications, and acknowledge Olinda's loyalty. After the fourth communiqué, which was no more useful than the first three, on June 27 he divested himself of his temporal power, turning it over to Valenzuela Ortiz, Field Marshal Cristóvão de Mendonça Arrais, and Senate officials,

> provided there is no bloodshed, which I protest 1,001 times, and which I have continuously protested, and for the benefit of the restoration effort and whatever else may happen, I run for no office directly or indirectly, because I want only peace and quiet for the vassals of His Majesty, may God protect him.[48]

If he had wanted to ensure bloodshed, the poor prelate could not have chosen a better course. Shielded by his complicity, the nobility surrounded Recife and hostility united with violence on both sides. Bombardment, sorties, recriminations, and circulars demonstrating the adversaries' wrongheadedness make up this entire uninteresting episode. The peddlers were led by João da Mota, a native of Alagoas, who had been promoted to captain because he was the officer of longest standing. He had no difficulty keeping up the fight, because the besieged peddlers knew that if this time they surrendered, the township's or vila's sacking would have fatal consequences. João da Mota was sufficiently calm, daring, enthusiastic, good-tempered, and spirited. Following the bishop's example, he set up a sort of ecclesiastic government consisting mainly of Augustinian and Carmelite friars. These friars, lettered and versed in canon law, were to counter the bishop's censures and excommunications. The prelate's messengers were never able to make their intimations felt, and consequently no one ever considered themselves excommunicated. The terrible arm failed to fire.

There were two battles in this campaign. The peddlers won the first one, the loyalists, the second. Despite his partisan fury, the chronicler from Olinda acknowledges a touch of Providence in the outcome of the two encounters:

> Both occasions were mysteries of Divine Providence that did not permit things to happen differently and that freed us from a greater evil, which, out of blindness, we failed to see. Because surely if our side had won the first battle, as we had wanted, we would have been carried off by the feat and without the protection [of Divine Providence] people in Recife would have been invaded by outsiders, who would immolate whomever they found. And if in the second battle they had beaten us, they would have likewise come to finish us off.[49]

The news of the first events reached Lisbon in February 1711. On the twenty-sixth of that month, the Overseas Council dealt with the information. Their reaction was vehement: "this is not only a most serious turn of events, it is the most important one up to now in the Portuguese nation." The variety of propositions and the virulence of the proposals showed just how upset the councilmen were. One member went so far as to suggest a minimum number of people who should receive the death penalty. Sebastião de Castro's flight to Bahia caused almost as much indignation as the shot and the uprising had. The governor had abandoned a post he had taken in the name of the king. Even if his life had been in danger, that was no reason to quit.

More and reassuring news arrived subsequently. The court learned of the bishop's taking over, his pardoning of the rebels, and the resumption of law and order following the upheaval. The meeting of April 8 shows how feelings had calmed down. However, it was not until June 1 that the government in Lisbon confirmed the pardon, ordered the arrest of Sebastião de Castro for abandoning his post, and had a new governor sent out, along with a chief magistrate, a judge, and some soldiers.

On October 6, Félix José Machado, the new governor, anchored far out from the port of Pau-Amarelo. The two sides immediately sent out representatives to explain their view of the current state of affairs. Only then must the new governor have learned of the siege of Recife and the following events. Machado demanded that João da Mota hand over the fortresses. He had the siege lifted and all of Dom Manuel's political authority reestablished. And only from Dom Manuel would he take the reins of power.

His acts demonstrated a healthy attitude, a willingness to put himself above the warring factions. It is quite possible that he could have preserved this objectivity throughout the entire process, had there been a means of reconciling the opposing sides, or of getting rid of the fundamental problem of determining who was really at fault. Was it the people from Olinda who had tried to kill Sebastião de Castro? Or was it those who had torn down the pillory? Those who had burned the list of voters? Or was it the peddlers who refused to obey the bishop's government? Those who manned the fortresses on their own authority? The ones who fired their cannons at their own country? The loyalists had been given amnesty by the king. The governor-general in Bahia had forgiven the peddlers, who, boastful and proud, claimed they needed no forgiveness. Instead they demanded gratitude and recompense.

The answer to the question of guilt would be easy if there were a third revolt, so it was not long before one side accused the other of planning one. The accusation was as absurd as the act of rebellion was impractical. Olinda had failed to receive any support north of Itamaracá or south of Santo Agostinho. It would garner even less support now that soldiers had come from Portugal and warships were anchored in the port. Recife had its status as a vila reinstated, the pillory had been rebuilt, and elections were held. What more could it want?

Nonetheless, the governor became convinced that people in Olinda were conspiring, so arrests, harassment, and trials began. Magistrates, both ouvidores and desembargadores, were called in to investigate. They not only displayed hateful partiality on behalf of the Portuguese; they sometimes had people arrested just to insult their adversaries and to amuse themselves with the people at hand. The bishop was ordered out of Olinda and down to the São Francisco. Owing to the rains he traveled slowly. One desembargador suggested he pick up his pace. If the highest ranking ecclesiastic did not escape these affronts, one can imagine what people with no immunity went through. The years 1712 and 1713 were calamitous.

At the end of 1713, Antônio de Albuquerque, after having governed Maranhão, Rio, São Paulo, and Minas Gerais, stopped off at Recife on his way back to Europe. He observed the state of misery and the tribulations of its inhabitants and, when he got to Lisbon, he explained how things really were.

Albuquerque's long years of service at such important posts gave weight to his words. A most benevolent decision was immediately made thanks to him. Royal letters dated 7 April 1714 reminded people that both the 1710 and the 1711 uprisings had been pardoned. There were to be no more investigations or arrests because of them. The only criminal uprising was the one in 1713.

Because they had been implicated in the 1713 rebellion, Bernardo Vieira de Melo and one son, Leonardo Bezerra and two of his sons, and Leão Falcão were kept in prison. Falcão was the impudent hothead who, even after Félix José Machado's arrival, took it upon himself to try to resist and rebel. He did this on the outskirts of Goiana, a powerful peddler stronghold.

After having been exiled to India, Leonardo Bezerra managed to return to Bahia, where he died. According to tradition, he would write to friends: "Do not cut down a single *quiri* in the woods. Try to save all of them so that at the right moment they can be broken on the sailors' backs." In Pernambuco one of the names given to the Portuguese was "sailor." A quiri was a type of tree whose wood was as hard as iron. If these words are authentic, that old insurgent must have been incurably optimistic, trusting as he did the republic or his country's independence to broken backs and broken clubs.

During all of this agitation, a book was published in Lisbon. Its title was *Cultura e opulência do Brasil por suas drogas e minas*, by André João Antonil, as one can read on the first page of the edition that was printed with the necessary license by the Deslanderina royal printer in 1711. Today we know that the pen name Antonil was an anagram of João Antônio Andreoni L (Luquense). Born in Luca, Tuscany, Andreoni came to Brazil in 1689 as a Jesuit inspector. Once his mission was over, he remained in the province. He was the rector in Bahia when Antônio Vieira died, in 1697. He was a high-ranking cleric (a provincial) when the Peddler War broke out. There are rumors, and probably some truth in them, that he was sympathetic to Olinda's cause.

Andreoni's book is divided into five parts. It deals with sugar mills and sugar, mines and livestock. Without elaboration in its terse and severe form, it piled number upon number and presented Brazil as it would seem to a penetrating researcher. The existence of 146 sugar mills operating in Bahia was made known. Their annual production was 14,500 crates of sugar. There were 246 sugar mills in Pernambuco that produced 12,300 crates and 136 in Rio that produced 10,220. The grand total was 36,020 crates, each weighing 35 arrobas or 525 kilograms and bringing in 2.535:142$800.

Bahia produced 25,000 bolts of tobacco, Pernambuco and Alagoas 2,500. Tobacco brought in 334:650$000 per year.

During the previous 10-year period, the amount of gold that was mined added up to 1,000 arrobas. The official annual figure was now 100 per year, but the real figure must have been around 300, one arroba per day, not counting Sundays and holidays.

To appreciate the number of cattle that needed to be raised, it is sufficient to remember that the thousands of bolts of tobacco had to be wrapped in leather before they were shipped out. On top of this, Bahia exported 50,000 cowhides [*meios de sola*], Pernambuco, 40,000, and Rio (counting those that came from Sacramento Colony [Uruguay]), 20,000. The total was 110,000 cowhides worth 201:800$000.[50]

And the 3,743:992$800 is not the only amount of Brazilian wealth that went to Portugal.

One must add to that amount:

the price of whaling contracts. In Bahia a six-year contract was auctioned off for 110,000 cruzados. In Rio a three-year contract went for 45,000 cruzados. In Bahia the year's contract for royal tithes, minus fees, went for almost 200,000 cruzados. A three year tithe contract in Rio was worth 190,000 cruzados, in Pernambuco, 97,000, in São Paulo, 60,000. Never mind the smaller captaincies, where tithe contracts also cost more. The six-year wine contract in Bahia went for 190,000 cruzados. A three-year contract in Pernambuco was worth 46,000. A four-year contract in Rio went for over 50,000. The 12-year salt contract for Bahia sold for 28,000 cruzados per year. The distilled liquor contract for local and foreign products together sold for 30,000 cruzados. The income from the Mint [Casa da Moeda] in Rio de Janeiro, which in two years minted 3,000,000 gold coins, gave the king an income of more than 600,000 cruzados since he buys gold at a price of 12 *tostões* [per oitava]. In addition, there are the quintos, measured in arrobas, that the king receives every year. He also receives 3,500 réis per head from the duties paid on slaves at customs houses in the ports of Bahia, Recife, and Rio de Janeiro. These blacks arrive in great numbers from Angola, São Tomé, and Mina on a yearly basis. And the ranches in Rio de Janeiro pay a 10 percent duty on their yearly imports, adding up to another 80,000 cruzados.[51]

The conclusions made from these scrupulously displayed figures could not be more modest. The number of churches should be increased, argued the sagacious Jesuit, because the population is growing so fast. Because the tithes are so great, competitions should be held so qualified people can be found to head and furnish vacant churches. Soldiers in towns and in maritime fortresses should be promptly paid, and they should be promoted according to their service records. The inhabitants' petitions should be respected, and the means of relief and accommodation that the town councils have so humbly proposed should be accepted.

If the plantation owners and the sugar and tobacco farmers are the ones who produce such worthy profits, it seems that they, more than anyone else, deserve to be favored and to find in the courts whatever can expeditiously relieve them from the delays owing to regulations, as well as from the burdens and expenditures coming from protracted lawsuits.[52]

The imperial government responded to the book in a fulminatory fashion. It was confiscated, and with such rigor that even today there are very few copies of the first edition. The pretext for this outrage was that the book would make Brazil's secrets known abroad. It is hard to see how this would be a problem. Sugar cane was planted and sugar was manufactured in other nations' colonies. Tobacco was also planted, livestock was raised, and mines were worked. What novelty might they learn from *Cultura e opulência do Brasil por suas drogas e minas*? The real truth is that the book revealed Brazil's secret to Brazilians. It proclaimed the colony's vitality; it justified its ambitions; and it made its grandeur obvious.

Under the severe architecture of those figures compiled by the worthy Jesuit, Brazil's secret was kept away from Brazilians. The secret was revealed, however. Under different disguises its outline began to emerge.

It rang out in dithyrambs praising the peerless riches of the country. It appeared in compilations or *nobiliarquias* that were dedicated to the noble families: in the compilation by Borges da Fonseca for Pernambuco, the one by Jabotão for Bahia, and especially in Pedro Taques's compilation for São Paulo.[53] These *nobiliarquias* linked Brazil's families to the premiere nobility of Spain, Italy, and Flanders. Because he lacked any sense of history, Loreto Couto gathered hundreds of names to demonstrate how Pernambuco was graced with virtues, letters, arms, and the women.

In the work of Loreto Couto, a Pernambucan Benedictine who wrote around 1757, one finds even more manifestations characteristic of this mentality: high praise and glorification of the native people contrasted [favorably] with [his portrayal of] early settlers coming from Portugal, as well as with more advanced peoples in the Old World.

As proof of the natives' moral virtues, he cites the names of Indians famous for their bravery and fidelity: Tabira, Camarão, and many other allies in the wars with the Dutch and in the conquest of the country. Among the manifestations of the natives' intellectual capacities, he points to the councils in which tribal elders would discuss the matters at hand, or their knowledge of illnesses and cures, and their traps for game and fish.

What did it matter that they were unaware of the true religion? Might they have adored a whale washed ashore, just like the old inhabitants of the Setúbal tidewaters and Beira? Might they have sacrificed a damsel and a swain every year?

> If the very repugnant errors of their beginnings in nature prove their barbarity, then it is necessary to declare the English, Danes, Swabians, and many Germans barbarians, since these nations share the prevalent notion that we do not sin by choice but by necessity. They believe that God makes us sin and we cannot help sinning.[54]

If they had been exposed to culture, they would have developed their intelligence.

> In our kingdom of Portugal, between the towns of Celorico and Trancoso there lived peoples who were as brutish and wild as untamed animals. They were so primitive that one family could not understand the language of another if they lived two leagues from one another. And for this reason they were judged by neighboring peoples to be wilder than the wildest of wild animals.[55]

Might they have been cannibals?

> We should not be surprised by these peoples' barbarity once we consider the descendants of Tubal and those of the other political factions that settled Portugal. These people sank to such levels of brutality that they killed and ate anyone they happened to capture from a neighboring faction—be it in a war, be it in a trap.[56]

Using similar arguments, he celebrates the virtues of língua geral and the natives' skin color. His ideas, put forth and argued discursively, also appear synthesized in the work of poets of the time. The surnames people adopted at the time of independence also reflect these nativistic notions: Araripe, Braúna, Canguçu, Guaicuru, Jucá, Montezuma, Mororó, Sucupira, Tupinambá and many others. Everywhere the Brazilian secret becomes apparent. We gradually distinguish ourselves from the Portuguese. The distinction is unconscious and timid in the beginning; conscious, resolute, and irresistible later on, thanks to our adaptation to the surroundings, the trees, the animals, and even the indigenous population.

With an air of triumph, the Benedictine writer waives the royal decree of 4 April 1755 and declares:

in this kingdom and in America my vassals who marry Indian women shall in no way be disgraced. Rather, they will be made worthy of my royal attention. Wherever they may set themselves up, they will receive preference for those posts and occupations that befit their status. Their offspring and descendants will be able and suited for whatever employment, honor, or distinction and will need no special permission [to go about their business]....[57]

This decree is but one episode in a long story that can be told in a few words.

Scarcely did Manuel da Nóbrega come ashore in Bahia in 1549 than he took up the Indians' cause. He sought their physical well-being as well as their spiritual growth and integration into Catholicism. His experience convinced him of the necessity of isolating natives from colonists, so as to achieve any sort of worthwhile and lasting results. It would be necessary to teach natives to appreciate the virtues of work; to guarantee their personal safety and economic independence. Neither Nóbrega nor any of his successors protested against the Indians' enslavement. All they demanded was that certain conditions be met for slavery to be permitted. They committed a capital but unavoidable error. How could they deny the right to enslave Brazilians if their contemporaries and forebears had been enslaving Africans for over two centuries?

In spite of all the snags created by indecision in Lisbon and by the passions in the colony, Nóbrega's work went on and, especially in the Amazon region, it thrived. The missionaries were in charge of administrating the worldly affairs of Indian villages, whose wealth and abundance exceeded that of white men's settlements. A constant topic of conversation was the Jesuits' wealth. And in fact their parsimony, their methodical management, and their personal disinterest were a sort of splendor whose secret they took with them, as time would tell.

With the passage of time these villages not only became states within a state, but churches within a church. The first bishop in Pará tried to put the missions under his jurisdiction, but the missionaries refused to submit. They were shielded by numerous papal privileges as well as by royal grants. Their arguments must have been weighty because the resolution to this conflict was many long years in coming.

On 24 September 1751 Francisco Xavier de Mendonça Furtado, who had been named governor-general of the state, assumed his post in Belém. He had been ordered to safeguard the Indians' freedom and to keep the missionaries in check. An excursion begun in February of the following year took him to the Indian villages between Marajó Island and the Strait of Pauxis. In Caiá he heard the speech of an Indian chief, and, satisfied that better times were on their way, he exclaimed: "And these are the men who they say have no judgment and who are capable of nothing! They can become a nation like any other, and this will be of great use."

Mendonça's correspondence during this time and later years harps on liberty for native peoples, on abusive missionaries, and on the real estate they possess, which was protected by incontestable laws. In February 1754, in a letter to Diogo de Mendonça Corte-Real, he reveals his conviction that the Indians cannot be civilized with ordinary help. His words were generic and made no specific reference to the Jesuits. His complaints were responsible for two laws dated 6 and 7 June 1755.[58] One law abolished the missionaries' role in managing Indian villages. The other reiterated the declaration of absolute liberty for natives. When and how to make these laws public was left to the governor-general.

Mendonça Furtado was responsible for demarcating the northern boundaries of the country. From the Indian villages he requisitioned hundreds of oarsmen who would be necessary for the undertaking. He also requisitioned quanties [alqueires] of manioc flour and other items necessary to keep these people alive for years. Modern Pará, served by steamboats, trading with both the New and the Old World, would be up to such demands. The Amazonia of old was not. It was busy gathering clove, sarsaparilla, and cacao. And it ate fish and was joyous when local agriculture produced enough for day-to-day consumption.

Mendonça seems not to have had a clear understanding of the situation. He attributed all the fatal complications to intrigues and to Jesuit ill will and perfidy rather than to the state of affairs at the time. The Jesuits were recidivistic and obstinate criminals, their monstrosity was beyond description. They had failed to make their domestic and economic laws conform to the urgent needs of Pombal's brother.[59] With the purpose of punishing such a heinous crime, the two perfect societies met and agreed that there was only one solution: eliminate the church within the church and the state within the state, which was what the Indian villages could not help but be.

On 5 February 1757, Mendonça published the law that ended the Jesuits' administration of the villages' worldly affairs. From that point on they were to be run by the state. The missionaries would continue to work as priests under the jurisdiction of the prelate. They all submitted, except for the Jesuits, whose constitutions prohibited such interference. They offered to work side by side with the state and the bishop, but the governor and the bishop turned down their proposal.

Mendonça composed a directorial dated 3 May 1757. It contained around 95 articles under which he would rule provisionally.[60] In this new order missionaries would be replaced by directors. On March 14 he explained his creation as follows:

> Since it is not possible for [the Indians] to go from one extreme to the other without some means of attaining that important goal, no better means occurred to me than that of putting a man with the title of director in each village. The director will not be there to teach them how to govern themselves. His sole mandate will be to teach them to do business and to work their land. From these most fruitful and interesting endeavors, these heretofore unfortunate men will, on their own, make a profit and of course become civil, Christian, and rich. And this will doubtlessly happen if the directors do their jobs.[61]

Immediately thereafter he promoted the larger villages to the status of vila and the smaller ones to *lugar* or "settlement." A contemporary, who, one suspects, was a Jesuit and not an eyewitness to the events, provides an interesting description of these innovations. His chronology is also somewhat off.

> It occurred to him to turn many of the Indian villages into vilas, with privileges similar to those in Portugal. He did this even though they were all, except for the church and the priest's house, little more than poor, rustic huts. He had a large pole erected in the middle of a square and called the site a pillory. After this he would choose from the savages some who, because of the look in their eyes or the size of their body, seemed better suited for the tasks he required. He made some of them councilmen, others he turned into judges. He told them they were as good as the Portuguese and that they should govern themselves without depending on, or subjecting themselves in any manner, to the missionaries. On top of this he had these new creations outfitted from head to toe. He sat them at his table, toasted them repeatedly, and told them, *inter pocula*, through a mouthpiece or interpreter, how they were to behave from then on, how they were to administer justice, etc. However, once the meal was over, and the party broken up, these Indians forgot everything Mister Mendonça had told them. Scarcely would they get beyond his sight, and they would take off their shoes and clothing and get drunk on that wine they call *mocòroròs*. As a sign of joy and satisfaction with the roles they had been given, they would all shout: "Wine from the king! Wine from the king!" thinking they were saying "Long live the king! Long live the king!" But once their spree was over and they came to, they became insolent not only with the missionaries, whom they no longer respected and whom they no longer followed even in spiritual matters; but also they treated their fellow Indians poorly. Indeed, they

treated them so poorly that, once the Jesuits and other priests in these villages had left and their replacements had come in, Mister Mendonça was obliged to send in some Portuguese with the title of director to govern them and keep them in line. And many of these Portuguese were loath to go to these new vilas without having with them at all times some soldiers to protect them from those barbarians' insults.[62]

After this Mendonça dealt with the law pertaining to the Indians' freedom. A papal bull had been passed on 20 December 1741 by Benedict XIV, at the insistence of Dom João V. It excommunicated *latae sententiae*, whoever, with whatever motive, might enslave a Brazilian Indian.[63] In the Marquis de Pombal's pamphlet, titled *Relação abreviada da república. . .*,[64] it says that the bishop of Pará, Dom Miguel de Bulhões, when he tried to carry out this papal order, found himself faced with a rebellion that for the time being impeded the apostolic decree. This allegation is absolute calumny. On 11 June 1757 Mendonça Furtado wrote:

> [the] bull was given to this prelate on Your Majesty's order, to be made public and observed in his diocese. He intended to carry out [your orders] when he arrived at this city, but was stopped for the same reasons I suspended the announcement of [Indians'] liberty. . . .[65]

The reasons for suspending the law to free the Indians were merely opportunistic considerations, as one can see in all of the governor-general's correspondence. There never was a rebellion. And the scribe was so aware that he was lying that he added:

> The same prelate chose not to inform the Court of such a singular upheaval, because during those times he feared a fact as scandalous as that would disturb said monarch's peace of spirit, since he was afflicted with the grave infirmity took his life on 31 July 1750.

On May 25 the bishop made the bull of Benedict XIV public.[66] On the twenty-eighth Mendonça made the law freeing the Indians public. These announcements caused no protest, and, let the truth be said, in spite of appearances, they were not obeyed.

The directorial, once the king approved it, remained in force from 1757 to 1798.[67] The misery it produced was appalling. Finally, Dom Francisco de Sousa Coutinho took pity on the Indians and had the directorial revoked. The redeeming measure was too late: the evil deed had been done. In 1850 Pará and Amazonas were less populous and less prosperous than they had been a century before. The brutal devastation and the suffering in those remote districts between the years of 1820 and 1836 are rooted in the ill-starred brainchild of Francisco Xavier de Mendonça Furtado. The laws withdrawing missionaries from village administration and liberating Indians were written originally only for the state of Maranhão. They were extended to the rest of Brazil by a charter dated 8 May 1758.[68] Here, as well as in the north, vilas sprang forth, all with legitimate Portuguese names. In the rest of Brazil, Indian affairs were no longer a matter of concern, and the violence against them was not as great as farther north. During the first decades of the nineteenth century, a writer in Pernambuco portrayed the situation as more absurd than baleful:

> The Indians have their own vilas and councils. Their judges cannot read, write, or make a speech. It is the scribe who makes up for all this, and he is often little more than a mulatto shoemaker or tailor. He directs those councils of quasi-irrationals according to his whims and using the following formula:
>
> On the eve of the day in which there is to be a town council meeting, the scribe leaves his house, always on horseback if it is far away. He spends the night in the judge's house. The first thing the judge does is take care of the scribe's horse. He takes it someplace where it can drink water, then he hobbles it in a place where it can graze comfortably.
>
> The scribe, meanwhile, is resting. He has become lord of the house, of the officious judge's wife and daughters. The judge has the scribe spend the night and sleep in the best part of his hut. Right at daybreak the judge dons old and borrowed ceremonial accouterments and at the proper time marches off to a shanty nicknamed the Town Hall. There the petitions that the scribe wrote the night before are read in the name of the presiding judge. Shortly thereafter the venerable senate meeting comes to an end and the senators appear once more in shirtsleeves or in undergarments, heading off to work.

The declaration of liberty and the directorial on behalf of the Indians were followed by other measures in which church and state collaborated. The Holy See named Cardinal F. de Saldanha inspector and general apostolic reformer of the Company of Jesus. On 15 May 1758 he wielded them a tremendous blow.[69] On 7 June 1758 the Patriarch of Lisbon suspended their right to preach and confess in his diocese. Making the most of some shots taken at the king, the Marquis de Pombal had the royal puppet sign a law that declared the Jesuits rebels and traitors. It stripped them of their citizenship and outlawed the Company of Jesus.

In the course of the following year hundreds of Nóbrega's successors still in Brazil were shipped off to Portugal. They had worked in Brazil for 200 years, and their influence must have been considerable. I say it "must have been" because given the present state of knowledge it is impossible to be more precise than that. During the time they prospered they only published Simão de Vasconcelos' redundant, deficient, and not always accurate chronicle, which only deals with the period from 1549 to 1570. What little can be found in general yearly chronicles as well as in other publications boils down to the few pages A. H. Leal gathered in the *Revista trimestral do Instituto Histórico*. Biographies, such as Anchieta's, Almeida's, Vieira's, and Correia's, have been next to useless. We urgently need a history of the Jesuits [in Brazil]. As long as none exists it is presumptuous to think someone can write the country's history.

Within the Jesuits' domains numerous and important documents must have been left to perish by neglect or by design. All that has been saved are the titles to their properties. Judging from some of the publications and documents given to Eduardo Prado and Studart, European Jesuit archives must be worth exploring.[70]

As long as no light is shed on these obscure matters, a definitive judgment concerning this famous religious order will be without foundation.[71] However it is, the attacks directed at the Jesuits are of little, indeed of very little, help. Instinctively our sympathies turn to Nóbrega, Anchieta, Cardim, Vieira, Andreoni, and their companions and disciples. They educated our youth; they founded American linguistics.

The attached chart [Table 9.1] was taken from Luís dos Santos Vilhena's four-volume *Recopilação de notícias sotero-politanas e brasílicas*, which was published along with two volumes of maps. Vilhena was a professor of Greek in Salvador at the beginning of the nineteenth century. His precious codex, which once belonged to the library of the Counts of Linhares, now belongs to José Carlos Rodrigues, who has kindly allowed this unpublished document to come to light.

It would be fitting to work up a similar document for the other Brazilian captaincies. But, for the time being, the following list of villages in existence before Pombal's revolution may be of some help.

The list for Pará and Amazonas is for the year 1751. It was composed by João Antônio da Cruz Diniz Pinheiro and published by J. Lúcio de Azevedo, in *Os Jesuítas no Grão-Pará*, Lisbon, 1901. There is more than one mistake in this work.

In Pará, Jesuits administered the villages of Caeté, Maracanã, Cabu, Vigia, Mortigura, Sumaúma, Araticu, Aricuru, Aricará—all on the Amazon River. On the Xingu River, they administered Itacuruçá, Pirauiri, and Aricará; on the Tapajós, they administered Tapajós, Borari, Cumaru, Santo Inácio, and São José. On the Madeira, Abacaxis and Trocano.

A Curious Chart Containing Uncommon Notice of Many Indian Villages Which, by Order of the King, Are Today's Vilas

#	Original Name	Bordering	Parish Vila	Religious Order	Name as Vila	Patron Saint	Diocese	Captaincy	District	Territory	Couples	Indians	Distance (in leagues) from Bahia
1	Juru	Lagarto	N.S. dos Campos do Rio Real	Jesuits	Távora	N.S. do Socorro	Bahia	Sergipe d'El-Rei	Sergipe d'El-Rei		60	Quiriris	50
2	Saco Dos Morcegos	Itapicuru Santa	Jesuits Ana dos Tucanos	Miran-dela	Ascensão de Cristo	Bahia	Bahia	Bahia	Considerable	100	Quiriris	65	
3	Cana Brava	Itapicuru	São João de Jerónimos	Jesuits	Pombal	Santa Teresa	Bahia	Bahia	Bahia	Negligible	110	Quiriris	60
4	Natura	Itapicuru	N.S. de Nazaré de Itapicuru	Jesuits	Soure	N.S. da Conceiçao	Bahia	Bahia	Bahia	Very Negligible	110	Quiriris	50
5	Ipitanga	Bahia	Santo Amaro	Jesuits	Abrantes	Espírito Santo	Bahia	Bahia	Bahia	6 leagues square	140	Tupis, Tupinambás Goianás, etc.	7
6	Serinhaém	Camamu	Assunção do Camamu	Jesuits	Santarém	S.Miguel, S.André	Bahia	Ilhéus	Ilhéus	Considerable	160	Paiaiá	30
7	Esala dos Ilhéus	São Jorge dos Ilhéus	Santa Cruz dos Ilhéus	Jesuits	Olivença	N.S. da Escada	Bahia	Ilhéus	Ilhéus		130	Tabajaras, Tupiniquins	50

#	Original Name	Bordering Vila	Parish Vila	Religious Order	Name as Vila	Patron Saint	Diocese	Captaincy	District	Territory	Couples	Indians	Distance (in leagues) from Bahia
8	Maraú	Camamu	São Sebastião do Camamu	Jesuits	Barcelos	N.S. das Candeias	Bahia	Ilhéus	Ilhéus		86	Tupiniquins	30
9	Grens	São Jorge dos Ilhéus	Santa Cruz da Vila de São Jorge	Jesuits	Almada vença	N.S. da Conceição	Bahia	Ilhéus	Ilhéus	Much	95	Grens	60
10	S. João dos Topes	Santa Cruz	N.S. da Pena	Jesuits	Trancoso Saint John	Rio de Janeiro	Porto Seguro	Porto Seguro			120	Tupinanbás Tupiniquins	70
11	Patatiba	Santa Cruz	N.S. da Pena	Jesuits	Vila Verde	Espírito Santo	Rio de Janeiro	Porto Seguro	Porto Seguro		80	Tupinanbás Jontutus	80
12	Reritiba	Guruparim	N.S. da Conceiçao	Jesuits	Benevente	N.S. da Assunção	Rio de Janeiro	Espírito Santo	Espírito Santo	12 leagues on coast	250	Tupinanbás	150
13	Reis Magos	Vila da Vitória	Serra	Jesuits	Almeida	Santos Reis Magos	Rio de Janeiro	Espírito Santo	Espírito Santo	Much	300	Tupinanbás	120
14	Poxino	São Jorge dos Ilhéus	S. Boa-Ventura do Poxino	Cleric	******	S. Boa-ventura do Poxino	Bahia	Ilhéus	Ilhéus				
15	Aramaris	S. João da Água Fria	Espírito Santo de Inhambuque	Cleric	******	S. Boa-ventura do Poxino	Bahia	Bahia	Bahia	Very Negligible	81	Quiriris	40

# Original Name	Bordering	Parish Vila	Religious Order	Name as Vila	Patron Saint	Diocese	Captaincy	District	Territory	Couples	Indians	Distance (in leagues) from Bahia
16 Mangu- inhos	S. João da Água Fria	Espírito Santo de Inhambuque	Cleric	******	S. Boa- ventura do Poxino	Bahia	Bahia	Bahia	Very Negligible	120	Caramurus	35
17 Conquista Da Pedra Branca	Marogo- gipe	Oiteiro Redondo de N.S. do	Cleric	******	S. Boa- ventura do Poxino	Bahia	Bahia	Bahia	Very Negligible	20	Quiriris	30
18 Another On the Same Site	Marogo- gipe Friaa	Oiteiro Redondo de N.S. do Desterro	Cleric	******	S. Boa- ventura do Poxino	Bahia	Bahia	Bahia	Very Negligible		Tapuias	30
19 Rodelas	Pambu	S. Antó- nio do Pambu	Italian Capuchines	*******	S. João Batista	Bahia	Sergipe	Jacobina	1 league	200 Souls	Periás	170
20 Porto da Folha	Vila Nova Real d'El-Rei	S. Antó- nio do Urubu de Baixo	Italian Capuchines	*******	S. Pedro	Bahia	Sergipe	Sergipe	1 league	250 Souls	Urumas	124
21 Pacatuba	Vila Nova Real d'El-Rei	S. Antó- nio de Vila Nova Real	Italian Capuchines	*******	S. Félix	Bahia	Sergipe	Sergipe	1 league	466 souls	Caxagos	106

#	Original Name	Bordering Vila	Parish Vila	Religious Order	Name as Vila	Patron Saint	Diocese	Captaincy	District	Territory	Couples	Indians	Distance (in leagues) from Bahia
22	Una Do Cairu	Vila Cairu	N.S. do Rosário Urubu de Baixo	Italian Capuchines	******	S. Félix	Bahia	Bahia	Ilhéus	1 league	160 Souls	Tupinambás	16
23	Itapicuru De Cima	Itapicuru	N.S. de Nazaré	Fransicans	******	S. António, N.S. da Saúde	Bahia	Bahia	Bahia	Less than 1 league	80	Tupinambás	45
24	Massacará	Itapicuru	S. João de Jerimoabo	Fransicans	******	Holy Trinity	Bahia	Bahia	Bahia	1 league	200	Quiriris and Catumbis	60
25	Bom Jesus Da Jacobina	Vila S. António de Jacobina	S. António	Fransicans	******	Bom Jesus	Bahia	Bahia	Jacobina	Very Negligible	100		80
26	Sai	Jacobina	S. António de Jacobina	Fransicans	******	N.S. das Neves	Bahia	Bahia	Jacobina	1 league Negligible	150	80	
27	Juazeiro	Jacobina	S. António	Fransicans	******	N.S. das Brotas	Bahia	Bahia	Jacobina		100	100	
28	Curral dos Bois	Vila Nova da Rainha or Penedo	Pambu	Fransicans	******	S. Francisco	Bahia	Bahia	Jacobina		80	100	

# Original Name	Bordering Vila	Parish Vila	Religious Order	Name as Vila	Patron Saint	Diocese	Captaincy	District	Territory	Couples	Indians	Distance (in leagues) from Bahia
29 Aldeia do Rio Real	Vila da Abadia	N.S. da Abadia	Carmelites	******	Jesus Maria José	Bahia	Sergipe	Bahia	Very Negligible	80	Quiriris	100
30 Japaratuba	Abadia	Jesus Maria José S. Gonçalo	Carmelites	******	N.S. do Carmo	Bahia	Sergipe	Bahia	Very Negligible	120	Boimé	65
31 Água Azeda	City of Sergipe	N.S. da Vitória	Carmelites	******	N.S. do Carmo	Bahia	Sergipe d'El-Rei	Sergipe d'El-Rei			Boimé	65
32 Massarandupio'	Sta. Luzia do Rio Real	S. Amaro de Ipitanga	Carmelites	******	S. António de Aguim	Bahia	Bahia	Bahia	6 leagues	240 Souls, 50 Couples	Tupis or Tupinambás	18
33 Santo Antó Da Aldei	Magarogipe	S. Bartolomeu	Cleric	******	S. António	Bahia	Bahia	Bahia			Tupis or Tupinambás	18
34 Jiquiriçá	Jaguaripe	S. António	Cleric	******	N.S. dos Prazeres	Bahia	Bahia	Bahia			Tupis or Tupinambás	18
35 Jaguaripe do Rio De Aldeia	Jaguaripe	Nazaré nio	Cleric	******	N.S. de Nazaré	Bahia	Bahia	Bahia			Tupis or Tupinambás	18
36 Aldeia do Salitre	S. António de Urubu de Cima	S. António nio	Cleric	******	N.S. Madre de Deus	Bahia	Bahia	Jacobina			Tupis or Tupinambás	134

Saint Anthony's Capuchines administered the Caviana villages located on Caviana Island. These were Menino Jesus, Socacas or Joanes, São José, Anaiatuba, Bocas, Urubucuara, Acarapi and Paru.

The Conceição or Saint Bonaventura Capuchines administered Mangabiras, Caiá, Conceição, Iari, Tuari, Uramucu. Saint Joseph's or the Piedade Capuchines administered Gurupá, Arapijó, Caviana, Maturu, Jamundá, Pauxis, Curuá, Manema, Suburiú, and Gurupatuba.

Carmelites administered villages in the Solimões region Coari, Tefé, Maneruá, Paraguari, Turucuatuba, São Paulo, and São Pedro. On the Rio Negro they ran Jaú, Caragaí, Aracari, Comaru, Mariuá, São Caetano, Cabuquena, Baratuá, and Dari.

The villages listed by Diniz Pinheiro add up to 63: 19 run by Jesuits, 12 by Saint Anthony Capuchines, 6 by Conceição Capuchines, 9 by Piedade Capuchines, 17 by Carmelites, and 1 by the Brothers of Mercy on the Urubu River.

In large part, the names given to villages once they stopped being administered by missionaries can be found in Baena's chorographic essay. It, however, needs critical revision, which, luckily, Manuel Barata has undertaken. He knows the history of the Amazon region very well. One document that would be helpful in resolving all doubts would be the *Mapa geral do bispado do Pará repartido nas suas freguesias* by Henrique Antônio Galuzi, an engineer who drew it up in 1759. It is in the National Library. However this map does not contain the villages' old names.

The R[oyal] C[harter] of 19 March 1693 entrusted the Indians of the south bank of the Amazon and beyond to the Jesuits. Saint Anthony's friars received the territory from Cape Norte and the north bank of the great river, which included the Jari and Paru Rivers, as well as the Indian village of Urubucuara, which the Jesuits had founded. The Piedade friars received the district of Gurupá and the neighboring villages along the north shore of the Amazon, from Trombetas River to the Negro River, as well as the Xingu.

According to Diniz Pinheiro, in Maranhão and its dependent captaincies there were 17 Indian villages: Aruazes and Paracatis in Piauí; two Araió and Araperu villages, along the Parnaíba River; a Tarabambé, a Gamela, a Tapijara village, known as São José, in Maranhão. In the Cumá Captaincy, São João, Maracu and Pinaré were administered by Jesuits; there was one village run by Carmelites and another by Brothers of Mercy.

A 1751 manuscript in the Instituto Histórico, *Évora* (8), lists villages of

Gueguê, Barbado, Caicaise, Aranhé, and Tupinambá Indians along the Itapicuru River. On the Pindaré River there were Marava Guajajara and Guajajara-açu villages. A letter of 12 February 1759 from the governor of Maranhão, Gonçalo Pereira Lobato e Sousa, to Diogo de Mendonça Corte-Real addresses the creation of several vilas. There is a copy of that document at the Instituto Histórico.

The villages in Pernambuco, from its borders with Minas Gerais through the backlands all the way to its coastal border with Piauí, can be found in *Informação geral de Pernmabuco*, which was organized in 1749, and which the National Library is in the process of publishing.[72]

In Pernambuco there were 54 Indian villages. In 17 of them língua geral was spoken; 6 of them were mixed; and there were others administered by Jesuits, Franciscans, Theresians, Carmelites, Benedictines, Italian and non-Italian Capuchines, Oratorians, and priests of Saint Peter's Habit. All of these villages spoke languages unrelated to língua geral. In what follows *l.g.* stands for língua geral; *J*=Jesuits; *F*=Franciscans; *Cm.*=Carmelites; *Cp.*=Capuchines; *Ci.*=Italian Capuchines; *B*=Benedictines; *O*=Oratorians; *H*=Saint Peter's Habit; *Th.*=Theresian; *NM*=no missionaries.

This is the order of villages set out in *Informação Geral de Pernambuco*:

In the vila of Recife there were the villages of Nossa Senhora da Escada, *l.g.*, *O*; in Igaraçu Limoeiro, *l.g.*, *O*; in Goiana Aratagui, *l.g.*, *O*; Siri *l.g.*, Cm.

Paraíba: In the city of Paraíba there were two: Jacoca, *l.g.*, *B*; Utinga, *l.g.*, *B*. In Mamanguape: São Miguel da Baía da Traição, *l.g.*, Cm.; Preguiça, *l.g.*, Cm.; Boa-Vista, Canindés, and Sucurus, *Th.*; Taipu, Cariris, *Cp.*; Cariri, Campina Grande, Cavalcantes, *H*; Brejo and Fagundes, *Cp.*. On the Piancó River there were: Panati and Tapuios, *Th.*; Curema, Tapuios, *Cp.*. On the Piranhas River: Pega and Tapuias, *NM*; on the Peixe River: Icó Pequeno and Tapuios, *NM*.

Rio Grande do Norte: Guajaru, *l.g.* and Paicus, *J.*; Apodi, Paiacus, *Th.*; Mipibu, *l.g.*, *Cp.*; Guarairás, *l.g.* J; Gramació, *l.g.*, Cm.

Ceará: Ibiapaba, *l.g.*; Acaracus, Irariú, and Anacés, *J.*; Tramambés and Tramambés *H*; Caucaia, *l.g.* J; Parangaba, *l.g.*; Anacés, *J*; Paupina, *l.g.*, *J*; Paiacus, Paiacus, *J*; Palma, Cacaia, *l.g.*, *J*; Quixeré, Cariú, Cariúané, Calabaça, and Icozinho, *Cp.*

Serinhaém: Una, *l.g.*, Cm.

Vila de Alagoas: Santo Amaro, *l.g.*, *F*; Gameleira, Cariris, and Uruás, *H*; Urucu, *l.g.*, *NM*. *Vila de Penedo:* São Brás, Cariris, Progés, *J*; Alagoa-

Comprida, Carapotiós, *NM*; Pão de Açúcar, *l.g.*; Chocós, *H*; Serra do Comonati, *l.g.*; Carnijós, H.

Ararobá Parish: Ararobá, Chururus, *O*; Carnijós (Panema River), Tapuias, *H*; Macaco, Paraquiós, *NM*.

Rodelas Parish: São Francisco do Brejo, Tapuios, *F*; Nossa Senhora da O' (Sorobabé Island), Porcás and Brancararus, *F*; Nossa Senhora de Belém (Cará Island), Porcás and Brancararus, *Ci.*; Beato Serafim, Porcás, and Brancararus *Ci.*; Beato Serafim, Porcás, and Brancararus, *Ci.*; Nossa Senhora da Conceição do Pambu, Cariris, *Ci.*; São Francisco de Aracapá, Cariris, *Ci.*; São Félix (Cavalo Island), Cariris *Ci.*; Santo Antônio de Irapuá, Cariris, *Ci.*; Nossa Senhora da Piedade (Inhamum Island), Cariris, *F*; Nossa Senhora do Pilar (Coripós Island) *F*; Nossa Senhor dos Remédios (Pontal Island), Tamaquiús, *F*; São Cristo de Araripé, Ichus, *Ci.*

Rio Grande do Sul (the old name for the western tributary of the São Francisco River): Aricobés, *l.g., F.*

The repetition of placenames is worked out in *Idéia da população de Pernambuco*, a manuscript organized under the government of José César de Menezes and now in the National Library.[73] The villages in Ceará that were raised to vilas have been studied by the indefatigable Baron Studart.

According to Joaquim Norberto, in his article in *Revista trimestral do Instituto Histórico*, (pp. 17, 109ff), in Rio there were the following villages: São Lourenço, São Barnabé, São Francisco Xavier, Nossa Senhora da Guia, São Pedro, Ipuca, and Guarulhos.[74] This interesting monograph has gathered elucidating documents on this matter. One can also profit from consulting *Regimento das câmaras Municipais* by Cortines Laxe, Rio, 1868. A. J. Macedo Soares has put out a revised and augmented second edition of this work.

Machado de Oliveira, in *Revista trimestral* 18, 200, registers the following names of villages for São Paulo: Pinheiros, Barueri, Ururari, Nossa Senhora da Ajuda do Itaquequercetuba, Emboú or Mbo, Itapecerica, and Conceição de Itanhaém.[75] The same author believes that along the Paranapanema River there were villages: São Xavier, Santo Inácio, and Encarnação.

The Indian villages in Santa Catarina, Rio Grande do Sul, Minas Gerais, Goiás, and Mato Grosso do not need to be listed.

10

Setting Boundaries

Popes Nicholas V, Calixtus II, and Sixtus IV gave the Portuguese Crown the lands and islands newly discovered under the aegis of Henry the Navigator and his immediate successors. It was a surprise for the Portuguese when the Catholic Monarchs of Spain received a similar concession after Columbus returned from his first voyage. In May 1493 Pope Alexander VI gave Spain all the land and islands discovered or to be discovered 100 leagues west of the Azores or Cape Verde Islands.

Dom João II protested this concession, alleging that the pope had infringed on Portugal's rights. After this protest he was able to enter into negotiations with the neighboring monarchs, with whom a treaty was drawn up in Tordesillas. The agreement signed on 7 June 1494 retained in principle what the Pope had declared. The world was to be divided into two hemispheres: one belonging to Portugal, the other to Spain. The number of leagues was changed, however. They were raised from 100 to 370, and the point where the counting would begin would be some unspecified island in the Cape Verde archipelago. The arrangement was merely formal and theoretical. Neither side knew what it was giving away or getting, or if it was winning or losing in this settlement.

Pedro Álvares Cabral's discovery of Brazil some years later had been preceded by Vicente Yáñez Pinzón's expedition to that region. But the Spaniards never alleged their primacy nor did they doubt that the Land of the Parrots belonged to Portugal. Their interests were located north rather than south of the equator. The south only became important after Dom Nuno Manuel's expedition.

The first doubts about the dividing line [between the two empires] arose concerning the Southern Indian Ocean. Magellan believed the Moluccas, treasured because of their spices, belonged to Spain. To prove it he undertook the voyage in which he discovered the strait that today bears his name. He carried through on Columbus's foggy and never fulfilled notion and traversed the Pacific Ocean to reach the East by sailing west. After Magellan's death, Sebastián del Cano concluded the incomparable circuit. When he reached Spain in September 1522, he displayed the same belief in his nation's rights [to those islands,] and he urged Spain to claim them. The Spanish court let itself be convinced. Between Spain and Portugal an irksome argument began in which one side argued for its priority on the basis of the discovery, and the other for the legitimacy of its control over the prestigious archipelago. The debate ended in the Zaragoza capitulation of April 1529. Admitting that the Moluccas legally belonged to the Spanish Crown, João III bought the rights to these Islands from Charles V, for 350,000 ducates. If later on it was determined that Spain had no right to them, the emperor would return the entire amount. The hemispheres would be divided 290.5 leagues east of the Moluccas. Each league would be 16.5 equatorial degrees in length.

Once the metal hatchet was raised in 1514, Solís's, Cristóvão Jacques's, Cabot's, and García's expeditions made the area around the River Plate important and brought the question of borders in America to the fore. Debates arose and dragged on and on concerning Martim Afonso de Sousa's expedition of 1530 to 1533. Portugal claimed the area through priority of discovery, Spain through legitimacy of domain. In September 1532, Dom João III expressed the idea of dividing the territory between Pernambuco and the River Plate into hereditary captaincies. In the allotments he finally made, owing to protests from Spain as well as because of Martim Afonso's astronomical observations, he stopped at 28.33° south latitude. He recognized that his domains extended no farther than that. The Spaniards, however, set their sights farther north. In 1534 Rui Mosquera established himself in Iguape. He bested Pero de Góis in an attack the latter made, and he sacked São Vicente. Several official documents of the time show the southern border of Portuguese territory to be at Cananéia and even at São Vicente.

With the union of the two kingdoms, the southern borders became less of an issue as attention was focused on the Amazon region. To counter the Dutch and English incursions, which up to then had been limited to Pará, Castelo Branco was founded. It seemed correct to put these newly conquered areas under the command of the Portuguese, since they were close at hand and better prepared to defend them. The creation of a separate government in Maranhão was a first step in this direction. Even more decisive was the creation of two hereditary captaincies, both of which were under the Portuguese Crown, but both of which lay in indisputably Spanish territory in letter and in spirit of the Treaty of Tordesillas. The captaincy of Cametá, which had been given to Feliciano Coelho de Carvalho, was bordered on the west by the right bank of the Xingu River. The Cape Norte Captaincy, which Bento Maciel Parente received, ended in the west at the Paru River. In 1639 Pedro Teixeira, on his way back from Quito, in the name of the king of Portugal took possession of the land situated between the Aguarico River (a tributary of the Napo) and the sea. He had no authority to do this, but later on his act would be invoked many times and accepted as title of ownership.

In the south settlement proceeded very slowly on Portugal's part. It followed the coast of Paraná and Santa Catarina and went on, slowly, even after 1640. For their part, the Spaniards did not bother to settle on the north bank of the River Plate. This lapse would be truly inexplicable if their right to settle there had not been in doubt. It could also be explained by their knowing that the area was inaccessible to the Portuguese.

If the Tape and Guairá reductions had survived, they would have proceeded eastward and reached the coast. If others had joined them, either the conflict could have been avoided or the victory would have gone to the Spanish. But the Jesuits only rebuilt their missions in Uruguay, and they oriented themselves toward Buenos Aires and Asunción, which, in turn, looked to the Andes and the Pacific.

On the other hand, Portuguese authors debated [where to set] the southern border according to the Treaty of Tordesillas. Some considered it to be at the outlet of the Plate, others at the Gulf of San Matias, in Patagonia. These debates became common knowledge. After the treaty was signed that recognized Portugal's independence, the king awarded a captaincy to one of Salvador Correia's grandsons.[1] Its southern border was the Plate Estuary. In 1680 the Sacramento Colony was founded on the northern bank of the River Plate, only 10 leagues from Buenos Aires.

Shortly after learning of Sacramento Colony's existence, the Spanish governor attacked the settlement and took it. When the news reached Europe it almost set off another war. Again people tried, but this time they were on firmer footing, to find the exact border stipulated by the Treaty of Tordesillas. Nothing was accomplished, however. Spain agreed to rebuild the fort and provisionally agreed to return the territory, so as to remove any friction from the debate, which would proceed on scientific grounds.

When the War of Spanish Succession broke out, the king of Portugal took sides with the Duke of Anjou, who in turn gave him the disputed territory north of the Plate. Later on Portugal switched sides and joined England on behalf of the pretender to the Austrian throne. This brought about another attack and another capture of Sacramento Colony, which remained in the hands of the enemy from 1706 to 1715. It had had, until then, a remarkable existence. Shortly after 1690 someone wrote:

> The new Sacramento Colony lives on by the grace of God. This is because they set it up as a closed presidio with men inside but without women. And in nowhere in the world have new populations arisen without men and women.

This nest was filled more with smugglers than with soldiers. It may have been the birth place of a sinister offspring—the gauchos. These long famous leeches originated on the north bank of the Plate and have yet to be totally civilized. The quantity of cowhides exported from Rio de Janeiro at the beginning of the eighteenth century cannot be explained merely by indigenous production nor by Argentine contraband. It also implicates the gaucho's summary killing of steers, which was the result of the abundance and relatively low value of bovine cattle. Horses bred like rabbits and there were wide open spaces on which they ranged.

The Treaty of Utrecht ordered the colony to be returned to Portugal. And it was returned, along with the surrounding territory, which included the entire northern bank of the Plate, according to the Portuguese. Whereas, according to the Spaniards, the surrounding area went no farther than the range of the cannons at the fortress. The Spaniards carried the day. The Portuguese tried to secure Montevideo, but their efforts came to naught. In 1735 the Spaniards again tried to take the colony and subjected it to a rigorous, 22-month siege. The fort's commander, Antônio Pedro de Vasconcelos, put up a heroic resistance, which forced the enemy to withdraw.

Sacramento Colony was to have been a point of departure for settlement starting at the Plate and running eastward to the seashore. This plan failed. The Portuguese were left with the other extreme: to settle the coast, then proceed inland toward the Plate. In other words, they would settle along the São Pedro River, which later became known as Rio Grande do Sul.

In February 1737 José da Silva Pais entered the channel that flows out of Lakes Patos and Mirim. At the place that seemed most appropriate he came ashore and built a fort. People began settle near this fort. From the Azores came several families who congregated at this primitive nucleus. The northern captaincies necessarily or voluntarily supplied not a few colonists.

Brazil's rapid expansion along the Amazon up to the Javari River, its expansion into Mato Grosso up to the Guaporé River, and its southern expansion necessitated facing head-on the matter of borders between Spanish and Portuguese possessions in the New and Old World. The matter had been constantly postponed, but it always came back to confront the two countries. The 1494 treaty had to be correctly interpreted. With this in mind the Iberian monarchs signed a treaty in Madrid on 13 January 1750.

In this document both parties acknowledged having violated the Treaty of Tordesillas. One had done it in Asia, the other in America. They began, however, by abolishing

> the line of demarcation set up in Tordesillas, because it was never determined which of the Cape Verde Islands would be used to begin counting out the 370 leagues, because of the difficulty of determining where to begin the dividing line on the northern and southern coasts of South America, and because of the moral impossibility of establishing a meridian line through the interior of the American continent.

On the same occasion they abolished all other conventions concerning borders, which would now be set by the treaty they were signing.

The line dividing the two domains, which until then had been in effect mainly on official documents, would be replaced by natural boundaries. Well-known land formations, such as the sources and courses of rivers or the most prominent mountains, would be used as landmarks. This would preclude any confusion or further dispute. Except for mutual concessions brought about by shared convenience, and to ensure that the outer reaches of each domain would be less subject to controversy, each side would keep whatever land it already held.

More importance was given to the use of rivers than to land. Both sides could use a river if both had settlements on its banks. If one side owned both banks, only it could use the river. In order to have exclusive use of the Plate, Spain traded Sacramento Colony for the missions along the Uruguay River. Two commissions were set up to determine the borders: one would head up the Amazon, the other would head up the Plate.

Francisco Xavier de Mendonça Furtado, the brother of the Marquis of Pombal, was the plenipotentiary and principal Portuguese commissioner of the Amazon Commission. As we have seen, he was already the governor of Pará when he was appointed to the border commission. On 2 October 1754, in the company of 796 people traveling in 25 boats, he set out for the Rio Negro. For his residence he chose the village of Mariuá, which was later called Barcelos. There he had dwellings built for the Spanish contingent, which would be headed by Don José de Iturriaga, whose general staff would be even larger. Iturriaga left Cádiz on 13 January 1754 and reached the Orinoco around the end of July. In 1756 he founded San Fernando de Atabapo as a stopover and way station for the great pilgrimage. From that point on he experienced such setbacks in the rugged, unpopulated backlands that, in spite of the explicit orders from his government and the extraordinary means it had given him, he spent years trying to reach his goal.

Mendonça's commission had to deal with three issues: the Negro, the Japurá, and the Madeira and Javari Rivers. Each one would require an exploration party. He took the necessary measures to organize them and, because Iturriaga had still not arrived, in 1756 he returned to Belém with the engineers brought in for the task. In Belém, other, more pressing matters absorbed his attention.

In January 1758, Mendonça received news of the impending arrival of the Spanish commission and once more set out for Barcelos. And, indeed, the following year Don José de Iturriaga arrived, along with his grandiose retinue of commissioners, mathematicians, engineers, and map makers. Almost simultaneously news arrived of Mendonça's being replaced both as governor of Pará and in the border commission. From then on Portugal's contingent would be led by Antônio Rolim de Moura, the governor of Mato Grosso. Rolim de Moura later became viceroy of Brazil and Count of Azambuja. On the same day and hour that Mendonça Furtado left for the capital, the Spanish commission returned to the Orinoco. At least this is how Baena tells the story.[2] Venezuelan and Colombian historians contest the meeting of Mendonça and Iturriaga, on better footing.

After so many years and so much trouble, not one step had been taken to carry out the ideal that had been nourished by the Treaty of Madrid. As far as Portugal's interests were concerned, this solution was not disadvantageous. Basing themselves on the doctrine of uti possidetis, they garnered tracts of land beyond which the Treaty of Madrid had given them, and their desire for land was satisfied.

During Mendonça's administration the captaincy of São José de Javari was established. The Crown had ordered Mendonça to put its capital along the Solimões River close to the western border. Mendonça found it more convenient to situate the capital on the Rio Negro. The Spaniards were far away from that point, as Iturriaga's slow march had proven. And from there Portugal could expand without setbacks. Furthermore, its relative proximity to Belém and to Portugal assured its overwhelming superiority. During Mendonça's tenure Fort Marabitanas on the Rio Negro and Fort São Joaquim were founded. Fort São Joaquim was at the confluence of the Uraricoera and Tacutu Rivers, which formed the headwaters of the Rio Branco.

According to its orders, the commission encharged with demarcating the southern region was to be divided into three parts. One would survey the terrain from Castilhos Grandes up to the Ibicuí harbor on the Uruguay River. Another would explore the Uruguay from the Ibicuí River up to the Pepiri-guaçu, and once it passed its watershed [*contravertente*], this contingent would head down the Iguaçu River until it marked the harbor on the Igureí River. These rivers are, respectively, eastern and western tributaries of the Paraná River. The third contingent was to map out the Igureí River along its entire course, then from its headwaters [*concabeçante*] it would go down to the Paraguay River, and then go up the Paraguay to the harbor of the Jauru River.

The second and third contingents carried out their tasks peacefully. The first was less fortunate. In exchange for Sacramento Colony and exclusive use of the Plate, Spain had given Portugal the Uruguay River and the seven nations of the Jesuit missions. The missions São Nicolau, São Miguel, São Luís Gonzaga, São Borja, São Lourenço, São João, and Santo Ângelo had been founded between 1687 and 1707, some of them from what was left of the reductions that had escaped the wrath of the mamalucos. To cede land with people on it is a painful amputation that continues even today. For people to give up their land and buildings and to take only what can be carried or carted away recalls Assyrian harshness. However, the two governments felt that this human outrage could be carried out with ease, if the Jesuits would help by using their influence on the Indians. The Jesuits believed they were up to the task and paid very dearly for this show of weakness, or vanity. The Indians belied or aggrandized the padres by revolting and showing that their catechism had not merely been a case of domestication. They had aquired an inner sense of self thanks to the Jesuits, who were held entirely responsible for a natural, human, and as such, inevitable rebellion.

The leaders of the commission for the southern borders (Gomes Freire de Andrada for Portugal and the Marquis of Valdelirios for Spain) met on the coastal border of Rio Grande do Sul in the beginning of September 1752. In October they began to work. In January the third marking point had been settled, and Gomes Freire left for Sacramento Colony, the Marquis for Montevideo. The first Luso-Spanish contingent went on with its task, which was supposed to take it up to the harbor on the Ibicuí. However, once it reached Santa Tecla, which was a satellite of the town of São Miguel and which was situated a bit north of the present-day city of Bagé, the band met up with armed Indians opposed to its further movement. The possibility of this had been foreseen, and there were orders from both governments to quell resistance with force of arms, since the Jesuits, as luck would have it, had been convinced of their own impotence.

Gomes Freire and Valdelirios met on Martim Garcia Island and decided to send emissaries to the missions to see if it might be possible to pacify the Indians. If they continued to be intransigent, Andoaegui, the governor of Buenos Aires, would send troops up the Uruguay River to São Borja, and Gomes Freire would proceed up the Pardo River to Santo Ângelo. After they took these two reductions, they would join forces. Andonaegui set off in March 1754, but the sorry state of his horses and other no less compelling reasons made him retreat to Daimán, close to the present-day city of Salto. Indians attacked the Spaniards there and lost 300 men, 230 of whom died. They also lost artillery, cold steel, and horses. Gomes Freire was less lucky. He was obliged to sign an armistice with the rebels on November 18.

It was obvious that the two armies would fare better if they were united. Gomes Freire set off from the Pardo River and at Sarandi, on the Rio Negro, he joined forces with Andonaegui. On 21 January 1756 they set off for the missions. About the only obstacles they encountered were those nature had created. The Indians, even though there were many of them, were poorly armed, poorly led, or without leaders. They could offer scant resistance, and they lost every battle. On May 17 São Miguel gave up without a fight, and the other towns followed this example. Now the trade could be made. Gomes Freire could take possession of the seven missions and turn Sacramento Colony over to Andonaegui. But this did not happen. Just as the original mamalucos had had, their heirs had one thing on their mind—destruction. In January 1759 Gomes Freire set sail for Rio and never returned.

Meanwhile, Fernando VI was on his deathbed, and next in line was

Carlos III, an enemy of the Treaty of Madrid since the time of his reign in Naples. One of Carlos III's first acts was to annul the treaty with the pact signed at the Pardo Palace on 12 February 1761. All the old acts governing borders were resurrected, beginning with the Treaty of Tordesillas, which had been disregarded by both sides, as had been publicly acknowledged a few years earlier. The Treaty of Madrid, precisely because it provided a solution for a centuries-old dilemma, had been violently attacked in both capitals, and the cordiality of the two monarchs who signed it was not echoed by their respective subjects. Now, both governments' representatives rightly condemned the treaty once they saw its results, which would have been easily avoided, were it not for the barbarous clause dealing with the seven tribes along the Uruguay River:

> substantially and positively stipulated in order to establish perfect harmony between the two Crowns and an unalterable union among their vassals, it has been seen that contrariwise [the Treaty of Madrid] has created and in the future would continue to create many and very frequent counterproductive controversies and challenges to such laudable goals.[3]

Portugal's insistence in not joining the famous family pact, which the Bourbons directed against England, unleashed hostilities in the peninsula as well as in South America. Pedro Cevallos, Andonaegui's successor in the Buenos Aires government, laid siege to Sacramento Colony in October 1762. He took it with little effort. He then set off for the shores of Rio Grande do Sul. This military excursion brought down the fort at Santa Teresa, close to the Chuí River. It also brought down the capital and the north shore of Lake Patos. An agreement signed at the Town of São Pedro on 6 August 1763 declared the port to be exclusively Spanish—in other words, closed to any other nation.

The treaty that was concluded in Paris on 10 February 1763 put everything back as it was before the war. Cevallos returned Sacramento Colony to the Portuguese, he kept Rio Grande, which left the Portuguese holding only the fortress on the Pardo River and the area around Viamão. Vertiz y Salcedo, the new governor in Buenos Aires, tried to snatch even these crumbs away from the Portuguese when he attacked along the Pardo in 1773. He was not as successful as he had hoped.

Portugal pretended to accept the hand Cevallos had dealt it, but it went about slyly preparing to exchange that hand for one that was more to its advantage. Without fighting, it reacquired São José do Norte, at the entrance to the harbor. It sent troops overland in dribs and drabs. A squadron entered the channel in spite of the enemy's fortresses. In March 1776, combined land and sea forces attacked and took the Spanish fortifications. In April the vila, or township, of São Pedro was evacuated. Spain had ruled for 13 years. The fortune of Porto dos Casais, today's Porto Alegre, dates from the time of Spanish rule.

Many of the Portuguese colonists who had been transplanted beyond the Chuí never returned to their old estates.

Scarcely did word of the reconquest of São Pedro River reach the Old World, than a fleet was put together in Spain to avenge this affront. The fleet was headed by Cevallos, who had been named viceroy of the newly created Viceroyalty of Rio de la Plata. He was to capture Santa Catarina, Rio Grande do Sul, and Sacramento. When the enemy showed its face, Santa Catarina gave up without a fight. Rio Grande was spared an attack by sea thanks to unfavorable winds. When it was about to be attacked by land, an order arrived to cease all hostility. Cevallos, as if he had a personal vendetta against Sacramento, that centuries-old bone of contention between the two peoples, refused to leave a wall standing. On 8 June 1777 he began with the fortress. Once it was demolished, houses were destroyed, and the port obstructed. The families that refused to return to Brazil were taken to Buenos Aires then relocated along the road to Perú.

With the death of José I and with the truculent Marquis of Pombal's loss of power, a queen ascended to the Portuguese throne for the first time ever. All of this must have added a note of reconciliation to the border treaty signed in Santo Ildefonso on 1 October 1777. In almost every aspect this treaty was similar to the Treaty of Madrid, but it was more humane and generous because it imposed no harsh exoduses.

The notion of uti possidetis, acknowledged in 1750 and annulled in 1761, prevailed once more. Were it not for the relative superiority of the Portuguese position in the disputed zones, an historian might conclude ironically that Spain's desire to hold onto the Philippines caused that country to make all the concessions that it did to Portugal.

The most notable modifications affected the southern border. Spain no longer agreed that Portugal should have the right to travel on the Uruguay River. For this reason it imposed a border in which Portuguese possessions would only touch the Uruguay east of the Pepiri-guaçu River. Following a principle set down in the Treaty of Madrid, whose article 22 did not permit hilltop border fortifications or towns, article 6 of the Treaty of Santo Ildefonso established that beginning with Lakes Mirim and Mangueira there would be sufficient space between the borders of both nations, albeit not necessarily as wide as the aforementioned lakes. In this space no towns will be built by either party [to this treaty], nor will either side build fortresses, outposts, or guardhouses for troops. Thus, these spaces shall be neutral and clearly set off with obvious markers letting the vassals of each nation know the point beyond which they must not go. To this end we shall seek rivers and lakes as fixed and unalterable boundaries. Otherwise, we shall use the peaks of the more prominent mountains, and they and their slopes will serve as a natural and dividing boundary where neither nation can enter, settle, or build fortifications.[4]

Four commissions were created to mark the border. The first would operate from the Chuí to the Iguaçu River; the second, from the Iguareí to the Jauru; the third, from the Jauru to the Japurá; and the fourth, from the Japurá to the Rio Negro. On Portugal's side, these divisions were under the command of the viceroy in Rio, and under the governors of São Paulo, Mato Grosso, and Pará. Actual work was limited to the area between the Chuí and the Iguaçu and from the Javari to the Japurá. The work went on through years of subtle arguments, delays, and inaction— as both sides blamed each other. The commissions under the governors of São Paulo and Mato Grosso never met up with their Spanish counterparts. One could say that [knowledge of] the geography of each region came out the winner since scientists explored rivers, described plants and animals, and sent curious specimens from the three kingdoms to the overseas establishment. One could say this, if that jealously guarded work had been made public.

Two episodes will show how the work proceeded. The Treaty of Madrid in articles 5 and 6, repeated in articles 8 and 9 of the Treaty of Santo Ildefonso, determined that the frontier above the Iguaçu harbor would go upward along the Paraná riverbed until the point where it was joined on the west by the Iguareí River. It would follow the Iguareí until it came to the next river flowing from the same headwaters, a tributary of the Paraguay River, perhaps called the Corrientes.[5]

According to Sá de Faria, a Portuguese who had gone to work for Spain, near the Iguaçu there is no river by the name of Iguareí that empties into the Paraná on the western side and that can serve as a boundary. And there is no river in Paraguay known as the Corrientes. It was then agreed that the border would begin at the Iguatemi, the first eastern tributary of the Paraná above the Sete Quedas area. Later on the viceroy of Brazil wrote to Buenos Aires and claimed that the agreement had depended on the non-existence of the Iguareí, which in fact existed—below the Sete Quedas area. Cândido Xavier had discovered it, and it corresponded to the Jejuí in Paraguay. The line dividing the two nations should run along the Iguareí and the Jejuí.

Félix de Azara, the Spanish commissioner, responded that the viceroy of Brazil was right. The agreement had been conditional and became null and void once the Iguareí was shown to exist. And it did exist: it is the Iaguareí, the Monici, or Ivinheima, and has a mighty counterpart in Paraguay that joins the Paraná at 22°. This, he added, will give us the only dry land in that region. We shall have meadows, clay pits, nitrate deposits, pastures, water holes, and forests. Shipments from Cuiabá and Mato Grosso will fall into our hands at the mouth of the Taquari, or farther up. We will be able to drain its wealth through dealings that will be to our advantage and cause us little harm. The famous establishments in Mato Grosso, Cuiabá, and the Paraguay Mountains are precarious for their illegitimate owners and with time will fall into our hands.

> It is not possible that we cannot take possession of the mines in Cuiabá and Mato Grosso, since we can attack them with competent force brought in on the best river in the world. And the Portuguese will not be able to retain those places, or even get to them, except on that tight and obstructed waterway, the Taquari River. And at that they will have to travel in canoes and face difficulties of which no one is ignorant.[6]

Were the Portuguese any better? A brief narration of the Chermont-Requena case will supply a satisfactory response.

The commission was to mark the border from the Javari to the westernmost mouth of the Japurá and then follow the Japurá upwards until it found a river that would safeguard the Portuguese establishments along the Rio Negro. The westernmost mouth of the Japurá gave rise to serious arguments because one side gave the name "mouth" to a channel which carried water from the Solimões River to the Japurá. Whereas the other side called the channel a "puncture", because it brought water to the Japurá rather than carrying it away. Concerning the river that should safeguard the Portuguese possessions along the Rio Negro, was it the Apaporis, the Comiari, the Enganos, or some other river? In view of the numerous waterways, imaginary or real, but that the Portuguese alleged existed, nothing was ever decided. At any rate, Tabatinga lay west of the westernmost mouth of the Japurá. It was actually west of the Içá River. And it was never included in the wildest claims of the Portuguese. When, however, Requena claimed possession of Tabatinga, Chermont refused to take such grave responsibility and deferred his authority to João Pereira

Caldas, who led that expedition. Pereira Caldas declared himself willing to hand Tabatinga over to the Spaniards if they would give him Fort São Carlos on the upper Rio Negro, which had been founded on Don José de Iturriaga's abortive commission during the first attempt at demarcation.

Requena spent 10 years haggling. Finally he received permission from his king to return to Europe, and the Portuguese king allowed him to come by way of Pará.

> Under order of the governor of Rio Negro, he was accompanied by Lieutenant Colonel José Simões de Carvalho, an engineer who had been secretly told to guide the trip in such a way that Requena would not see a single town nor be able to make topographic notations of any part of the Amazon region. The governor of Pará had him billeted at the Val de Cães Ranch, where he was almost under house arrest until he set off for Europe. When he came to Belém on official business, he was permitted to come only at night and in the company of a regular army officer. During these visits he was also received by noteworthy citizens, who, according to the governor's wishes, treated him with great ceremony.

In sum, the commissioners of the two contracting powers were put to good use. Whoever might affirm their bad faith may or may not be right; either opinion would, however, be superficial. The terms of the treaties lent themselves to more than one interpretation. The maps brought from Portugal did not correspond to the lay of the land. Neither the maps nor the terrain were responsible for contrived interpretations. Each public servant tried to put his best foot forward, i.e. each one tried to advance his career. In the schools of neighboring countries, when students learn these individuals' names, they also inherit a hatred for Brazil propagated by their teachers. Fortunately, in Brazil we are no longer prisoners of inferior passions typical of fossilized colonials.

Portugal came out ahead because it had created the independent captaincy of Mato Grosso immediately after the 1750 treaty,[7] as well as the subordinate captaincy of Rio Negro shortly thereafter. From Vila Bela one could see that the Portuguese faced a two-fold problem. They would have to absorb the navigation on the Madeira River, which would paralyze hostilities coming from nearby Moxo and Chiquito Indian villages. This was mainly done by Count Azambuja. They would also have to extend their domain beyond the Xarais area, up to where the Paraguay River never floods. This would limit the possibility of surprises and attacks and guarantee navigation to São Paulo. To this end Luís de Albuquerque founded Corumbá and Coimbra, and Caetano Pinto founded Miranda. In the subordinate captaincy Mendonça Furtado understood the importance of the Negro and Branco Rivers. By choosing Barcelos as the capital, he set out clearly the path his successors were to follow. Both in Mato Grosso and in Rio Negro there were minor, unimportant conflicts in which the Spaniards fared no better than the Portuguese, who went on in their original manner of understanding and applying the principle of uti possidetis.

The inane border disputes were still going on in 1801, when war broke out between Portugal and Spain. The treaties lapsed ipso facto. José Borges do Canto, a deserter from a dragoon regiment, and Manuel dos Santos Pedroso, under orders from no one, gathered a handful of adventurers and attacked the seven nations along the Uruguay River. They went, they saw, they conquered. The Ibicuí River once more became a boundary.

After this, there were no more disputes between the two Iberian capitals over American borders.

The account of the borders with France and Holland, from the Rio Branco in the west to Cape Orange in the east, can be told in a few words.

The captaincy of Cape Norte, given to Bento Maciel Parente, ended along the shoreline at the Vicente Pinzón River, which the Indians called the Oiapoque. Scarcely had the French planted roots in Cayenne than they cast greedy eyes over the Amazon River, demanding it as their southern border.

To shore up their claims, in 1697 they took the Portuguese forts at Araguari, Toeré, and Macapá—which the Portuguese quickly recaptured. A provisional treaty signed in 1701 made the territory neutral, but the Treaty of Utrecht gave it back to the Portuguese. According to the unequivocal article 8, his Most Christian Majesty gave up:

> in the strongest and most authentic terms and with all the clauses that are required, both in his name and in those of his descendants, successors, and heirs; all and whatever right or claim he can or may have on the lands known as Cape Norte and situated above the Amazon and Iapoc or Vicente Pinsão Rivers, without reserving or retaining any portion whatsoever of said lands, so that they may be from this day on possessions of His Portuguese Majesty.[8]

This disposition, owing to its clarity, left no room for doubt. However, the French were able to perpetuate doubt by discovering another Vicente Pinzón River and another Oiapoque, which enabled them to draw as near as possible to the Amazon, their real and constant objective. They managed to do this during the French Revolution and the Empire. The Treaty of Paris (23 Thermidor V [between July 19 and August19]) drew the border along the Caloene River up to its headwaters and from there the border continued as a straight line up to the Rio Branco. The Treaty of Badajoz (6 June 1801) moved the border to the Araguari River, beginning at the outlet farthest from Cape Norte up to the headwaters and from there to the Rio Branco. The Treaty of Madrid (29 September 1801) set the border on the Carapanatuba River from its outlet to its headwaters, from where it would follow the contour of the mountain range dividing the waters up to the nearest point on the Rio Branco, which was around 2.33° north latitude. The Treaty of Amiens, 27 March 1802, brought the border back to the Araguari.[9] All of these treaties lapsed with the Treaty of Fontainebleu, which dismembered Portugal and occasioned the transfer of the Portuguese court to Brazil.

After having passed the Branco and having reached the Rupunini River around the year 1750, the Portuguese approached the Dutch possessions. However, they never had contact or conflict with the Dutch, nor was there ever any [border] agreement between the two capitals.

11

Three Centuries Later

Three centuries after its discovery, Brazil had a population of more than one million. If the people were spread out evenly over the land that Lisbon claimed was hers, each individual would have two or three square kilometers.

There were people living along the coast from Marajó Island down to the Chuí, as well as along both shores of the Amazon, from its mouth up to Tabatinga and the Javari River. Along its tributaries in this basin, settlements were erected close to harbors, preferably near the muddy water streams. The Rio Negro settlements were different because concerns about the border pushed natural expansion farther inward, up the Madeira, Tapajós, and Tocantins Rivers, which flow from Goiás and Mato Grosso. Beginning at Piauí, the coastal line had as parallels one or more interior lines of settlements on the banks of rivers and on the plateaus along the Parnaíba, the São Francisco, and the Paraná, as well as in the regions between these rivers. These lines were constantly interrupted. It would be better to call them points along which lines could be drawn.

By observing settlers' geographic distribution, one can see two easily distinguishable trends. Spontaneous settlement tended toward continuity and sought the periphery in the west, north, and south. The voluntary trend, which was determined by governmental measures and by the desire for land or strategic advantage, came out scattered and disconnected. It started on the periphery and took off in opposite directions. In the gold fields the irregular distribution of mineral deposits produced a scattering of centers at first and was later corrected, where correction was possible.

Most of the population was racially mixed. And the mixtures varied in composition according to each locale. In the Amazon region the Indian element prevailed. Mamalucos abounded, mulattos were rare. In the cattle-raising regions there were few blacks, and many Indians were assimilated. On the coast and in the mining districts blacks were in ascendance, with all possible derivatives from this base. South of the Tropics the percentage of whites rose. Of the three irreducible races, each one originating on a different continent but forced to live side by side, pure Africans were there in greatest numbers owing to the waves of them brought in every year by slave traders.

In the Amazon lowlands the predominance of water and forests hampered agriculture and the raising of livestock. Farming was done only around the larger settlements, and it was limited to sugar cane, coffee, some cereal crops, and manoic. Manioc was made into water flour [*farinha d'água*], which withstood humidity better. *Tucupi* or *manipuera* [spiced manioc juice] was used to make a well-liked sauce. It was also used raw to catch birds. Bovine cattle were raised on Marajó Island, near the Paru River, in Óbidos, along the Tapajós, and on the fields along the Rio Branco; but were not enough to satisfy local appetites. Even fewer horses were raised. Boats were almost the only means of transportation. They ranged from *montaria* canoes (the horse's true heir as the name "montaria" suggests) to the huge canoes that carried hundreds of arrobas at a time, and that were sent upstream by the prevailing winds during part of the year.

People ate fish. Fresh fish was caught daily using the various and ingenious processes inherited from the natives. Mullet, Piracu, and manatees were [dried] and preserved in salt. People also ate turtles, which became more and more abundant farther west, either because that was how they were originally distributed or because the devastation process had not yet reached that area. Turtles were the cows of the Amazon. People called them river cattle. They could be corralled by the hundreds. They produced a butter substitute. One species' egg yolk was drunk like milk in coffee. Its oil, besides being eaten, was also used for lighting. These turtles' shells were not shiny and therefore could not be used to make delicate objects. They were, however, used as bowls.

Extraction of forest produce: cacao, parsley, piassaba palm, and clove kept the masculine population busy during parts of the year marked by high or low water levels of the inland sea. During these periods, the village population was reduced to old men, women, and children. Women, often showing their artistic talents, made pottery and painted vessels fashioned from gourds. They also spun thread and wove cloth. The *seringeira* or rubber plant was known and used for manufacturing household objects such as the syringes for which it was named or for waterproofing boots and cloth. Not by a long shot was anyone aware of how important rubber would become once modern processes of polymerizing it were discovered.

During the time of Pombal, Friar João de São José described the situation which came to pass in Pará after his writing:

> They ordinarily seem not to worry about the state. If they have a hammock, manioc flour, and a pipe, they are satisfied. Frugality at the table is permitted if it is in line [*coerente*] with the amount of drinking. As far as the rest is concerned, it can be summed up in the following verse or quatrain:

> Life in Pará
> Is a life of ease:
> Gulp down your food,
> Rock off to sleep.[1]

Going from the Amazon Basin to the cattle raising area, the lack of forests and the scarcity of water became immediately obvious. There was only forest on the banks of the mightiest rivers, on some humid lowlands, and on mountains around 1,000 or more meters in height. Water, except for the permanent rivers, was found only in *ipueiras* [river overflows] and swamps, at springs, and at natural wells that varied in size and constancy. Otherwise, water had to be found in the earth's breast. It was easy to find in the dry beds of rivers, elsewhere finding water was an arduous and frustrating task. Generally, water was hardly tasty, owing to the saline quality of the ground that filtered it. The soil's salinity, the abundance of juicy grass, and the accommodating nature of the open fields determine whether bovine cattle will proliferate. They ranged freely most of the time. During calving time cows were brought into corrals because of the special care calves would require, as well as for milking and the production of cheese and *requeijão*, or farmer cheese. If the weird product people kept in jugs, which they would heat before pouring the contents out, deserved to be called butter, it was not worth much.

Cattle did not merely graze on the open range. They lived in the thickets and on the mountains. Cowboys chased after them. They used a rod with spikes located at various points along its length, or they merely grabbed steers by the tail to knock them down and catch them. According to Koster:

On the man's approach, the ox runs off into the nearest wood; and the man follows as closely as he possibly can, so that he may take advantage of the opening of the branches which is made by the beast, as these quickly close again, resuming their former situation. At times the ox passes under a low and thick branch of a large tree, then the man likewise passes under the branch, and that he may do this, he leans to the right side so completely, as to enable him to lay hold of the girth of the saddle with his left hand, and at the same time his left heel catches the flap of the saddle. Thus with the pole in his right hand, almost trailing upon the ground, he follows without slackening his pace, and being clear of this obstacle, again resumes his seat. If he can overtake the ox, he runs his goad into its side, and if this is dexterously done, he throws it. Then he dismounts, and ties the animal's legs together, or places one foreleg over one of the horns, which secures it most effectually. Many blows are received by these men, but it is seldom that deaths occur.[2]

Popular tradition had celebrated some of the more famous rogue steers, such as Surubim, or "Channel Cat," Geralda's Passion, and the great Espaço. (That is, "Espaço" or "spaced" because his horns were widely spaced, and not "Space" [espácio] as José de Alencar called him and others repeated afterwards.)

Sílvio Romero published the following ballad in the voice of the steer known as Geralda's Passion:

> The chase was long and mighty ugly
> On Chapada Mountain Trail.
> I'd found out, but 'twas too late,
> There was a cowboy on my tail.
>
> Before me lay a tree trunk
> On the slope down to the gulch:
> The horse went underneath it,
> The horseman sailed above.
>
> I picked up speed and ran
> Down the river route.
> The horse rolled down the gully.
> The cowboy hit the dirt.[3]

Equine cattle were well suited to the backlands, but did not proliferate the way bovines did because they could not find proper fodder. Perhaps the lack of food rather than the lack of breeding is responsible for Brazilian horses' small size. At any rate, their ability to work is without comparison, and their small size made them well suited for chasing through the brambles. Trips always came to a halt during the hottest periods of the day. And the horses were not shod, since their hooves were hard enough to withstand the flinty ground. Mules were almost, if not entirely, absent in the beginning. There were few sheep and goats. And goats only began to be raised during the last 30 years [of the colonial period], once people recognized the superior quality of their skin.

Meat was naturally part of the food supply, but in proportions smaller than one might imagine. A steer had great relative value because with Bahia and Pernambuco nearby there were great markets for them. Besides, the Parnaíba and São Francisco backlands, and the streams originating at the same points, produced the cattle that supplied and overran Minas Gerais, Goiás, and, indirectly, Mato Grosso. Supplying those areas with cattle made beef even more expensive because it strained the source. And one should not forget the calamitous droughts. All this means that people ate jerky made from beef or from the meat of smaller animals, preferably sheep.

In the beginning nothing was planted, since people considered the land to be sterile. Later on, beans, corn, manioc, and even sugar cane were introduced. Even today there are three festive times during the backlanders' year: the fresh corn harvest, the manioc harvest, and cane grinding time. When dried corn was not used exclusively to feed horses, it was toasted or popped and used to make cuscus from time to time. It was also used to make *aluá*, an insipid fermented beverage. Fresh corn was either boiled or roasted, or made into *pamonha* corn cakes, or *canjica* mush (very different in the northern and southern regions of Brazil). For several weeks fresh corn relieved the monotony of the other meals. *Farinhada*, a dish made from soft manioc flour, *beijus*, pancakes made with coconut or greens, tapiocas, and other puddings [*grudes*], and the jovial scenes in which manioc roots were scraped made for days of conviviality and cordiality. During grinding time, sugar cane was roasted, there was cane juice or *garapa* to drink, almond paste, rapadura, and molasses.

These festivities, except for the corn festival, which was probably inherited from the Indians, presupposed the existence of "big houses" where wealthy proprietors lived. They also entailed the existence of slaves who worked the land. Nearby lived the free but dedicated tenant farmers. Often, because of futile disagreements between the owners of two big houses, issues arose that could put entire populations up in arms. Typical of this phenomenon are the fights between the Montes and the Feitosas in Ceará. The mechanical inventions, which in the eighteenth century revolutionized the textile industry and increased the use of cotton, caused cotton to be planted in the remote backlands, whose standard of living rose.

The owners of big houses, just as all males did, except when they traveled, went around wearing only undergarments and a shirt. The shirt generally had rosaries, relics, and prayers carefully sewn on it. They wore a scapular around their neck. On solemn occasions, when visitors were received, the plantation owner wore a kimono, a long frock coat [*timão*], or a robe. According to Koster, "when a Brazilian takes to wearing one of these long gowns, he begins to think himself a gentleman, and entitled, consequently, to much respect."[4] Women's household garb consisted of blouses and skirts; the short jacket or *casebeque* was a late arrival. Single women slept together in a gynoceum called a *camarinha* or "little chamber." They did not show their face to outsiders. It was common for a bride and a groom to set eyes on one another for the first time at their wedding. Necklaces were the most highly prized [female] adornment, and the number of them a woman had was somewhat indicative of her status. Peddlers penetrated into distant briar patches and brought golden jewels, cloth, and household utensils. When these objects were traded for cattle, they would rent people to round the cattle up, and they could go back [to the city] with many head of cattle. The same thing happened with tithe collectors and even with traveling churchmen. One phenomenon of that region that still exists are the fairs—of cattle or whatnot. Some of these fairs begat towns.

The cattle raising region began a little above the mouth of the São Francisco. It ran along the river's banks until it reached the border with Minas Gerais. It extended up and beyond the Tocantins and Parnaíba watersheds and, in a weakened state, it reached the upper Itapicuru. It took in the streams of all the rivers on the slope between All Saints Bay and Tutóia. In spots it came very close to the seashore. At Ilhéus and Porto Seguro the Espinhaço Mountains and their coastal forests separated cattle from the sea. In Pernambuco something similar happened. Since the lines of communication ran parallel to the São Francisco River at greater or lesser distances, the great bulk of backlanders found it easier and more to their advantage to deal with Bahia. Between the two provinces an area varying in length and width was left deserted. The road between Pajeú and Capibaribe, which dates from the early years of the nineteenth century, remedied this anomaly.

As we have seen, one can ascribe to Pernambuco the outer backlands from Paraíba to the Acaracu River in Ceará. Bahia's are the inner backlands, from the São Francisco River up to southwest Maranhão. Between the residents of one or another region there must have been some more or less detectable differences. They may be determined some day, when missionaries' and superior court judges' [*corregedores*] accounts are made public. At any rate the similarities among the inhabitants of both backland regions are greater than those among any other inhabitants of Brazil.

Along the São Francisco, Bahians, Pernambucans, and Paulistas met up with one another. To the south and to the west one can determine fairly well the farthest reaches of the two currents by marking the places where high points are no longer preferred for settlement. This area is well beyond the points where there is a danger of flooding and where water mills are used.

Preference for building houses in the lowlands, the use of the water mill or *monjolo* to crush dried corn, corn as a habitual foodstuff (eaten as southern style *canjica*, as *fubá* or Indian meal, or fermented before the final roasting), or the preference for pork over beef indicate the presence of Paulistas or their descendants. At the root of all these scattered offshoot populations is the lack of salt, which precluded the rapid development of bovine cattle and which even today is not used to season *angu* or canjica (local corn meal mush). Pork, despite the huge local market, later on became an export item, as salt pork [*toucinho*] or on the hoof.

For the rough, hilly country, mules imported from beyond the Uruguay River worked better than horses. They were more steady, more sure-footed and resistant. Trips were not divided as they were in the north. They dragged on slowly from sunup to sundown. Mounts were shod. On the most traveled roads, next to trading posts that sold corn, there were blacksmiths whose services constantly required using the terrible cauldrons.

Gold, once the initial hubbub had passed, was almost entirely left to panners. Iron mining, which, according to Eschwege,[5] had been learned from Africans, showed little promise owing partly to outmoded techniques, but mainly because of the lack of firewood, which had been misused wantonly. Agriculture, in addition to the normal cereal crops, profited from the planting of cotton. Cotton from Minas Novas was especially appreciated for its high quality. Coffee planting began relatively late, once people recognized the superiority of the mountain regions over those along the shore near Rio. From its very beginning coffee planting assumed its enduring characteristics.

Auguste Saint-Hilaire[6] asked one of his countrymen who knew the area what coffee planters spent their money on. He answered:

As you can see, it's not on building beautiful houses nor on furnishing them. They eat rice and beans. Their clothes cost them very little. Nor do they spend money on their children's education. Indeed, their children wallow in ignorance. They are entirely unaware of society's pleasures. But their money comes from coffee, and coffee cannot be gathered except by blacks. It is, then, on the purchase of blacks that all their income is spent, and their increased wealth is used to satisfy their vanity rather than to increase their pleasure. They do not live luxuriously. Nothing advertises their wealth. However, in the surrounding area everyone knows how many slaves and how many coffee trees planters have. They stand tall and are pleased and satisfied with themselves, even though they can hardly be distinguished from poor people—were it not for the vain renown that extends a few shotgun shots beyond their houses.[7]

Setups this meager and bereft may have been the norm in recently tamed areas, but in areas that had been settled for longer periods the spectacle was quite different. Martius wrote:

For the far-off coffee plantations between Vila Rica and the edge of the diamond region, all help from society at large is missing. Each wealthy planter is, for that reason, obliged to train his slaves to do everything that is needed. Thus it is common that at every plantation there are all sorts of tradesmen: shoemakers, weavers, sawyers, blacksmiths, masons, potters and brick makers, hunters, miners, gardeners; as well as all of their equipment and tools. Supervising everything is the overseer or *feitor*, who is usually a mulatto or a trustworthy black. The daily routine is determined as it is in convents. The owner simultaneously performs the duties of agent of the king [*regedor*], judge, and doctor on his property. Often there is a clergyman on the premises or one comes from the surrounding area to celebrate Mass in the plantation's private chapel.[8]

Since some friars played prominent roles in early rebellions, Lisbon severely prohibited the establishment of monasteries in the three gold producing captaincies. And, peculiarly, it was unwavering in this prohibition. The friars of Saint Peter's Habit were brought from abroad in great numbers. Later on, once the diocese of Mariana was created under Dom João V and Pope Benedict XIV, these friars were ordained in Ribeirão do Carmo.

After Dom Joaquim Borges de Figueiroa was named Bishop of Mariana in 1782, innumerable individuals have been needlessly and wantonly ordained. There are today some cases of men being made into priests who had learned a mechanic's trade and who had served as foot soldiers. Even though the governor of the bishopric, Dr. Francisco Xavier da Rua, under the aegis of said bishop, had ordained all the priests that were necessary, they were not enough to prohibit his successor, Dr. José Justino de Oliveira Godim, from ordaining 101 candidates in three years. He did this needlessly, disregarding their illegitimate births and their status as mulattos. Dr. Inácio Correia de Sá, who succeeded José Justino in governing the bishopric, ordained 84 candidates in less than seven months. One of these was in debt to the royal treasury.[9]

The ease with which priests were ordained only began to disappear during the nineteenth century.

One quickly understands why there were so many religious celebrations by taking into account the overabundance of priests, the many religious brotherhoods, the general appeal of music, the proximity of towns in the region where the yellow metal was first extracted, the numerous idlers supported by indigenous hospitality and indifference, and the lack of public entertainment. Processions were especially noteworthy because of their lavishness, their many symbolic figures, and their theatricality and buffoonery. Far off in Traíras, Goiás, Pohl[10] attended a feast of Santa Ifigênia, the blacks' patron saint, which was complete down to the last detail: there was an emperor, an empress, cannon blasts, incense burners waved before the rulers, jousts on horseback, lances, auctions, etc.[11]

Mineiros and Paulistas seemed quite different in appearance. According to Martius:

> Mineiros are generally slim and trim, with a narrow chest, long neck, a somewhat elongated face, bright, black eyes, with black hair on their heads and chests. They possess a natural noble pride and outwardly appear mild-mannered, affable and intelligent. They are sober and seem to like their gentlemanly way of life. In all their features they look more like the ardent Pernambucans rather than like the weighty Paulistas. Their local dress is different from the Paulista's. Normally they wear a short coat made from cotton or black Manchester [wool?], a white vest with gold buttons, velvet or wool [Manchester] pants, long, white, leather boots fastened by buckles above the knee. A wide-brimmed felt hat protects them from the sun. Out of doors their inseparable companions include a sword, often a musket, and an umbrella. Even the shortest trips are traveled on the backs of mules. Their stirrups and reins are made of silver, as is the metal butt of the dagger Mineiros carry below the knee in their boots. On these journeys women are carried in sedan chairs by blacks or animals. Or they sit on a seat fastened to the mule. They wear long blue riding garb and round hats.[12]

The Paulistas' short stature, their straight [*corrido*] hair, their pale faces, and penetrating eyes betray their American background, according to Eschwege, who, contrary to Martius, adds:

> Their courage, their indifference to danger, their agility and their spirit of initiative, their scorn for toil, and their thirst for vengeance testify to their savage background on their mothers' sides; just as their manners and their vivaciousness of spirit betray their Portuguese ancestry on the part of their fathers.

However, even though Martius described Paulistas as weighty [*pesadão*], he was only referring to their physical appearance, since he had just written:

> Paulistas are known throughout Brazil for their extreme frankness, their fearlessness, and their storybook love for adventure and danger. Mixed in with this is their passionate temperament, which allows them to become enraged and vengeful. Their pride and inflexibility are feared by their neighbors. . . . Many Paulistas are free from cross with Indians. Mamalucos, according to their degree of mixture, have skin that ranges from almost coffee color, to yellow, or almost white. More than anything else, what betrays an Indian mixture is a wide face, with prominent cheekbones, black, not large eyes, and a certain furtiveness in their looks. Tall but broad in stature, strong features, a sense of freedom and boldness, brown or from time to time blue eyes that are full of fire and daring, thick, straight, black hair, abundant musculature, forthright and rapid in movement—these are the main features that characterize the look of a Paulista. In general their character can be described as melancholic, and choleric. . . . In no other part of Brazil are there so many cholerics and hysterics as there are here.[13]

He goes on:

> In São Paulo men and women always travel on horseback, or on mules. Often a man will have a woman riding behind him, on his mount's hindquarters. Riders wear wide-brimmed brown felt hats, a blue poncho, which is long and wide, in the middle of which there is a hole to fit it over one's head. They wear dark cotton jackets and pants; long, undyed boots which are tightened at the knee by a strap and a snap. They carry long, silver-handled knives stuck in their boots or in their sashes. They use these knives for eating and for other tasks. Women wear long overcoats and round hats. According to a current proverb, the men, not the women, are highly regarded in Bahia; in Pernambuco it is the women not the men who are admired; and in São Paulo it is both men and women. From time to time in this province one hears people say: if we were not the first to discover the gold mines, we would still be well thought of in the country

thanks to canjica and hammocks, because we picked them up first from the Indians.

São Paulo canjica, also known as *preguiça* "sloth" or *negro velho* "old black man," was prepared by the water mill. It was prevalent in the areas where there was moving water, and it was not necessary to use mortars and pestals to grind corn. In the northern backlands, where such abundance of water was not common, *munguzá*, canjica's northern counterpart, was only eaten in the big houses, and slaves did the grinding.

Martius credits Paulistas with having discovered the medicinal properties of indigenous plants without the help of the Indians. Beginning at Pindamonhangaba people with goiters became noticeable. And in general Paulistas carried this trait wherever they went.

> Often their throats are totally engulfed by the large swelling. However they seem to consider this deformity a mark of beauty. Indeed, it is not rare to see women with enormous goiters decorated with gold and silver. They sit in plain view in front of their houses with a pipe in their mouth or spinning cotton.[14]

At the beginning of the [nineteenth] century, Paulistas began to awaken from their hibernation owing to the mines and from the great exoduses mines had caused in São Paulo. Agriculture once more came to life. There were numerous sugar mills and distilleries. People still doubted that the climate was suitable for large-scale cotton and coffee planting. The most important source of income was in the transport industry: from Mato Grosso, Goiás, parts of Minas Gerais, and from the southern backlands. The famous Sorocaba fair was already in operation.

People in Goiás were known as "Paulistas minus vitality." They were known to be adverse to marriage.

According to some statistics taken from the work of Pohl for the year 1804, there were 7,273 white people, 15,585 mulattos, 7,992 blacks, 19,285 slaves—a total of 50,135 inhabitants. Discounting the 24,371 females and the 7,868 female slaves, about whom he gives no information, there were 809 married white women, 1,668 married mulatto women, and 575 married black women—a total of 3,052 married women. There were 2,663 single white women, 6,639 single mulatto women, 4,179 single black women—a total of 13,481.[15] With this synopsis we can see that there were numerous African elements in the population.

People in Cuiabá to a certain extent resembled Mineiros. Within them lay a bloodthirsty streak, which they may have learned from the

Guaicuru Indians. It burst forth during the period of the regency, and it has come forth with greater frequency since the proclamation of the republic, in 1889. People living along the Paraguay and Guaporé Rivers were weak and sickly.

There were many cattlemen living on the open fields of Paraná, but the real pasturelands of the south were in Rio Grande do Sul.

Except for the still unpopulated slopes of the mountain range and a few scattered forests and some stretches along the rivers, the entire territory was covered with succulent grasses that were propitious for the raising both of steers and of horses. And there was no need to distribute salt. There was abundant water year round. There were no drought years. There were no thorny thickets or *catingas* typical of other, less favored regions. The ratio of horses to steers was far greater than in the north. Suffice it to say that there were herds of mustangs: wild, ownerless horses. And owners only knew their horses by their brand. They killed mares for their hides. For long journeys a single mount was not sufficient; one took a herd.

How different this is from the northern backlands, where there were few horses, all of whom were well known and well studied. A saddle horse was trained to step, to trot, to joust, to canter, and to execute all the other speeds and styles for which there are capable trainers. A horse was almost a family member!

When settlement began these animals were already swarming in the area. They had come from the destroyed Jesuit missions. People took whatever they needed. The use of bolas and lassos, adapted from the Charrua Indians, obviated the violent chases through the backland thickets of Bahia and Pernambuco. The price of cattle was to an extent negative. There was too much for the local population and nowhere to export it. To consume it wantonly seemed an act of prudence, since it [the remaining cattle] could be more easily tamed, and the pastures would not be overburdened. Roundups were all that were needed once the situation became stable. And people considered them more fun than work.

Aires de Casal writes:

> It was all-out war against calves, and normally one did not suffice for two comrades' dinner. If both of them wanted tongue, they considered it more fitting to kill a second calf than to share the first one. There were men who would kill a steer in the morning to eat roast kidneys. And they would not be bothered carrying around a slab of meat for dinner, so wherever they would end the day, they would kill a steer that caught their eye. There was no banquet in which a recently born calf was not served.[16]

Little by little, people stopped eating salt, manioc flour (gulped down in Pará), and any other accompaniments. The scarcity of firewood made it necessary for people to eat their meat almost raw. It was singed in fires made from animal droppings or twigs, and almost always eaten without chewing. People believed maté had the power to lessen the ill effects of this diet. Maté first made its appearance in the Guairá backlands and was propagated by the Jesuits.

The slightly undulating surface, the almost omnipresent open fields, the ease with which food was secured, and the abundance of mounts kept people on the move. They traveled mainly during the summer—when it rarely rained, when the rivers had little water, and the number of fords increased. The importance of fords in captaincies without bridges can be seen in the countless passages providing place-names. They sometimes used *pelotas*, or fragile leather-covered canoes to cross rivers. So in passing let it be known that there was also a leather age in this region.

People slept in the open air. Their mount's gear was used as a bed. They would stretch out the *carona*, a leather blanket used under the saddle. They put a sheepskin over the carona. And on top of this they would sleep, wrapped up in their poncho with their head sticking out and using the saddle as a pillow.

Since the border, a most disputed border, went through that region, the tendency toward nomadism became marked. Both sides wanted to expand into the other's territory, and both entered the neutral area, where neither had a right to be, but where they constantly trespassed, especially those from Rio Grande do Sul. There were not many all-out battles, but there were almost daily surprise attacks, whippings [*arreatas*], single encounters, and incursions by smugglers. People from Rio Grande do Sul inevitably became adventurers and soldiers. They only respected the military. They gave Saint-Hilaire the title of colonel. They called anyone a *baiano* or a hillbilly [*maturango*] if they could not ride well or lasso from a horse.

This semibarbarous dissipation changed thanks partly to a growth in population and thanks partly to the droughts in the North. Ceará could no longer furnish the meat to which some of the people on the coast had become accustomed, so they tried eating jerky from Rio Grande do Sul. It is said that people from Ceará played a role in the founding of São Francisco de Paula, later known as Pelotas, a city in Rio Grande do Sul. A source of wealth had been found. The price of cattle went up, and ranches, which also in these parts were set up on the high points, began to have a modicum of organization. As meat-drying operations were set up, blacks were brought in, and their numbers attained several dozen thousand. Some cattle ranches brought in thousands of cruzados, which were squandered in betting and gambling.

Around 1803 in Bahia, nearly 40 ships, 250 tons apiece, were used in bringing jerky from Rio Grande do Sul. Round trips between the two places took nearly two years. From Bahia they took brandy, sugar, china, European merchandise (mainly British and German). They exchanged these goods for contraband silver in Montevideo and Maldonado. While this was going on, the crews were busy loading leather and dried meat. When the ships reached Bahia, they retailed the meat at two *vintens* [coins of minute value] per pound. Disposing of their cargo in this fashion, rather than unloading it, they were able to spend at least five months in port. According to Lindley, had they not done this, they could have made three trips during the time one was made.

Agriculture was never totally neglected. Wheat production rose to thousands of alqueires. Other grains were grown, as well as manioc. To keep free-ranging cattle away, cattle guards [*velados*] were opened and live fences made of cactus or elderberry bush, or others made from cattle skulls and horns were set up. Still, the agricultural strip occupied an insignificant area, which only widened once German immigrants arrived. The decay of wheat farming has been explained by certain counterproductive measures taken by the central government and by the deterioration of the seeds themselves owing to rust. There must have been deeper causes, since wheat farming has seemed impossible to bring back.

Saint-Hilaire, who visited the region, describes the rural Rio Grandean as lively, ruddy, generally white, reasonably tall, lacking in intellectual curiosity, rural in manner, incredibly voracious and, if not cruel, somewhat insensitive. He speaks of revelry every time a steer was dressed:

> The idea that in a short time one will be able to stuff oneself with meat is one of the reasons for rejoicing, but not the only one. An even greater source of merriment is just to kill and quarter a cow, independent of being able to satisfy one's gluttony immediately. Still, it is my duty to confess that this passion is one of those that prevail among the inhabitants of the Rio Grande Captaincy.[17]

The same author made an observation that explains an entire set of facts that have obtained since the Regency. The Mineiros, he asserts, are not tied to their land. Indeed, no particular habit keeps them there, and they are not upset if they have to leave. He adds that their natural intelligence guarantees them easy means of subsistence wherever they may go.

The inhabitants of Rio Grande do Sul, on the other hand, never leave their soil, because anywhere else they would be obliged to give up their constant horseback riding, and nowhere else would they find meat in such great abundance.

In the make-up of the Rio Grandean enter Azoreans, northerners, most of them from São Paulo, and not a few Spaniards who immigrated or were incorporated. More than ever, Spanish and Portuguese have intertwined along the southern border. There were few mulattos. One noticed a certain youthful ardor that was missing in the other captaincies. Their battle with animate creatures had effects very different from those of people's battles with the masses of vegetation and inclement cosmic forces in the north.

On the seashore poor fishermen eked out a meager living. The whaling outfits provided work during only one part of the year, and only at a few places. Large-scale fishing, such as that in Porto Seguro and elsewhere, did not displace importing dried fish, of which cod was one of the more popular varieties.

Universal smuggling operations mocked all measures to suppress contraband.

Rural landowners, with better equipment, as well as with more spacious and better furnished houses, went on growing cash crops for foreign markets. They wasted the wealth of the land and were indifferent to cultivation of basic foodstuffs and to forming internal markets. One victim of this rapacious agriculture was African slavery, which also condemned agriculture to stagnation and retreat. There were repeated crises in agriculture. Rises in price disguised but did not extinguish its central defect.

The old settlements like Igaraçu and Porto Calvo, founded within reach of riverboat traffic, died out as these boats increased their draft. Commercial prosperity demanded ocean contacts. The great commercial centers were São Luís do Maranhão, Recife, Bahia, and Rio.

Faced with Europeans, blacks, and their pure or mixed descendants, in the coastal cities the poor Indian disappeared. Color prejudice died a slow death as can be seen in the segregated battalions such as the Henriques, who were all black. Some religious brotherhoods were restricted to blacks, tans, or whites. Each group had its particular patron saint, such as Our Lady of the Rosary, Saint Benedict, and Saint Gonçalo Garcia. Prejudice was not sufficiently strong to stop or even minimize racial mixture. Prejudice was more a half-effaced tradition than it was a vital force.

Slaves did all the household work. There were always too many of them. Still, one got by with little. Thanks to barnyard animals, abundant shellfish, cheap fish, and ingenious and varied confections, prodigality was as widespread as was the lack of foresight in that primitive economy. Some of the slaves were employed in tasks of transportation on land and water. Some learned trades. Others, by paying their owners a fixed amount, sought occupations that appealed to them. They sometimes spoke in African languages. They formed secret guilds. And they practiced sorcery. With their native joy, their persistent optimism, and their animal sensuality, they withstood the burden of slavery.

They never threatened the established order in any serious way. And the porters made the streets happy places to be. John Luccock writes:

> slaves [are] sent into the streets, with empty baskets and long poles, to seek employment for their owner's benefit. Heavy goods were conveyed between two, by means of these poles laid upon their shoulders; then a pair of slings was attached, by which the load, raised a little above the ground, was carried to its place of destination. If the burden were too heavy for a couple of men, four, six, or even more united, and formed a gang, over which one of the number, and generally the most intelligent of the set, was chosen by them to be their captain, and to direct the labour. To promote regularity in their efforts, and particularly an uniformity of step, he always chaunted an African song to a short and simple air; at the close of which the whole body joined in a loud chorus. This song was continued as long as the labour lasted, and seemed to lighten the burden, and to cheer the heart.[18]

Mulattos, by nature unruly and quarrelsome, could be contained for a time by acts of despotism, but immediately afterwards they resumed their original rebelliousness. Their festivals were less cordial than the blacks', and not infrequently ended in altercations. From their numbers came murderers and professional thugs. As they grew in number, they failed to acknowledge and finally erased racial distinctions. They had enough strength to break with the reigning conventions and to live as their restless nature demanded. The feminine element among mulattos, with its particular wiles and provocative sashaying, was especially effective in this leveling process. Spix and Martius recorded the following ditty in Bahia.

> A pretty mulatto gal,
> She don't need to pray.
> With all them sexy movements,
> Her soul's already saved.[19]

Social conventions oppressed white people. Pretentious civil servants who came from overseas had the same haughty disdain for the land and for its inhabitants. So did the coarse and scarcely honest businessmen. And they were mere agents for their countrymen who, in turn, were nothing more than agents for the British. Wary capitalists, impoverished descendants of wealthy, wasteful fathers, members of religious brotherhoods [*irmãos das almas*], the mulattos themselves when their repeated mixtures allowed them to pass for white—all these people went about in public like melancholy automatons.

According to Luccock:

> the whole population seemed tongue-tied; there was no playfulness of boyhood, no sprightliness of youth, no obstreperous shouting of the more advanced in years. . . . The first general shout, uttered by the people in my hearing, was on the birth-day of the Queen, in 1810. It followed the *feu de joie* fired on that occasion, and was a suppressed huzzah, not cold, but timid; it seemed to ask whether it might be repeated.[20]

From his residence, at the corner of Rua do Ouvidor and Rua da Quitanda, in Rio, he witnessed a scene that he describes as follows:

> precisely on this spot, every unhallowed morning, the Attorneys, together with the under officers of the law, met to transact business. . . . The generality of those who composed it, were dressed in old, rusty, black coats, some of them well patched, and so ill adapted to the height and form of the wearers, as to excite a suspicion that they were not the first who owned them; their waistcoats were of gayer colours, with long embroidered bodies, large flaps and deep pockets; their breeches were black, so short as scarcely to reach either to the loins or the knees, where they were fastened with square buckles of mock brilliants; their stockings of homespun cotton, and their shoe-buckles enormously large. Their heads were covered with powdered wigs, surmounted by large, fantailed, greasy hats, in which was usually placed a black cockade. The left thigh bore a very old and shabby dirk. It was amusing to observe, with what punctilious ceremony these gentlemen, and their subalterns, addressed each other; how exactly in order they bowed, and held their dirty hats; with what precise forms, and cool deliberation, they combined to pick the pockets of their clients.[21]

Education was tantamount to expunging pupils' vivaciousness and spontaneity. At home boys and girls went about naked until the age of five. For the next five years their dress consisted of a shirt. If, on the other hand, they went to church or out on a visit, they would dress with all the formality of an older person, differing only in their clothes' dimensions. Few learned to read. Given the scarcity of books, reading was done from manuscripts, which explains the loss of so many precious documents.

Only the friars, following the example of people of color, obeyed the dictates of temperament without fear of scandal, or, indeed, in the interest of scandalizing. Friar Caetano Brandão, the Bishop of Pará, was to write that:

> One of the reasons for social decay is that there are many monasteries but few clerics. Because they cannot perform all their religious duties, they soon use this fact to shirk even the simplest ones. And there you have them: idle and absolutely useless, both to the Church and to the state.[22]

Up to the beginning of the Second Empire, when they were replaced by lawyers graduated from the academies in São Paulo and Olinda, priests enjoyed their prestige as the genuine representatives of [refined] thinking. Few of them possessed the virtues of their vocation, but because this was so common, it was scarcely noticed. Some of them broke away from the exclusivity of Latin and learned French and English. They engaged in the study of natural science. They espoused the ideas of the Encyclopedists. They waxed enthusiastic concerning the tragedies of the French Revolution and were familiar with the theories of Adam Smith.

There were freemasons among them. And freemasons existed in small numbers elsewhere, among the Portuguese and Brazilian officers who had traveled abroad. They did not meet in lodges. Because no one dared declare himself to be a mason, the population, let it be said, could not know who they were, but they were crazed by fear of them. Bloodcurdling accounts of their sacrilegious abominations were circulated. A favorite rumor was that they delighted in stabbing crucifixes. In spite of or owing to their dearth, they garnered a modicum of influence and were able to help Thomas Lindley escape from prison. He had been jailed for smuggling. [He also recorded some impressions of Brazilians]:

> The chief amusements of the citizens are the feasts of the different saints, professions of nuns, sumptuous funerals, the holy or passion-week, &c. which are all celebrated in rotation with grand ceremonies, a full concert, and frequent processions. Scarcely a day passes that some one or other of these festivals does not occur; and thus is presented a continued round of opportunities for uniting devotion and pleasure, which is eagerly embraced, particularly by the ladies. On grand occasions of this kind, after coming from church, they visit each other, and have a more plentiful dinner than common ... during and after which they drink unusual quantities of wine; and, when elevated to an extraordinary pitch, the guitar or violin is introduced, and singing commences: but the song soon gives way to the enticing *negro dance*. ... a mixture of the dances of Africa, and the fandangoes of Spain and Portugal. It consists of an individual of each sex dancing

to an insipid thrumming of the instrument, always to one measure, with scarcely any action of the legs, but with every licentious motion of the body, joining in contact during the dance in a manner strangely immodest. The spectators, aiding the music with an extemporary chorus, and clapping of the hands, enjoy the scene with undescribable zest.[23]

Women rarely appeared in public. They attended early morning Masses. Some of them rode in sedan chairs carried by stately blacks in fine livery. There were no carriages. Most of their time was spent indoors where they went about half undressed: in shirt sleeves, without stockings or footwear. They heard fairy tales or fresh gossip from their servants. They combed their hair, and delighted in having their scalps scratched. They embroidered, they made lace and sweets, they crooned sentimental songs, they talked to neighbor women from the gardens in back of their houses, and they passed the time of day with female street venders or devout women. Or, hidden behind a discrete screen or jalousie, they tried to find out what was going on outside. Unmarried women whose wedding days seemed long in coming got fat. The happiest were those who found "a house of 'Wooster', when the hen sang louder than the rooster."

Luccock describes the women of Rio:

the ornaments of these females have a pleasing effect, and set off the charms of a face, the features of which are round and regular, of a black, lively, inquisitive eye, a smooth and open forehead, a mouth expressive of simplicity and good temper, furnished with a white and even set of teeth; united with a moderately handsome figure, a sprightly laughing air, and a demeanour gay, frank, and unsuspicious. Such is the common appearance of a young lady, about thirteen or fourteen years of age; . . . at eighteen, in a Brazilian woman, nature has attained to full maturity. A few years later she becomes corpulent, and even unwieldy; acquires a great stoop in her shoulders, and walks with an awkward waddling gait. She begins to decay, loses the good humour of her countenance, and assumes, in its place, a contracted and scowling brow. The eye and the mouth both indicate that they have been accustomed to express the violent and vindictive passions, the cheeks are deprived of their plumpness and colour, and at twenty-five, or thirty at most, she becomes a perfectly wrinkled old woman.[24]

Men gambled, frequented cafés, went out to eat, and talked. Their conversation consisted, almost entirely, of gossip. They used the most homey of affairs for interminable malicious commentary. Everyone had a nickname. Not even death was respected. If someone with a saintly reputation were to die, [or] if a particular body failed to rot, people became restless and the demand for relics assumed the most imprudent proportions. If, on the other hand, it was rumored that some soul had gone to the devil, prodigious rumors spread like wildfire. Houses became haunted and people reacted to the proximity of outer darkness by crying and gnashing their teeth. This still goes on in rural areas.

In Rio and, with slight differences, in other coastal cities, most of the houses were single-storied. The front room was large and had a floor. In back of it were the bedrooms, the kitchen, and the garden. In the few two-storied houses, the first floor was usually a store. The family would get together on the back veranda. Women sat on mats, men leaned on whatever, or they walked around. There they would eat at an old table set up on two saw horses and surrounded by wooden stools and from time to time a chair or two. The main meal was at midday, and at that time the man and the woman of the house, as well as their children, sat down to eat. More commonly, however, they would squat on the ground and eat in that position. Moist food was served in tureens or gourds. Dry food was served in baskets. They ate off cheap plates made in Lisbon [*pratinhos de Lisboa*]. Only men ate with knives. Women and children ate with their hands.[25]

According to Luccock:

> When a gentleman calls upon another, if he be not intimate at the house, he goes thither in full dress, with a cocked hat, with buckles in his shoes and at the knees, and with a sword or dirk by his side. Having reached the bottom of the stairs, he claps his hands as a signal to attract attention, and utters a sort of sibilant sound, between his teeth and the end of his tongue. . . . The servant, who attends the call, roughly inquires in a nasal tone, who is it? and being told, retires to inform the master of the house. . . . If he be a friend, or one so well known as to be received without ceremony, the master quickly comes to him, and ushers him into the Sala [living room], making loud protestations of the pleasure given him by the visit, mixing his complimentary speeches with a great number of bows. Before business is entered upon, if that be the object, repeated apologies are offered for the free mode, in which the visitor is received.
>
> Should the call be a ceremonious one, a servant is sent to conduct the visitor to the Sala, from which, as he enters, he often sees the persons who were in the room, escaping at the other door. Here he waits alone, it may be half an hour, when the gentleman appears in a sort of half dress. They both bow profoundly, at a distance; after a sufficiency of skill in this science has been displayed, and thus time gained to ascertain each other's rank and pretensions, they approach; if unequal, with corresponding dignity and respect; if supposed to be nearly equals, with familiarity. The business is then entered upon, and dispatched at once.[26]

The visitor was entreated to consider the house his own, Pohl noted. If he shows he likes something, custom demands that it be offered to him and that he be asked to accept the trifle.

Streets were narrow, unpaved, unlit, or lit with [lamps burning] fish oil. Water and sewage were left to private initiative. Bodies were buried at the churches. The lack of epidemics can only be explained by the scanty population. Public sanitation was taken care of by rain water, sunlight, and diligent buzzards. The public promenade or *Passeio Público* and the aqueduct were notorious exceptions to this rule.

After the first attempts at industry were brutally extinguished, the only tradesmen left in the cities worked on commission and were paid only for their labor. Saint-Hilaire observed that:

> When tradesman made a little money, they would stop working until it was all spent. They only possessed the most necessary of tools and almost never supplied raw material. People had to furnish leather for the shoemaker, thread for the tailor, and wood for the carpenter. They were lent money to buy these things, but they almost always spent the money and the work was not completed or it was only finished after considerable time had passed. If someone wanted something done, they had to begin far in advance. Let us suppose that it was some carpentry work. It was first necessary to employ some friends to procure the necessary wood in the country. Then one had to make a hundred calls at the carpenter's house, one threatened, and at times this was to no avail. I asked an honest man in São Paulo what he did when he needed a pair of shoes. "I order them," he said, "from several shoemakers at the same time. Among them there is usually one who, pressed for money, will resign himself to making them."[27]

Tradesmen in Rio put on airs of knowing all the tricks of their trade, but they did not even know the basics. Luccock reports that one time when he lost a key, he sought and finally found a worker who would attend to his plight.

> He detained me a long time, but to compensate for the delay, made his appearance at last in full dress, with a cocked hat, shoe and knee buckles, and other corresponding paraphernalia. At the door of the house he still loitered, wishing to hire some black man to carry his hammer, chisel, and another small instrument. I suggested that they were light, and proposed to carry a part, or the whole, of them myself; but this would have been as great a practical solecism as using his own hands. The gentleman waited patiently, until a negro appeared; then made his bargain, and proceeded in due state, followed by his temporary servant. The task was soon finished, by breaking the lock, instead of picking it; then the man of importance, making me a profound bow, stalked off with his follower.[28]

Craftsmen never formed professional guilds as they did in Europe. There were too few of them for that. And, if they were in the cities, they could support themselves with a single occupation, but in places where the population was less dense, they needed seven trades to get by. Even in the cities slave tradesmen competed with them.

The lack of guilds affected other classes. There continued to be historically noteworthy moral individuals, but their efforts, from the start debilitated by the vastness of the territory, had expired because the leveling absolutism failed to honor these individuals' privileges. If we except some brotherhoods and charity organizations, such as the *casas de misericórdia*, which remained vital and praiseworthy, collective operations were almost always fleeting: barn-raisings [*mutirão*], fishing expeditions, roundups, fairs, and novenas. Between the state and the family there was neither interaction nor coordination capable of establishing any tradition. And there was no definitive advancement. An individual might try something new and actually succeed. But if he left it to someone else, or if he died, it all came to naught. A few years later someone else might try it again, only to reap the same ephemeral result.

There was no such thing as social life—there was no society. Public affairs were also not of interest and went unheralded. At best, according to Lindley,[29] people knew whether or not they were at war. Even though they called one another by patriotic names such as *patrício* or *paisano*, it is even dubious whether or not they felt they were citizens of a captaincy, much less of a state. One or another reader of a foreign book might speak of the possibility of future independence, especially after the United States of America was founded and Portugal's sorry weakness was exposed.

No one asked, however, how such vaguely conceived independence might be attained. Practical and concrete matters were so contrary to the people's nature. They preferred to digress over what they would do after they became independent by some as yet undefined means, by a set of unforeseen events, as in fact happened. Once more the intellectual sloth of Bequimão and the Recife peddlers prevailed!

Our five ethnographic groups were actively linked by a common language and passively linked by their religion. They were shaped by the environmental circumstances of five different regions. They were intensely enthusiastic about the country's natural resources. They were adverse to or scornful of the Portuguese, but did not think especially highly of one another either. After three centuries, this is how we were.

Notes

The notes for this translation are an amalgam of selected footnotes added to later editions of *Capítulos de história colonial* by José Honório Rodrigues and notes added to the translation itself by Professor Stuart Schwartz [SBS]. The list of sources has been extracted from the information in the notes to the Brazilian editions. Owing to at times inconsistant data in the footnotes and the limitations of some of the finest research libraries, it has not always been possible to supply all the bibliographical data (e.g., dates, publishers, and pages) researchers have come to expect in historical works.

Chapter One: Indigenous Antecedents

1. Wilhelm Ludwig von Eschwege (1777–1855) has been called the "father of Brazilian geology." Born in Germany and educated at the University of Göttingen, he was employed as a geologist and mineralogist by the Crown of Portugal. He came to Brazil in 1810 and remained there for more than a decade. He published more than 20 scientific works on Brazilian geology, but Abreu here refers to his study of the decline of Brazilian mining, especially in Minas Gerais. This book, *Pluto brasiliensis* (Berlin: G. Reiner, 1833) contained much historical information. There is a useful modern edition in Portuguese. See *Pluto brasiliensis*, 2 vols., ed. trans. Domício de Figueiredo Murta, Mário Ferri, (Belo Horizonte: Itatiaia, 1979). [SBS]

2. Emil August Goeldi (1859–1917), a Swiss naturalist who went to Brazil in 1884, lived and worked in the Amazon region. He founded and directed the Natural History Museum of Belém now named for him. He was chiefly instrumen-

tal in assembling teams of scientists to study the Amazon region. His own scientific work centered on diseases of the flora and fauna. [SBS]

3. João Capistrano de Abreu, "O descobrimento do Brasil," in *Livro do Centenário, 1500–1900* (Rio de Janeiro: Imprensa Nacional, 1900), 1: 54.

Chapter Two: Exotic Factors

1. The privileges of citizens of Oporto can be found in João Francisco Lisboa, *Obras*, 2 vols. (Lisbon: Tipografia M. Moreira & Pinheiro, 1901), 2: 170–171.

2. Damião de Góis, *Fides, Religio, Moresque Aethiopum sub Imperio Preciosi Ioanis*, 2d ed. (Paris: Cristianum Wechelum, 1542).

3. A. de Sousa Silva Costa Lobo, *História da sociedade em Portugal do século quinze* (Lisbon: Imprensa Nacional, 1903).

4. André João Antonil was the pseudonym for Giovanni Antonio Andreoni (1649–1716), an Italian Jesuit who served in Brazil and became an important official of the Jesuits in that country. His remarkable book, *Cultura e opulência do Brasil por suas drogas e minas* (Lisbon, 1711), described in detail the sugar, tobacco, and cattle economies of the colony as well as the mining zones. The Portuguese Crown, fearing that the details about Brazil's mineral wealth might invite foreign attack, withdrew the book from publication. It was Abreu who, in 1886, was the first to identify Andreoni as the author of the book. The best modern edition of the book is the bilingual (Portuguese and French) version by Anrée Mansuy, ed., *Cultura e opulência do Brasil por suas drogas e minas* (Paris: Institut des Hautes Etudes de l'Amerique latine, 1968). [SBS]

Chapter Three: The Discoverers

The interpretation of the Portuguese voyages of discovery and exploration has been considerably altered and enriched since Abreu wrote. The major works of Portuguese scholars, such as Vitorino Magalhães Godinho, *Os descobrimentos e a economia mundial*, 2d ed., 4 vols. (Lisbon, 1984) and António de Silva Dias, *Os descobrimentos e a problemática cultural do século xvi* (Coimbra, 1973), are now essential reading. A good summary in English is provided by Bailey W. Diffie and George D. Winius, *Foundations of the Portuguese Empire, 1415–1580* (Minneapolis: University of Minnesota Press, 1977). [SBS]

1. *Livro do Centenário*, 63–72, especially 63, 65, and 72–73.

Chapter Four: The First Conflicts

1. Concerning the names *Maïr* and *Peró* see Cândido Mendes de Almeida, "Por que razão os indígenas do nosso litoral chamavam aos franceses "Maïr" e aos portugueses "Peró?" *Revista do Instituto Histórico e Geográfico Brasileiro* 41, no. 2 (1878): 71–141.

2. Pero Lopes de Souza, *Diário da navegação que foi à terra do Brasil em 1530 sob a capitania-mor de Martim Afonso de Sousa, escrito por seu irmão Pero Lopes de Sousa*, ed. Francisco Adolfo Varnhagen (Lisbon: 1839), 58.

3. The part of the letter Diogo de Gouveia wrote from Roen to Dom João III on 29 February 1532 can be found in Francisco Adolfo Varnhagen, *História geral do Brasil*, 3d ed. (Rio de Janeiro: Laemmert & C. Editores, 1907), 1: 143. It was first published in Francisco Adolfo Varnhagen, *Primeiras negociações diplomáticas* (Rio de Janeiro, 1845), 135.

CHAPTER FIVE: HEREDITARY CAPTAINCIES

1. This letter can be found in Varnhagen, *História*, 1: 165–167 and in Varnhagen, *História da colonização portuguesa do Brasil*, 3 vols. (Porto: Litografia Nacional, 1924), 3: 160–161.

2. *Fonti Italiane per la Storia della Scoperta del Nuovo Mondo* (Rome, 1893), 293.

3. *História da colonização*, 3: 311. See also Costa Rubim, *Revista do Instituto Histórico e Geográfico Brasileiro* 24 (1861): 175–196 and Capistrano de Abreu, "História pátria," *Kosmos* (April, 1905).

4. Marie Armand Pascal M D'Avezac, *Considérations géographiques sur l'histoire du Brésil* (Paris, 1857), 30–31.

CHAPTER SIX: CROWN CAPTAINCIES

1. Duarte Coelho's letters of 1546 and 1549 were published by J. B. Fernandes Gama, *Memórias históricas da província de Pernambuco*, 4 vols. (Pernambuco, 1844), 1: 70–82. Other letters, from the years 1534, 1542, 1548, and 1550 have been published in *História da colonização*, 3: 309 ff. See also F. A. Pereira da Costa, "Donatários de Pernambuco e governadores seus locotententes," *Revista do Instituto Arqueológico e Geográfico Pernambucano* (1896); Luís de Sousa, *Anais de Dom João III*; Capistrano de Abreu, "História pátria," *Kosmos* (July 1905).

2. According to the *Regimento* [by-laws and statutes], Tomé de Sousa was governor of the lands of Brazil, captain of the lands and fortress of Bahia, and capitão-mor of the fleet that brought him to Brasil. See *História da colonização*, 3: 345.

3. Cf. A. Thevet, *Les singularités de la France-Antarctique* (Paris, 1557), 2.

4. Capistrano de Abreu, "Trabalhos dos primeiros jesuítas do Brasil," *Revista do Instituto Histórico e Geográfico Brasileiro* 57, no. 1 (1894): 212–247.

5. José de Anchieta, "Informação dos primeiros aldeamentos da Bahia," in *Cartas* (Rio de Janeiro: Academia Brasileira de Letras, 1933), 377.

6. Pero de Magalhães Gandavo, "Tratado da terra do Brasil," in *Coleção de notícias para a história e geografia das nações ultramarinhas*, 4? vols. (Lisbon: Academia Real das Ciências de Lisboa), 4: 198, 199.

CHAPTER SEVEN: FRENCHMEN AND SPANIARDS

1. The "Dialogos das grandezas do Brasil" was a seventeenth-century manuscript describing the flora, fauna, colonization, peoples, and politics of Brazil in a series of dialogues between an imaginary newcomer and an old Brazil hand. Utilized by Varnhagen for his *História geral do Brasil*, the authorship of the manuscript remained a mystery until Capistrano de Abreu, using textual evidence and references, identified the author as Ambrósio Fernandes Brandão. There is an excellent modern version by José Antônio Gonçalves de Mello, *Diálogos das grandezas do Brasil* (Recife: Imprensa Universitária, 1966) and a fine English-language translation and edition by Frederick Arthur Holden Hall, William F. Harrison, and Dorothy Winters Welker, eds., *Dialogues of the Great Things of Brazil* (Albuquerque: University of New Mexico Press, 1987). [SBS]

2. Diogo de Campos Moreno, "Jornada do Maranhão," in *Memórias para a história do estinto Estado do Maranhão*, ed. Cândido Mendes de Almeida, 2 vols. (Rio de Janeiro, 1874), 2: 188–89.

3. Claude d'Abbeville, *Histoire de la mission des pères capucins en l'isle de Maragnan* (Paris, 1614), 180v–181.

4. Campos Moreno, "Jornada," 225, 230.

5. *Os Diálogos das grandezas do Brasil* were published in their entirety by Francisco Adolfo Varnhagen in *Revista do Instituto Arquelógico e Geográfico Pernambucano* 28, 31, 32, 33 (1883–87).

CHAPTER EIGHT: FIGHTING THE DUTCH

1. Duarte de Albuquerque Coelho, *Memorias diarias de la guerra del Brasil* (Madrid, 1654), 191v, 195–195v.

2. G. Barlaeus, *Rerum per octennium in Brasilia* (Amsterdam, 1647), 37. The Latin means: "[Calabar was] tortured. He paid for his desertion on the gallows, and, in a public spectacle in testimony of his infidelity and lowliness, he was dismembered. See Gaspar Barléu, *História dos feitos recentemente praticados durante oito anos no Brasil*, trans.. Cláudio Brandão (Rio de Janeiro: Ministério da Educação, 1940), 39.

3. Johann Maurits of Nassau, the governor of Dutch Brazil, brought naturalists, artists, and scholars in his entourage. Among the most distinguished were the humanist Caspar van Barele (Barlaeus), whose *Rerum per Octennium in Brasilia* (Amsterdam, c.1647) detailed Nassau's government in Brazil and is still prized today for its wonderful engravings and maps. George Marcgrave (or Marcgraf) was a brilliant naturalist and was also brought to Brazil by Nassau. He collaborated with Nassau's physician Wilhelm Pise (Piso) in producing the *Historia naturalis Brasailiae* (Leiden, 1648), a work that included astronomy and natural history and that was accompanied by many illustrations. [SBS]

4. João Fernandes Vieira's Testament can be found in *Revista do Instituto Arquelógico e Geográfico Pernambucano* 3, 25 (1869): 144–149.

5. Rafael de Jesus, *Castrioto lusitano* (Lisbon: 1679), 567–568.

6. Pierre Moreau, *Histoire des derniers troubles du Brésil* (Paris, 1651), 197–198.

7. Cf. Manuel Calado, *O Valeroso Lucideno e triunfo da liberdade* (Lisbon, 1648) and Diogo Lopes de Santiago, "História da guerra de Pernambuco e feitos memoráveis do mestre de campo João Fernandes Vieira," *Revista do Instituto Histórico e Geográfico Brasileiro* 38 (1875): 249–336; 39 (1876): 97–195, 323–409; 40 (1877): 411–504; 41 (1878): 143–181, 387–429; 42 (1879): 91–104, 157–198; 43 (1880): 5–79, 191–255.

Chapter Nine: The Backlands

1. Antonio Ruiz de Montoya, *Conquista espiritual* Madrid, 1639, 46v.

2. Ibid. 45v.

3. Ibid. 6.

4. For more information on Don Luis Céspedes Xeria, see "Relación de los sucesos ocorridos durante el viaje que hizo el gobernador del Paraguay Don Luis de Céspedes Xeria desde Mardrid hasta llegar a la ciudad de Asunción," *Anais do Museu Paulista* (1925), 2, 15–221, and Afonso de E. Taunay, "A viagem de Dom Luís de Cépedes Xeria," *Revista do Instituto Histórico e geográfico Brasileiro* 84: 449–478. Montoya, 45v.

5. Montoya, 92v–93.

6. Ibid., 93v.

7. Varnhagen, *História geral*, 156–157.

8. In Spanish America, the *encomienda*, a grant of Indians who were required to pay tribute, was given to individual Spaniards during the conquest. These grants were hereditary but were increasingly limited by the Spanish Crown. [SBS]

9. The Bahian expedition of the Paulistas was detailed in an unpublished contemporary work that has subsequently been published. See Stuart B. Schwartz, ed., *A Governor and his Image in Baroque Brazil. The Funeral Eulogy of Afonso Furtado de Castro do Rio de Mendonça*, trans. Ruth Jones (Minneapolis: University of Minnesota Press, 1979). [SBS]

10. Pedro Taques, *Nobiliarquia paulistana*, 32, part 1, (1869), manuscript, Instituto Histórico e Geográfico Brasileiro, 249–251.

11. According to M. E. Azevedo Marques, São Paulo's backlands vilas were founded on the dates listed below.

Moji das Cruzes	3 September 1611
Parnaíba	14 November 1625
Tabuaté	5 December 1650
Jacareí	1653
Jundiaí	14 December 1655
Guaratinguetá	13 February 1657
Itu	18 April 1657

Sorocaba   3 March 1661

Pindamonhangaba 10 July 1705

These dates, however, need to be revised. See Azevedo Marques, M. E. *Apontamentos históricos, geográficos, biográficos, estatísticos e noticiosos da província de São Paulo*, ? vols. (Rio de Janeiro, 1879),I.

12. "Informação do Estado do Brasil e de suas necessidades," *Revista do Instituto Histórico e Geográfico Brasileiro* 25 (1862): 473.

13. "Relação do Jácome Raimundo de Noronha, sobre as coisas pertencentes à conservação, e aumento do Estado do Maranhão, "*Anais da Biblioteca Nacional* 26, (n.d.): 435–441.

14. Cf. letters transcribed by Bernardo Pereira Berredo, *Anais históricos do Estado do Maranhão* (Lisboa, 1749), 448–460. Vieira's letter can be found in *Cartas do Padre António Vieira*, ed. Lúcio de Azevedo (Coimbra, Portugal: Imprensa da Universidade, 1925), 1: 579–583.

15. Cf. Varnhagen, *História geral*, 3: 339–341.

16. Domingos Teixeira, *Vida de Gomes Freire de Andrada* (Lisbon: 1727), 426.

17. Capistrano de Abreu, "Caminhos antigos e povoamento do Brasil," *Jornal do comércio* (12, 29 August and 10 September 1899) Cf. Abreu, *Caminhos antigos e povoamento do brasil* (Rio de Janeiro: Sociedade Capistrano de Abreu, 1930), 108–109.

18. Cf. Varnhagen, *História geral*, 5: 339–340.

19. "Roteiro do Maranhão e Goiás pela Capitania do Maranhão," *Revista do Instituto Histórico e Geográfico Brasileiro* 62, no. 1 (1900): 60–161.

20. Cf. André João Antonil, *Cultura e opulência do Brasil por suas drogas e minas* (Lisbon: Oficina Real Deslanderina, 1711), 188–189.

21. "Informação do Estado do Brasil e de suas necessidades," *Revista do Instituto Histórico e Geográfico Brasileiro* 25 (1862): 465–478.

22. Cf. Antonil, *Cultura*, 183–185.

23. "Informação geral da Capitania de Pernambuco, 1749," *Anais da Biblioteca Nacional* 28 (1908): 343–344.

24. First created in Brazil in 1532, these municipal judges were chosen annually by the town councils to deal with civil cases involving less than 400 reis. They were especially important in small outlying districts where there were no permanent judicial officers. [SBS]

25. (Rio de Janeiro: Academia Brasileira de Letras, 1930), 63.

26. Orville Derby, "Os primeiros descobrimentos de ouro nos distritos de Sabará e Caeté," *Revista do Instituto Histórico e Geográfico Brasileiro* (1899–1900): 282–285.

27. Códice 51-VI-24, fols. 460–467, Biblioteca da Ajuda (Lisbon). Cf. "Informação sobre as minas do Brasil," *Anais da Biblioteca Nacional* 57 (1939): 178–180.

28. *Tratado descritivo do Brasil em 1587* (Rio de Janeiro: Laemmert, 1851). See also, *Revista do Instituto Histórico e Geográfico Brasileiro* 14 (1851): 364.

29. See Capistrano de Abreu, "Subsídio para a história das minas," *Revista do Instituto Histórico e Geográfico Brasileiro* 63 (1901): 5–13, especially 12.

30. Cf. Antonil, *Cultura*, 130.

31. Cf. José João Teixeira Coelho, "Instruções para o governo da Capitania de Minas Gerais," *Revista do Instituto Histórico e Geográfico Brasileiro* 15 (1852): 445.

32. Cf. Antonil, *Cultura*, 131.

33. Cf. Ibid., 140–41.

34. Cf. Ibid., 139–40, 145.

35. José Barbosa de Sá, "Relação das povoações de Cuiabá e Mato Grosso de seus princípios até os presentes tempos," *Anais da Biblioteca Nacional* 23 (1904): 5–58, especially 24.

36. J. M. P. de Alencastre, "Anais da Província de Goiás," *Revista do Instituto Histórico e Geográfico Brasileiro* 27 (1864): 37.

37. J. Pandiá Calógeras, *As minas do Brasil e sua legislação*, 3 vols. (Rio de Janeiro: Imprensa Nacional, 1904), 1: 221–224.

38. Teixeira Coelho, "Instruções," 257ff.

39. Wilhelm L. von Eschwege, "Extrato de uma memória sobre a decadência das minas de ouro da Capitania de Minas Gerais e sobre vários outros objetos montanísticos," In *História e memórias da Academia Real das Ciências de Lisboa*, 4? vols. (Lisbon: História e memórias da Academia Real das Ciências de Lisboa, 1868), 4: 222–23.

40. Johan B. Spix and Karl von Martius, *Reise in Brasilien*, 2 vols. (Munich: 1825, 1828), 1: 364.

41. Cf. Alberto Lamego, *Mentiras históricas* (Rio de Janeiro: n.p, n.d.), 152, and Varnhagen, *História geral*, 3: 370.

42. Manoel da Fonseca, *Vida do venerável Padre Belchior Pontes* (Lisbon: 1752). Cf. *Revista do Instituto Histórico e Geográfico Brasileiro* 3 (1841): 266.

43. Sebastião da Rocha Pita, *História da América Portuguesa*, 18 vols, 42 (Lisbon: 1730), 9: 553.

44. Fonseca, *Vida*, 274.

45. Domingos de Loreto Couto, "Desagravos do Brasil e glórias de Pernambuco," *Anais da Biblioteca Nacional* 25 (1903): 196. See also "Narração histórica das calamidades de Pernambuco," *Revista do Instituto Histórico e Geográfico Brasileiro* 53, no. 2 (1890): 24.

46. Fernandes Gama, *Memórias históricas*, 4: 64.

47. Ibid., 68. Cf. "Narração histórica," 49.

48. See Fernandes Gama, *Memórias históricas*, 4: 88–89, 92.

49. See "Guerra civil ou sedições de Pernambuco," *Revista do Instituto Histórico e Geográfico Brasileiro* 16 (1853): 93. Varnhagen (*História*, 3: 398) believes this is the work of Father Antônio Gonçalves Leitão or Father Manuel Rodrigues Neto, who sided with Olinda. Cf. Manuel dos Santos, "Narração histórica das calamidades de Pernambuco sucedidas desde o ano se 1707 até o de 1715," *Revista do Instituto Histórico e Geográfico Brasileiro* 53, no. 2 (1890): 1–307.

50. Antonil, *Cultura*, 96, 101, 163, 122–123, 135, 144, 190–191.

51. Ibid., 192.

52. Ibid., 193.

53. Antônio José Vitoriano Borges da Fonseca, "Nobiliarquias pernambucanas," *Anais da Biblioteca Nacional*, 2 vols. (1935): 47–48. Antônio de Santa Maria Jaboatão, "Catálogo genealógico das principais famílias que procederam de Albuquerques e Cavalcantes em Pernambuco e Caramurus na Bahia (1768)," *Revista do Instituto Histórico e Geográfico Brasileiro* 52, no. 1 (n.d.): 5. Cf. Pedro Taques de Almeida Paes Leme, "Nobiliarquia paulistana," *Revista do Instituto Histórico e Geográfico Brasileiro* 22–25 (1869–1872); Afonso d'E Taunay, *Pedro Taques e seu tempo* (São Paulo, 1922). Taunay and Augusto da Siqueira Cardoso reprinted the *Nobiliarquia* in a special volume of *Revista do Instituto Histórico e Geográfico Brasileiro* for the year 1926.

54. Loreto Couto, "Desagravos do Brasil," 45.

55. Ibid.

56. Ibid., 42.57. Ibid, 54–55

57. Ibid., 54–55.

58. Antônio Delgado da Silva, *Coleção da legislação portuguesa*, ? vols. (Lisbon: 1830), 1. For Mendonça's correspondence see "Correspondência dos governadores do Pará com a Metrópole, primeira série—1752–1757," *Anais da Biblioteca e Arquivo Público do Pará*, 5 vols. (Belém do Pará: n.p.), 2(1902), 3(1904), 4(1905), 5(1906). The letter of February 14 appears in *Anais . . . do Pará*, 3: 167–168.

59. This is a reference to Francisco Xavier de Mendonça Furtado (1700–1769), who was governor of Grão Para e Maranhão.

60. Delgado da Silva, *Coleção*, 1.

61. See "Correspondência dos governadores," *Anais* 4 (1905): 186.

62. *Resposta apologética ao poema intitulado O Uruguay, composto por José Basílio da Gama* (Lugano, 1876), 46–48. See also "Refutação das calúnias contra os jesuítas contidas no poema 'Uruguay' de José Basílio da Gama," *Revista do Instituto Histórico e Geográfico Brasileiro* 68, no. 1 (1907): 112.

63. The papal bull, "Immensa pastorum principis," can be found in *Coleção dos breves pontifícios e Leis Régias* (Rio de Janeiro?: Impressa da Secretaria de Estado, n.d.), 4.

64. *Relação abreviada da república que os religiosos jesuítas das províncias de Portugal e Espanha estabeleceram nos domínios ultramarinos das duas monarquias* (n.p.: n.d.), 35.

65. "Correspondência dos governadores," *Anais* 5 (1906): 227.

66. *Coleção dos breves*, n.p.

67. Lisboa, *Obras*, 2: 333.

68. Delgado da Silva, *Coleção*, 1.

69. Cf. *Coleção dos Breves*.

70. Guilherme, Baron of Studart was a prolific regional historian who concentrated on his native Ceará. He was a friend of and corresponded regularly with Abreu.

71. To a large extent this need was filled by the works of the Jesuit historian Father Serafim Leite. His monumental *História da Companhia de Jesus no Brasil,* 10 vols. (Lisbon, 1938–50) has filled the gap that Abreu perceived. A large general study of the Jesuits within the Portuguese empire is Dauril Alden, *The Making of an Enterprise: The Society of Jesus in Portugal, Its Empire, and Beyond, 1540–1750* (Stanford: Stanford University Press, 1996). [SBS]

72. "Informação geral, 1749," 117–496. For information on the Indian villages, see 419–422.

73. "Idéia da população da Capitania de Pernambuco," *Anais da Biblioteca Nacional* 40 (1923): I–III.

74. Joaquim Norberto de Sousa e Silva, "Memória histórica e documentada das aldeias de índios na província do Rio de Janeiro," *Revista do Instituto Histórico e Geográfico Brasileiro* 17, 3d Ser. (1894): 109.

75. J. J. Machado de Oliveira, "Notícia sobre as aldeias de índios da Província de São Paulo desde o seu começo até a atualidade," *Revista do Instituto Histórico e Geográfico Brasileiro* 8 (1868): 204.

CHAPTER TEN: SETTING BOUNDARIES

1. Alberto Lamego, *A Terra Goitacá à luz de documentos inéditos,* ? vols. (Paris, 1913), 1: 120–123.

2. Antônio Ladislau Monteiro Baena, "Resposta ao presidente da Província do Pará, em 20 de março de 1844 sobre os limites do Brasil com a Venezuela," *Revista do Instituto Histórico e Geográfico Brasileiro* 7 (n.d.) 329–337. See also Artur César Ferreira Reis, *Limites e demarcações na Amazônia brasileira* (Rio de Janeiro: Imprensa Nacional), 2: 92–93, 105–107.

3. José Maria da Silva Paranhos Júnior, Barão de Rio Branco, *Questão de limites Brasileiro-Argentina,* 4? vols. (Nova Iorque, 1894), 4: 71–72.

4. Ibid., 82.

5. Ibid., 3–21.

6. Félix de Azara, "Correspondencia ofical e inédita sobre la demarcación de límites entre el Paraguay y el Brasil," in *Colección de obras y documentos,* ed. Pedro de Angelis (Buenos Aires: Imprenta del Estado, 1836), 44.

7. Cf. Varnhagen, *História geral,* 5: 370.

8. Cf. José Maria da Silva Paranhos Júnior, Barão de Rio Branco, *Frontières entre le Brésil et la Guyanne Française* (n.p.; 1899), 184–190, 199.

9. Ibid., 236.

CHAPTER ELEVEN: THREE CENTURIES LATER

1. Friar João de São José, "Viagem e visita do sertão em o Bispado do Grão-Pará em 1762 e 1763," *Revista do Instituto Histórico e Geográfico Brasileiro* 9 (1869): 223.

2. Henry Koster, *Travels in Brazil* (Philadelphia: Carey & Son, 1817), 201.

3. Sílvio Romero, *Cantos populares do Brasil,* (Rio de Janeiro: Livraria Clássica de Alves & Cia, 1897): 76–77.

4. Koster, *Travels,* 81.

5. Wilhelm L. von Eschwege, *Pluto Brasiliensis* (Berlin: n.p., 1833), 514.

6. Auguste de Saint-Hilaire (1779–1853) was a French naturalist remembered primarily for his penetrating and detailed descriptions of his travels throughout southern and western Brazil. He was an accurate observer who wrote with considerable style and grace and his nine volumes of travels are still widely appreciated for his detailed observations and for his ability to interpret what he saw. Although a naturalist with particular interest in the flora of Brazil, his works always paid considerable attention to the human dimension and social relations. See, for example, *Voyages dans l'intérieur du Brésil; seconde partie: Voyage dans le district des diamans et sur le littoral du Brésil* (Paris: Librarie Gide, 1833). [SBS]

7. Auguste de Saint-Hilaire, *Segunda viagem do Rio de Janeiro a Minas Gerais e a São Paulo (1822),* trans. Afonso d'E. Taunay, 5? vols. (Brasiliana, n.d.), 5: 198–199.

8. Spix and Martius, *Reise,* 2: 417.

9. Teixeira Coelho, "Instruções," 311–312. Cf. Varnhagen, *História geral,* 4: 383.

10. Johann Emanuel Pohl (1782–1834) was born in Bohemia and educated at the University of Prague. He came to Brazil in 1817 as part of a large scientific expedition sent by Francis I of Austria and was assigned to investigations of mineralogy and botany. He collected over 4,000 botanical specimens and published *Plantarum Brasiliae icones et descriptiones hactenus inedital* (Vienna, 1827–31). He traveled through Rio de Janeiro, Minas Gerais, and Goiás between 1817 and 1821 and he published an account of his travels, *Reise im Innern von Brasilien,* 2 vols. (Leipzig, 1832–37). The book was particularly important for its descriptions of Goiás, the Brazilian "Far West" that was little known at the time. There is a translation into Portuguese. See *Viagem no interior do Brasil,* ed. Mário Guimarães Ferri, trans. Milton Amado and Eugênio Amado, (Belo Horizonte: Itatiaia, 1976). [SBS]

11. J. E. Pohl, *Reise im Innern von Brasilien,* 2? vols. (Vienna: 1837), 2: 72–76.

12. Spix and Martius, *Reise,* 1: 318–319.

13. Ibid., 221–223.

14. Ibid., 240–253.

15. Pohl, *Reise,* 1: 373.

16. M. Aires de Casal, *Corografia brasílica,* ? vols. (Rio de Janeiro: 1817), 1: 142.

17. Auguste de Saint-Hilaire, *Voyage à Rio Grande do Sul* (Orleans, 1887), 104, 142, 252, 318.

18. John Luccock, *Notes on Rio de Janeiro and the Southern Parts of Brazil* (London, 1820), 108.

19. Spix and Martius, *Reise,* 2: 711.

20. Luccock, *Notes,* 109. See Saint-Hilaire, *Voyage,* 533.

21. Luccock, *Notes,* 102.

22. Friar Caetano Brandão, *Pastorais e outras Obras* (Lisbon: Impressão Régia, 1824), n.p.

23. Thomas Lindley, *Narrative of a Voyage to Brazil* (London, 1805), 275.

24. Luccock, *Notes*, 112–113.

25. Ibid., 112, 118.

26. Ibid., 121–122.

27. Auguste de Saint-Hilaire, *Voyage dans les Provinces de Saint Paul et de Sainte-Catherine*, ? vols. (Paris: Bertrand, 1851), 1: 289.

28. Luccock, *Notes*, 107.

29. Lindley, *Narrative*, 78.

Bibliography

Abreu, Capistrano de. "Caminhos antigos e povoamento do Brasil." *Jornal do Comércio* (12, 29 August; 10 September 1899).

———. "O descobrimento do Brasil. O povoamento do solo. Evolução social." In *Livro do Centenário, 1500–1900*, 1–78.

———. "Subsídio para a história das minas." *Revista do Instituto Histórico e Geográfico Brasileiro* 63 (1901): 5–13.

———. "História pátria." *Kosmos* (April 1905).

———. "História pátria." *Kosmos* (July 1905).

———. "Trabalhos dos primeiros jesuítas do Brasil." *Revista do Instituto Histórico e Geográfico Brasileiro* 57, no. 1 (1894): 212–247.

———. *Caminhos antigos e povoamento do brasil.* Rio de Janeiro: Sociedade Capistrano de Abreu, 1930.

Aires de Casal, M. *Corografia brasílica.* 2 vols. Rio de Janeiro: 1817.

Albuquerque Coelho, Duarte de. *Memorias diarias de la guerra del Brasil.* Madrid, 1654.

Alencastre, M. P. de. "Anais da Província de Goiás." *Revista do Instituto Histórico e Geográfico Brasileiro* 27 (1864): 229–349.

Anchieta, José de. "Informação dos primeiros aldeamentos da Bahia." In *Cartas.* Rio de Janeiro: Academia Brasileira de Letras, 1933.

Antonil, André João. *Cultura e opulência do Brasil por suas drogas e minas.* Lisbon: Oficina Real Deslanderina, 1711.

Azara, Félix de. "Correspondencia ofical e inédita sobre la demarcación de límites entre el Paraguay y el Brasil." In *Colección de obras y documentos,*. edited by Pedro de Angelis. Buenos Aires: Imprenta del Estado, 1836.

Azevedo Marques, M. E. *Apontamentos históricos, geográficos, biográficos, estatísticos e noticiosos da Província de São Paulo*. 2 vols. Rio de Janeiro, 1879.

Barbosa de Sá, José. "Relação das povoações de Cuiabá e Mato Grosso de seus princípios até os presentes tempos." *Anais da Biblioteca Nacional* 23 (1904): 5–58.

Barlaeus, Gaspar. *Rerum per octennium in Brasilia*. Amsterdam, 1647.

Barléu, Gaspar. *História dos feitos recentemente praticados durante oito anos no Brasil*. Translated by Cláudio Brandão. Rio de Janeiro: Ministério da Educação, 1940.

Borges da Fonseca, Antônio José Vitoriano. "Nobiliarquias pernambucanas." *Anais da Biblioteca Nacional* 47–48 (1935).

Brandão, Caetano. *Pastorais e outras obras*. Lisbon, Impressão Régia, 1824.

Calado, Manuel. *O valeroso Lucideno e triunfo da liberdade*. Lisbon, 1648.

Calógeras, Pandiá. *As minas do Brasil e sua legislação*. 3 vols. Rio de Janeiro: Imprensa Nacional, 1904.

Campos Moreno, Diogo de. "Jornada do Maranhão." In *Memórias para a história do estinto Estado do Maranhão*, edited by Cândido Mendes de Almeida, 2 vols. Rio de Janeiro, 1874.

Códice 51–VI–24, fols. 460–467, Biblioteca da Ajuda, Lisbon.

Coleção de notícias para a história e geografia das nações ultramarinhas. 4? vols. Lisbon: Academia Real das Ciências de Lisboa.

"Correspondência dos governadores do Pará com a Metrópole, primeira série— 1752–1757." *Anais da Biblioteca e Arquivo Público do Pará*, 5 vols. Belém do Pará: n.p., 2(1902), 3(1904), 4(1905), 5(1906).

Costa Rubim, "Title Unknown." *Revista do Instituto Histórico e Geográfico Brasileiro* 24 (1861): 175–196.

D'Abbeville, Claude. *Histoire de la mission des pères capucins en l'isle de Maragnan*. Paris, 1614.

D'Avezac, Marie Armand Pascal M.. *Considérations géographiques sur l'histoire du Brésil*. Paris, 1857.

Delgado da Silva, Antônio. *Coleção da legislação portuguesa*. ? vols. Lisbon: 1830.

Derby, Orville. "Os primeiros descobrimentos de ouro nos distritos de Sabará e Caeté." *Revista do Instituto Histórico e Geográfico Brasileiro* (1899–1900): 282–285??.

Diálogos das grandezas do Brasil. Edited by Francisco Adolfo Varnhagen. *Revista do Instituto Arquelógico e Geográfico Pernambucano* 28, 31, 32, 33 (1883–87).

———. Rio de Janeiro, Academia Brasileira de Letras, 1930.

Eschwege, Wilhelm L. von. *Pluto Brasiliensis*. Berlin, 1833.

———. "Extrato de uma memória sobre a decadência das minas de outro da Capitania de Minas Gerais e sobre vários ouros objetos montanísticos." In *História e memórias da Academia Real das Ciências de Lisboa*. 4? vols. Lisbon: 1868.

Fernandes Gama, J. B.. *Memórias históricas da Província de Pernambuco*. 4 vols. Pernambuco: Typographia de M. F. de Faria, 1844. (Reprint, Chicago, 1977.)

Fernandes Vieira, João. "História pátria. Testamento de J. F. Vieira." *Revista do Instituto Arquelógico e Geográfico Pernambucano* 3, no. 25 (1869): 144–149.

Ferreira Reis, Artur César. *Limites e demarações na Amazônia Brasileira.* 2 vols. Rio de Janeiro: Imprensa Nacional, n.d.

Fonseca, Manoel da. *Vida do venerável Padre Belchior Pontes.* Lisbon, 1752.

———. "Levantamento em Minas Gerais no ano de 1708 [Extrato da vida do Padre Belchior de Pontes, Escrita pelo Padre Manoel da Fonseca, e naturais de São Paulo." *Revista do Instituto Histórico e Geográfico Brasileiro* 3 (1841): 266.]

Fonti Italiane per la Storia della Scoperta del Nuovo Mondo. Rome: 1893.

Góis, Damião de. *Fides, Religio, Moresque Aethiopum sub Imperio Preciosi Ioanis.* 2d ed. Paris: Cristianum Wechelum, 1542.

"Guerra civil ou sedições de Pernambuco." *Revista do Instituto Histórico e Geográfico Brasileiro* 16 (1853): 5–134.

"Idéia da população da Capitania de Pernambuco." *Anais da Biblioteca Nacional* 40 (1923): 1–111.

"Immensa pastorum principis." In *Coleção dos breves pontifícios e leis régias.* Rio de Janeiro?: Impressa da Secretaria de Estado, n.d.

"Informação geral da Capitania de Pernambuco, 1749." *Anais da Biblioteca Nacional* 28 (1908): 117–496.

"Informação do Estado do Brasil e de suas necessidades." *Revista do Instituto Histórico e Geográfico Brasileiro* 25 (1862): 465–478.

"Informação sobre as Minas do Brasil." *Anais da Biblioteca Nacional* 57 (1939): 159–186.

Jesus, Rafael de. *Castrioto lusitano.* Lisbon: 1679.

Koster, Henry. *Travels in Brazil.* Philadelphia: Carey & Son, 1817.

Lamego, Alberto. *Mentiras históricas.* Rio de Janeiro: n.p, n.d.

———. *A Terra Goitacá à luz de documentos inéditos.* ? vols. Paris, 1913

Lindley, Thomas. *Narrative of a Voyage to Brazil.* London, 1805.

Lisboa, João Francisco. *Obras.* 2 vols. Lisbon: Tipografia M. Moreira & Pinheiro, 1901.

Livro do centenário, 1500–1900. 4 vols. Rio de Janeiro: Imprensa Nacional, 1900.

Lopes de Santiago, Diogo. "História da guerra de Pernambuco e feitos memoráveis do mestre de campo João Fernandes Vieira." *Revista do Instituto Histórico e Geográfico Brasileiro* 38 (1875): 249–336; 39 (1876): 97–195, 323–409; 40 (1877): 411–504; 41 (1878): 143–181, 387–429; 42 (1879): 91–104, 157–198; 43 (1880): 5–79, 191–255.

Lopes de Sousa, Pero. *Diário da navegação que foi à terra do Brasil em 1530 sob a capitania-mor de Martim Afonso de Sousa, escrito por seu irmão Pero Lopes de Sousa.* Edited by Francisco Adolfo Varnhagen. Lisbon: 1839.

Loreto Couto, Domingos de. "Desagravos do Brasil e glórias de Pernambuco." *Anais da Biblioteca Nacional* 25 (1903): 5–214

Luccock, John. *Notes on Rio de Janeiro and the Southern Parts of Brazil.* London, 1820.

Machado de Oliveira, J. J. "Notícia sobre as aldeias de índios da Província de São Paulo desde o seu começo até a atualidade." *Revista do Instituto Histórico e Geográfico Brasileiro* 8 (1868–2d ed.): 204–254.

Magalhães Gandavo, Pero de. "Tratado da terra do Brasil." In *Coleção de notícias para a história e geografia das nações ultramarinhas*. IV.

Mendes de Almeida, Cândido. "Por que razão os indígenas do nosso litoral chamavam aos franceses "Maïr" e aos portugueses "Peró?." *Revista do Instituto Histórico e Geográfico Brasileiro* 41, no. 2 (1878): 71–141.

Monteiro Baena, Antônio Ladislau. "Resposta ao presidente da Província do Pará, em 20 de março de 1844 sobre os limites do Brasil com a Venezuela." *Revista do Instituto Histórico e Geográfico Brasileiro* 7. N.d.

Moreau, Pierre. *Histoire des derniers troubles du Brésil*. Paris, 1651.

Noronha, Jácome Raimundo de. "Relação do Jácome Raimundo de Noronha, sobre as coisas pertencentes à conservação, e aumento do Estado do Maranhão." *Anais da Biblioteca Nacional* 26, (1905: 435–441).

———. and Pereira Berredo, Bernardo. "Title Unknown" *Anais históricos do Estado do Maranhão*. Lisbon: 1749, 448–460.

Pereira da Costa, F. A. "Donatários de Pernambuco e governadores seus loco-tenentes." *Revista do Instituto Arqueológico e Geográfico Pernambucano* 48 (1896): 3–28.

———. "Capitães-mores governadores loco-tenentes dos donatários de Pernambuco," *Revista do Instituto Arqueológico e Geográfico Pernambucano* 50 (1897): 59–91.

Pohl, J. E. *Reise im Innern von Brasilien*. 2 vols. Vienna: 1837.

"Refutação das calúnias contra os jesuítas contidas no poema 'Uruguay' de José Basílio da Gama." *Revista do Instituto Histórico e Geográfico Brasileiro* 68, no. 1 (1907): 93–224.

Relação abreviada da república que os religiosos jesuítas das províncias de Portugal e Espanha estabeleceram nos domínios ultramarinos das duas monarquias. N.p. n.d.

"Relación de los sucesos ocorridos durante el viaje que hizo el gobernador del Paraguay Don Luis de Céspedes Xeria desde Madrid hasta llegar a la ciudad de Asunción." *Anais do Museu Paulista* 2 Parte Segunda (1925): 15–221.

Resposta apologética ao poema intitulado O Uruguay, composto por José Basílio da Gama. Lugano, 1876.

Rocha Pita, Sebastião da. *História da América Portuguesa*. 18 vols. Lisbon, 1730.

Romero, Sílvio. *Cantos populares do Brasil*. 2d ed. Rio de Janeiro: Livraria Clássica de Alves & Cia, 1897.

"Roteiro do Maranhão e Goiás pela Capitania do Maranhão." *Revista do Instituto Histórico e Geográfico Brasileiro* 62, no. 1 (1900): 60–161.

Ruiz de Montoya, Antonio. *Conquista espiritual*. Madrid, 1639.

São José, João de. "Viagem e visita do sertão em o Bispado do Grão-Pará em 1762 e 1763." *Revista do Instituto Histórico e Geográfico Brasileiro* 9 2d Ed. (1869): 43–107, 179–227, 328–375, 476–527.

Saint-Hilaire, Auguste de. *Segunda Viagem do Rio de Janeiro a Minas Gerais e a São Paulo 1822.* Translated by Afonso d'E. Taunay São Paulo: Companhia Editora Nacional, 1938.

——. *Voyage dans les Provinces de Saint Paul et de Sainte-Catherine.* ? vols. Paris: Bertrand, 1851.

——. *Voyage à Rio Grande do Sul.* Orleans, 1887.

Santa Maria Jaboatão, Antônio de. "Catálogo genealógico das principais famílias que procederam de Albuquerques e Cavalcantes em Pernambuco e Caramurus na Bahia 1768." *Revista do Instituto Histórico e Geográfico Brasileiro* 52, no. 1 (1889): 5–484.

Santos, Manuel dos. "Narração histórica das calamidades de Pernambuco sucedidas desde o ano de 1707 até o de 1715." *Revista do Instituto Histórico e Geográfico Brasileiro* 53, no. 2 (1890): 1–307.

Silva Paranhos Júnior, Barão de Rio Branco, José Maria da. *Questão de limites Brasileiro-Argentina.* 4? vols. Nova Iorque, 1894.

——. *Frontières entre le Brésil et la Guyanne Française.* N.p., 1899.

Soares, Gabriel. *Tratado descritivo do Brasil em 1587.* Rio de Janeiro: Laemmert, 1851.

Soares, Gabriel. "Tratado descritivo do Brasil." *Revista do Instituto Histórico e Geográfico Brasileiro* 14 2d ed. (1879): 1–330.

Sousa, Luís de. *Anais de Dom João III.*

Sousa e Silva, Joaquim Norberto de. "Memória histórica e documentada das aldeias de índios na província do Rio de Janeiro." *Revista do Instituto Histórico e Geográfico Brasileiro* 17 N.d.

Sousa Silva Costa Lobo, A. de. *História da sociedade em Portugal do século 15.* Lisbon: Imprensa Nacional, 1903.

Spix, Johan B. and Martius, Karl von. *Reise in Brasilien.* 2 vols. Munich, 1825, 1828.

Taques, Pedro. "Nobiliarquia Paulistana." Manuscript, Instituto Histórico, lata 22, n. 489.

——. "Nobiliarquia Paulistana." *Revista do Instituto Histórico e Geográfico Brasileiro* 32, Part 1, (1869): 175–200, 209–261; 33, Part 1 (1870): 5–112, 157–242; 33, Part 2 (1870): 27–185, 149–334 (mispaginated); 34, Part 1 (1871): 5–115, 141–253; 34, Part 2 (1871): 5–46, 129–194; 35, Part 1 (1872): 5–132, 243–384; 35, Part 2 (1872): 5–79.

Taunay, Afonso de Escragnolle. "A viagem de Dom Luís de Cépedes Xeria." *Revista do Instituto Histórico e geográfico Brasileiro* 84: 449–478.

——. *Pedro Taques e seu tempo.* São Paulo, 1922.

Teixeira, Domingos. *Vida de Gomes Freire de Andrada.* Lisbon, 1727.

Teixeira Coelho, José João. "Instruções para o governo da Capitania de Minas Gerais." *Revista do Instituto Histórico e Geográfico Brasileiro* 15 2d ed. (1888): 255–481.

Thevet, A. *Les singularités de la France-Antarctique.* Paris, 1557.

Varnhagen, Francisco Adolfo. *Primeiras negociações diplomáticas,* Rio de Janeiro: 1845, 135.

———. *História geral do Brasil.* 3d ed. 5 Vols. Rio de Janeiro: Laemmert & Cia. Editores, 1907.

———. *História da colonização portuguesa do Brasil.* 3 vols. Porto: Litografia Nacional, 1924.

Vieira, Antônio. *Cartas do Padre António Vieira.* Edited by Lúcio de Azevedo. 3 vols. Coimbra, Portugal: Imprensa da Universidade, 1925.

Index